JEWISH AND CHRISTIAN TEXTS IN CONTEXTS AND RELATED STUDIES

Series

Executive Editor
James H. Charlesworth

Editorial Board of Advisors

A Commentary on
the *Gospel of Thomas*

From Interpretations
to the Interpreted

Petr Pokorný

t&t clark

NEW YORK • LONDON

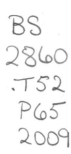
2009

The Scripture quotations contained herein are from the New Revised Standard Version Bible, copyright © 1989 by the Division of Christian Education of the National Council of the Churches of Christ in the U.S.A., and are used by permission. All rights reserved.

www.continuumbooks.com
www.tandtclarkblog.com

T & T Clark International, 80 Maiden Lane, New York, NY 10038

T & T Clark International, The Tower Building, 11 York Road, London SE1 7NX

T & T Clark International is a Continuum imprint.

Printed in the United States of America on 30% postconsumer waste recycled paper.

A catalog record for this book is available from the Library of Congress.

ISBN 9780567027443

Contents

PREFACE

The English translation used in this commentary is that of the Berliner Arbeitskreis für Koptisch-Gnostische Schriften (Hans-Gebhard Bethge, Christina-Maria Franke, Judith Hartenstein, Uwe-Karsten Plisch, Hans-Martin Schenke, and Jens Schröter), which is a slightly revised version of the translation in the edition "Das Thomas Evangelium/The Gospel according to Thomas (Coptic text, German and English translations)," in Kurt Aland, ed., *Synopsis quattuor evangeliorum* (Stuttgart: Deutsche Bibelgesellchaft, 519–46). I preferred this solution to translating the *Gospel of Thomas* from Coptic (and Greek) into a language in which I was not educated. I owe appreciation to my colleagues in Berlin who allowed me to use their translation, whose preparation I was able to follow for a number of years. I thank, in particular, Hans-Gebhard Bethge, who was in regular contact with our Coptic working group at the Center of Biblical Studies of the Academy of Sciences and Charles University in Prague. Since the Berlin edition does not include the translation of the Greek version (where it is preserved), translations of portions of the Greek text that are different from the Coptic translation are mine.

The Greek and Coptic expressions are transcribed according the *SBL Handbook of Style* (Peabody, MA: Hendrickson, 2004). However, we transcribe the Coptic *djandja* as *č,* and *kyima* as *q.*

When biblical texts are presented in our translation, they are from the *New Revised Standard Version of the Bible* (New York: American Bible Society, 1989).

If the page number of the commentary on the *Gospel of Thomas* is not indicated when it is quoted in a footnote, the note refers to the comment about the given saying.

Thanks and Dedication

This commentary originated in the spring of 2007 at the Center of Theological Inquiry in Princeton, New Jersey, and is based on my former Czech and German Gnostic and Coptic studies, which were a by-product of my exegetical work in the New Testament. Much inspiration came from the Berliner Arbeitskreis für Koptisch-Gnostische Schriften (chairs Hans-Martin Schenke [deceased 2006] and Hans-Gebhard Bethge), from the Institute for Antiquity and Christianity in Claremont, California (James M. Robinson), and from the Dead Sea Scrolls Project of Princeton Theological Seminary (James H. Charlesworth). I dedicate this book to all of these institutions and to my colleagues who do their research there.

I am indebted to Pavel Moskala, who read the manuscript, and especially to Anna Bryson Gustová. The book could not have appeared without her thorough and intelligent correction of my English.

Abbreviations

A, B	In part A of the commentary section, we reproduce the meaning of the given saying in the context of the *Gospel of Thomas*. In part B, we discuss the historical and other hermeneutical issues.
ANRW	*Aufstieg und Niedergang der römischen Welt*. Edited by H. Temporini and W. Haase. Berlin: de Gruyter, 1972–.
BAK	Berliner Arbeitskreis fur Koptisch-Gnostische Schriften
BETL	Bibliotheca ephemeridum theologicarum lovaniensium
ca.	Lat. *circa*, probable, about
cf.	Lat. *confer,* compare
f., ff.	following verse(s)
FRLANT	Forschungen zur Religion und Literatur des Alten und Neuen Testaments
FS	Festschrift (from German) volume in honor of X
JSNTS	Journal for the Study of the New Testament: Supplement Series
log.	logion, logia (saying, sayings)
LXX	Septuagint
MPG	Migne, Patrologia graeca [=Patrologiae cursus completus: Series graeca]. Edited by J.-P. Migne. 162 fols. Paris, 1857–1886.
NHC	Nag Hammadi Codices
NHD	German translation of Nag Hammadi Codices (and comments by the authors of this translation; see preface)
pap	papyrus
Politeia	*Politeia, Respublica, Constitution of an Ideal State* (Plato, 427-347 B.C.)
P.Oxy.	Oxyrhynchus papyri
par., parr.	parallel(s)
Q	the source of Jesus' sayings used by Luke and Matthew
S	the group of sayings including elements of social ethics
SJLA	Studies in Judaism in Late Antiquity
WMANT	Wissenschaftliche Monographien zum Alten und Neuen Testament
WUNT	Wissenschaftliche Untersuchungen zum Neuen Testament
ZNW	*Zeitschrift für die neutestamentliche Wissenschaft*

Jewish and Early Christian Writings

Adv. haer.	*Adversus haereses* (Irenaeus, 115-ca. 202)
Apol.	*Apology* (Justin Martyr)
1–2 Clement	The letters of Clement (of Rome) to the Corinthians (first and second centuries A.D.)

Comm. Ps.	*Commentarius in Psalmos, Commentary on Psalms* (Didymus the Blind, 313–398)
Corp. Herm.	*Corpus Hermeticum,* various tractates ascribed to the god Hermes, originating between the first century B.C. and the third century A.D.
De opif. mundi	
	De opificio mundi, On the Creation (Philo of Alexandria, ca. 25 B.C.–45/55 A.D.)
De somn.	*De Somniis, On Dreams* (Philo of Alexandria, ca. 25 B.C.–45/55 A.D.)
Didache	*Didache,* the Teachings of the Apostles from the end of the first century A.D.
Didascalia	Church order (originally Syrian) and pastoral admonitions from third century A.D.
Epideixis	*Epideixis, Demonstration* (Irenaeus, 115-ca. 202)
4 Esra	*The Revelation of Esdras,* fictional Jewish (-Christian) apocalypse from the beginning of the 2nd century A.D.
Exc. ex Theod.	
	Excerpta ex Theodoto [biblical commentaries] (Hippolytus, 170-ca. 236
GosPhil	*Gospel of Philip*
GosTh	*Gospel of Thomas*
Herm.	*Shepherd of Hermas,* Christian apocalypses, end of the first to beginning of the second century (*Sim. = Similitudes, Parables*)
Hist. Eccl.	*Historia Ecclesiae* (Eusebius)
Homil. Lat. in Jerem.	
	Homilia Latina in Jeremiam, Homily on Jeremiah (Origen)
Leg. alleg.	*Legum allegoriae* (Philo of Alexandria, ca. 25 B.C.–45/55 A.D.)
Od. Sol.	*Odes of Solomon,* late first or early second century A.D.
Panarion	*Panarion* (*Medical Box*), *Against Heresies* (Epiphanius, ca. 315-403)
Philos.	*Philosophumena* (Hippolytus, 170-ca. 236)
Pist. Soph.	*Pistis Sophia,* Gnostic text, 250-300
Quod deterius	
	Quod deterius potiori insidiari soleat, Commentary on Genesis 4:8-15 (Philo of Alexandria, ca. 25 B.C.–45/55 A.D.)
SibOr	*Sibylline Oracles,* Jewish (second century B.C.–second century A.D.) and Christian (later) prophecies and apocalypses
Sim.	*Similitudes, Parables* (Shepherd of Hermas)
Strom.	*Stromata,* sermonic essays (Clement of Alexandria, ca. 160-215)

Sigla in the Translation
of the Coptic and Greek Text

[ ]   square brackets = unreadable or missing part of the manuscript
( )   parentheses = added words for better understanding the text
< >   angle brackets = improvement of scribal errors
*   beginning of a new page in the manuscript

I. Introduction

1. The Discovery and Its Description

Discovery

The discovery of the mysterious *Gospel of Thomas* evoked great expectations. Many people speculated about its acceptance into the Bible as the fifth Gospel. Such expectations evoked further questions: Who would proclaim it? Would it be the pope in Rome, or the pope in Rome and the World Council of Churches in Geneva? After a few years of investigation these hopes proved to be premature. The *Gospel of Thomas* does not include any independent information about Jesus' life and, as to his teaching, the *Gospel of Thomas* is so deeply influenced by ideas from the beginning of the second century that it is very difficult to define and isolate the authentic core. In the eighties and nineties of the last century, however, several scholars realized that the *Gospel of Thomas* still may contribute to our knowledge (1) of the piety of early Christianity, (2) of the teaching and message of Jesus, and (3) of the ways in which Jesus' teaching has been transmitted. That is why scholars have begun a new period of studies of this peculiar text. This new interest in the *Gospel of Thomas* continues to the present, and this volume documents that interest.[1]

The *Gospel of Thomas* has been preserved as a part of a collection of books belonging to a heterodox (sectarian) Christian group. The collection consisted of thirteen codices, which were discovered shortly after World War II in Upper Egypt, in the province of Kena, near the town called Nag Hammadi in an isolated part of Egypt: in the west and the north are the sheer cliffs of the Gebel el Tarif; in the south and east, the Nile river. It is an uncontrolled area, in which blood feuding was a reality in the twentieth century and complicated the investigation of the site where the codices were discovered. This is one of the reasons why the *Gospel of Thomas* was published only in 1956.[2] A facsimile edition of the whole collection appeared under the auspices of UNESCO; the *Gospel of Thomas* was in the second volume, which was published in 1974.[3] All of the preserved parts of the collection (twelve codices plus eight leaves from a thirteenth) contain tractates and religious and speculative texts. At the present time we have three critical editions of the *Gospel of Thomas*. One appears in the series Nag Hammadi Studies (Nag Hammadi Codex II,2–7);[4] another is in the series Texte und Untersuchungen;[5] and the most

---

1. About the biblical canon today, see Metzger 1987, 167ff., esp. 272 (the *Gospel of Thomas*).
2. P. Labib, *Coptic Gnostic Papyri in the Coptic Museum at Old Cairo, Vol. I* (Cairo, 1956), 80–99; the first edition of the Coptic text dates from 1959 (Guillaumont 1959).
3. See Robinson 1974 in the bibliography.
4. Koester 1989, 37–128.
5. Leopoldt 1967.

recent is in Kurt Aland's edition of the *Synopsis Quattuor Evangeliorum.*[6] Short but reliable information about the discovery and fate of the manuscripts in the twentieth century comes from James M. Robinson[7] and is published in the introduction to the English translation of the Nag Hammadi collection.[8] Together with the Dead Sea scrolls, the Nag Hammadi[9] codices are the most important discovery of ancient texts in the second part of the twentieth century.

From the fact that the *Gospel of Thomas* has been preserved in a Coptic translation within a set of texts that may belong to a Christian Gnostic library, we may deduce that the readers of some versions of this translation were viewed as unorthodox by the mainstream church of the fourth century. This does not mean that the *Gospel of Thomas* is a Gnostic book. It means only that for the Gnostics it may have been attractive or, at least, acceptable.

Description

The *Gospel of Thomas* is a part of the second codex of the Nag Hammadi library according to our modern numeration, where it is found between page 32, line 10, and page 51, line 28. According to the unified subdivision of its text[10] the *Gospel of Thomas* consists of 114 sayings.[11] The title "The Gospel according to Thomas" was added at the end. In our commentary we use the numbers of the Coptic sayings even when discussing the Greek parallels.

Most of the sayings are introduced by the words "Jesus says" (Greek: *legei Iēsous*; Coptic: *peče Iesous*). A few sayings are missing this introduction; in some cases, however, a saying can in fact be a logical consequence of the previous one (e.g., 59 and 60) and the division into two *logia* has to be ascribed to the judgment of the modern editors. Ancient collectors are responsible for instances where several sayings are linked by introductory phrases into one unit (e.g., log. 13 or 61).

The papyrological description of the codex is of secondary significance for this commentary. Still, it is important to know that the Coptic translation has been written as a codex, not as a scroll. The codex form is a predecessor of our book form. A codex consisted of sheets that could be covered with writing on both sides (pages). Unlike a scroll, the pages could be turned, and the orientation in the book

---

6. Bethge 1996.

7. Robinson 1997.

8. Robinson, ed., 1996.

9. They were called also Chenoboskion papyri, according to the name of the nearby Hellenistic town.

10. It was introduced in the first edition of the Coptic text prepared by a team of scholars— Guillaumont et al. 1959. The best of the older critical commentaries, that of R. Kasser 1961, took it over and it was accepted by the whole scholarly community..

11. In the last generation of critical editions the sayings are subdivided according to their inner semantic units. We have adopted this division, together with the translation from the Berliner Arbeitskreis für Koptisch-Gnostische Schriften (Hans-Gebhard Bethge, Christina-Maria Franke, Judith Hartenstein, Uwe-Karten Plisch, †Hans-Martin Schenke, Jens Schröter).

form facilitated reading.[12] Also the price was not so high, since the consumption of the papyrus or parchment was lower. Christians promoted this book shape, which was used originally only for notebooks. The oldest manuscripts and fragments of Christian (New Testament) texts we have at our disposal are codices or parts of them. Unlike Christians, Jews copied the Law and Prophets on scrolls.

Attestation

Scholars knew about the *Gospel of Thomas* even before its full text had been published. Cyril, the bishop of Jerusalem (d. 386), warned against it in his catecheses and ascribed it to one of the followers of Mani.[13] This is inaccurate information, however, because the most ancient text in which the *Gospel of Thomas* is mentioned originates from the beginning of the third century—a time when Mani had just been born.

Nevertheless, from Cyril's notice, we may deduce (1) that the *Gospel of Thomas* influenced the church of his time; (2) that Manicheans liked it or at least used it; and (3) that it was not commonly used in Christian worship. This means that the *Gospel of Thomas* was one of the books whose impact would have been limited by the formation of the Christian canon and its defined list of individual elements (books, epistles, etc.).

The oldest mention of the *Gospel of Thomas* originates from Hippolytus of Rome, who mentioned that the Naassenes used to read the *Gospel of Thomas*.[14] He also quotes a saying from it (Hippolytus *Philos.* 5.7.20f.),[15] which, surprisingly, is not identical to any saying from the preserved versions. Logion 3 from the Coptic translation would be the most similar text, and Hippolytus may have reproduced it from memory. The other possible explanation is that the *Gospel* circulated in several (slightly) different versions. Hippolytus's quotation includes a Gnostic idea. However, since the saying is not part of the text attested in our accessible Coptic translation, it cannot be understood as a document showing the Naassene origin of the *Gospel of Thomas*; it only illustrates how the Gnostics tried to adapt this collection of sayings for their use.

Text

The most important documents related to the existence of the *Gospel of Thomas* are two fragments of its original Greek text, which were discovered more than a hund

---

12. The codices were not bound but consisted of several quires (folded papyrus sheets), which had been preserved in various covers; in the case of Nag Hammadi texts the covers were of leather.

13. MPG 33,500B and 593A.

14. Naassenes were a Gnostic group, the name of which is derived from the Hebrew word for serpent (or dragon)—*nāchāš*. For some Gnostic groups the serpent from Genesis 3 was a positive hero, something like Prometheus, who brought the humans knowledge, which the gods kept for themselves. Another similar group was called Ophits, from the Greek *ofis*, "snake."

15. See below, on the layers of the *Gospel of Thomas*.

red years ago near the former Hellenistic town of Oxyrhynchus (present-day Behnesa) in Egypt. They were published by B. P. Grenfell and A. C Hunt in 1898 (P.Oxy. 1) and 1904 (P.Oxy. 654 and 655).[16] Even though the prologue to the *Gospel of Thomas* was included in papyrus 654, in the period after its publication the fragments were not identified as a part of the *Gospel of Thomas*, because it was not expected that a collection of sayings could be a gospel. A gospel was supposed to include narratives. So it was only after the Coptic[17] translation of the full text of the *Gospel of Thomas* had been published that the French scholar Henri Charles Puech made the public aware that the Greek fragments from Oxyrhynchus were part of the *Gospel of Thomas* in its original language.[18]

The Oxyrhynchus papyri have a parallel (often not a word-for-word) in these Coptic sayings:

    prologue to log. 7 = P.Oxy. 654
    log. 26 to 33 + 77 (second part) = P.Oxy. 1
    log. 36 to 39 (40?) = P.Oxy. 655

Paleographically (according to the type of the letters), the Oxyrhynchus papyri are dated to the beginning of the third century. This means that the *Gospel of Thomas* must have been known in Upper Egypt at about 180 A.D., at the latest. The manuscript of the Coptic translation originates from the fourth century, from the time of the foundation and first development of Pachomian monasteries. A very probable hypothesis supposes that the codices of Nag Hammadi had been for a long time preserved in one of them.

Since P.Oxy. 655 contains sayings that are not influenced for the most part by the special theological interests of the Thomas group, James M. Robinson proposed the interesting theory that P.Oxy. 655 was a small collection of ancient sayings of Jesus, older than the sayings-source Q. It was later included in the *Gospel of Thomas*. Unfortunately, this interesting theory cannot be supported by any other evidence, but the hypothesis confirms our belief that the *Gospel of Thomas* was composed from various sources. The idea of the author of the *Gospel of Thomas* was that a collection of sayings was the original form of conserving the traditions about Jesus.

Similar groups of sayings with Synoptic parallels are included into other parts of the *Gospel of Thomas*: e.g., the beatitudes in sayings 54 or 68 and 69. Nevertheless, saying 37, which is attested in P.Oxy. 655, is not typical of ancient tradition about Jesus.

---

16. Grenfell and Hunt 1898; and iidem 1904.

17. It is an impure kind of Sahidic Coptic (the Coptic of Upper Egypt) and is considered to be a special dialect.

18. Nonetheless, G. Garitte supposed that Coptic was the original language and that the Greek fragments were a translation from Coptic. See the discussion in *Museon* 73 (1960) and the report by Wilson 1995, 331. Garitte's hypothesis was not substantiated. On the hypothesis that Syriac was the original language, see below in part 4 of the introduction.

Impact in Antiquity

The *Gospel of Thomas* was obviously popular and circulated widely. Only the formation of the Christian canon of Scriptures and its use in the liturgy and as a counterpart to the Law and the Prophets limited its influence, so that it gradually lost its position in Christianity.

Even so, its impact is astonishing. As we have mentioned, Hippolytus of Rome quoted it at the beginning of third century in Rome. Puech found a quotation of logion 5 on a linen band of an Egyptian mummy from the fifth century,[19] and a great part of the *Gospel of Thomas* was discovered in Chinese Eastern Turkmenistan among the so-called Turfan fragments, which had a Manichean background.[20] This means that it spread from Syria to Rome, Egypt, and even to the border of China.

We have already mentioned Syria, or its northern foreland Osroene (Edessa being the center), as the area with which most of the writings ascribed to Thomas are linked.[21] The *Gospel of Thomas* also most probably originated from this part of the Near East. Some scholars have objected that an originally Greek collection could not have originated in Osroene, because the majority of its Semitic inhabitants spoke Syriac,[22] which in the second part of the second century gradually replaced Aramaic as the literary language. We shall discuss the hypothesis of a possible Syriac original version of the *Gospel of Thomas*; however, we must not forget that, for example, the *Acts of Thomas* were also written in Greek, and the Gospel of John, which may originated in the same area, was likewise written in Greek. At that time, many people of Semitic origin received their education in Greek.

2. The Gospel of Thomas as Literature

The Literary Shape—Wisdom, Prophecy?

It is surprising that the book which was introduced as "Hidden Words of the Living Jesus," and which at its end bears the title "The Gospel according to Thomas"[23] (page 51, lines 27–28) is not the same type of literature as the biblical Gospels —the four canonical biographies of Jesus. Since at the beginning of the second century, Christians called each of these "gospel" (Greek: *euangelion*) and added "according to Mark," "according to Luke," "according to Matthew," or "according to John."[24] The *Gospel of Thomas* is similarly called *Gospel according to Thomas* (NHC II/2);

---

19. See the commentary that follows.

20. Now they are deposited in Berlin.

21. H. Drijwers 1970, 28ff.

22. This is the thesis of M. Desjardins from *Toronto Journal of Theology* 8 (1992): 121–33, here 127 (according to the report by G. J. Riley 1994, 238f.).

23. For practical reasons we shall usually call it simply the *Gospel of Thomas*.

24. These titles do not belong to the original text, of either of them; however, they originated as early as the beginning of the second century; see Hengel 1984.

and in the same codex from Nag Hammadi as the third tractate (NHC II), we find the *Gospel according to Philip* (NHC II/3). However, as we have mentioned, the canonical Gospels and both of these latter "Gospels" are strikingly different. The canonical Gospels belong to the literary genre of biography, even if they represent its special subgenre; but the *Gospel of Thomas* is a collection of sayings of the "living Jesus." The *Gospel of Philip* is in some respect similar to that of Thomas, even though it is more of a collection of meditations and several statements are expanded into short tractates. As we shall see, the *Gospel of Philip* represents a later Gnostic development from the third century.

As in all collections of sayings, the *Gospel of Thomas* lacks not only a narrative frame but also clearly definable argumentation. The individual sayings are grouped according to key words, which are usually common to two (e.g., world—log. 27 and 28) or at most to four (life and death—log. 58–61a; the kingdom of the Father—log. 96–99; seeking and finding the kingdom—log. 1–5) neighboring logia.[25]

Various attempts have been made to reconstruct an overarching structure; but what we know for certain are only the signals at the beginning and at the end that make the reader aware of the meaning and crucial significance of his reading: "These are the hidden words which the living Jesus spoke. . . . Whoever finds the meaning of these words will not taste death" (*incipit*[26] and log. 1) and, at the end, "The one who has found the world and has become wealthy should renounce the world" (log. 110); and "whoever is living from the Living One will not see death" (log. 111:2). Or compare a saying from the beginning: "The kingdom is inside you and outside you" (log. 3:3) with another from the end: "Rather the kingdom of the Father is spread out upon the earth, and people do not see it" (113:4). Another overarching idea is that of the soul and flesh, as summarized in logion 112. It has its opposite member in logion 7, on the "happy lion." The theme of finding and understanding (or finding as understanding) is also common to the beginning and the end. To find the meaning of Jesus' words of eternal wisdom means at the same time that the readers/hearers discover their own hidden divine substance (log. 76) and understand the visible world as substantially aiming toward death. Reading the Gospel means, therefore, to renounce the mortal and, from the point of eternal wisdom, already-dead world (log. 56). The reading process is the process of conversion.[27]

From a purely literary point of view, the *Gospel of Thomas* belongs to the same genre as Proverbs, Ecclesiastes, Wisdom of Solomon, Ecclesiasticus, or Pseudo-Phocylides in Jewish tradition or the Letter of James in the New Testament.

---

25. For a survey of such small clusters, see Fallon and Cameron 1988, 4206f., and Patterson 1993, 100–102. Tripp (1980–81) attempted to identify larger groups of sayings (see Fallon and Cameron 1988, 4207); as a reconstruction of an aim of the *Gospel of Thomas,* it is nothing more than hypothetical, since he grouped the sayings according to the religious themes that terminologically are not represented in the Gospel text. For deciphering an overall structure of the *Gospel of Thomas,* see Meyer 1991, 168.

26. "The opening sentence."

27. See Beardslee 1972, 95f.

The tradition of collecting the sayings of wise men was common in Jewish (e.g., Sayings of the Fathers = *Pirqe Abōt, Pseudo-Phocylides*) as well as in Greek settings (*logoi sophōn*). The *Gospel of Thomas,* however, has a special function, similar to that of prophetic sayings from Scripture. The apostle Paul must have known a collection of Jesus' sayings as oral tradition. He quoted from this collection when it was necessary to solve some problem in the name of Jesus as the Risen Lord (Greek: *kyrios*). These sayings had special authority. Like the Old Testament prophets and obviously like the other Christian prophets, Paul selected and quoted the appropriate words of the Lord, such as we read, for example, in 1 Cor 7:10: "To the married I give this command—not I but the Lord." Obviously, written collections of sayings, such as the sayings source Q, played a similar role in some early Christian groups.[28] The Christian prophets quoted words from the stored treasure when discussing the topical problems of the community and proclaimed them as interpreters who were inspired by God himself.[29] Their community accepted them as the voice of the Lord.[30] When Paul said that he received the words constituting the Lord's Supper "from the Lord" (*parelabon apo tou kyriou* [1 Cor 11:23]) he has the Lord Jesus in mind, whom he never met. He learned these words from the oral tradition, just as he learned the formula of faith in 1 Cor 15:3b–5 (see *parelabon* = "I took over," in 15:3), and he considered his conversion at Damascus as divine authorization of the eucharistic tradition, which he learned from the apostles. Such collections of dominical sayings differed from collections of proverbs. The Christian analogy of sapiential books is the Letter of James rather than the collection Q or the *Gospel of Thomas.* We mention the differences between the *Gospel of Thomas* and the sapiential genre as a preliminary hint at the main problem of interpreting the *Gospel of Thomas* at the beginning of the twenty-first century.

In the thirties or forties of the second century, Bishop Papias of Hierapolis in Asia Minor (Phrygia) wrote the "Expositions of Dominical Sayings" (*Logōn kyriakōn exēgēseis*")—that is, of the orally transmitted words of Jesus (Eusebius, *Hist. Eccl.* 3.39.1).[31] The collections of Jesus' sayings have been a treasure from which an appropriate word could have been quoted according to the inspiration and experience of a Christian prophet.[32]

In his study about the tradition of the Lord's sayings, J.-M. Robinson discussed the similarities between the tradition of the sayings of the Lord and the genre of Q,

---

28. See a similar use of the Sayings of the Lord in *2 Clem* 6:1: "The Lord says. . . ."

29. This is the way in which the prophets in Israel spoke, when they introduced such sayings by *ne'ūm adonai,* "the Word of the Lord." This use functioned also in the prophecy of Jesus' disciples: see Migaku Sato, *Q und Prophetie* (WUNT 2/29; Tübingen: Mohr Siebeck, 1988), 408. It was E. Käsemann who first analyzed the function of the apocalyptic prophetic sentences of the sacred Law ("Sätze des heiligen Rechtes"), in idem, *Exegetische Versuche und Besinnungen II* (2d ed.; Göttingen: Vandenhoeck & Ruprecht 1965), 69–82.

30. Schürmann 1968, 52–65.

31. According to Körtner 1983, 157ff., 205, the *logoi* of the Lord were the stories about Jesus, that is, probably sayings that have been put into the frame of a story in the sense of the ancient *chreia* as a rhetorical unit.

32. The Q-disciples "were . . . bearers of traditions as well as prophets"; see Sato, *Q und Prophetie,* 408.

the common source of Matthew and Luke.[33] Q was a collection that was oriented to proclaiming the new laws of the kingdom of God or the concrete way of salvation. Robinson's general statement about such collections as mediators of Jesus' authority is, at its core, still valid.[34] As to its genre, the *Gospel of Thomas* belongs to the tradition represented by Q, by the small collections of Jesus' sayings included in the Gospels, such as in the parables from Mark 4, by the apocalyptic words of Mark 13, by the special source of the Gospel of Luke (mostly parables),[35] by a part of the *Book of Thomas* (*the Contender*) (NHC II/7), by the *Dialogue of the Savior* (NHC III/5), by the collection of Papias mentioned above, by the collection represented by P.Oxy. 1224, and by other sources.

Our first statement is therefore negative: The *Gospel of Thomas* does not belong to the same genre as the canonical Gospels, and to analyze the function of its genre is a decisive step in understanding the *Gospel of Thomas* as a whole.

The Gospel as Oral Message and as Book

The canonical Gospels likewise contain sayings of Jesus.[36] They too are related to Jesus as the Risen Lord, but their frame is a narrative that refers predominantly to Jesus' earthly life. They are influenced not only by the Greek literary genre of biography as represented, for example, by Plutarch or, in the Jewish Hellenistic area, by Philo's biography of Moses, but first of all by the biblical narrative—by the Law and Prophets as well as by the narrative texts from the Greek version of the Hebrew Bible, the Septuagint. It is necessary to define the specific "historical" features of the canonical Gospels to understand the difference between them and the *Gospel of Thomas*.

In early Christianity, "Gospel" (*euangelion*, good news) became a term denoting short confessions proclaiming Jesus' new presence in Christian communities and in the world after Easter. The apostle Paul, who wrote his incontestably authentic letters in the fifties and early sixties of the first century, is the earliest witness to this practice. He often speaks about the gospel, but only in a few cases does he also mentioned its content. This occurs especially in 1 Cor 15:1 (referring to 15:3b–5),

---

33. James M. Robinson, "LOGOI SOPHON: Zur Gattung der Spruchquelle Q," in Helmut Köster and James M. Robinson, *Entwicklungslinien durch die Welt des frühen Christentum* (Eng., *Trajectories through Early Christianity*) (Tübingen: Mohr Siebeck, 1971), 67–106, here 89ff.

34. The collections have been adapted in the second century A.D. In the *Secret Book of John* (NHC II/1; III/1; IV/1, BG 2; Irenaeus *Adv. haer.* 1.29) the sayings have been transformed into a dialogue between the risen Jesus and his disciples. However, in the first part, the main problems of faith are being discussed in a speech of Jesus. Also, the *Dialogue of the Savior* is arranged in a similar way. In this way it was possible to interpret the individual sayings as answers to topical questions; see Koester 1990, 32f.

35. Kim Paffenroth, *The Story of Jesus according to L* (JSNTS 147; Sheffield: Sheffield Academic Press, 1997), 149ff.

36. In the Gospel of Mark they represent about 30 percent of the text; in Matthew and Luke even more; and in the Gospel of John, Jesus' speeches are shaped as extensive literary units.

in Rom 1:1 (1:3–4), and in 1 Thess 1:5 (1:10). The common denominator of these quite different formulas is the "resurrection" (Rom 1:4; "was raised" 1 Cor 15:4). Consequently, the gospel (*euangelion*) is a message about Jesus' resurrection, and the biblical Gospels tell the story of Jesus as pre-history of the oral gospel, of his new presence on the Spirit. The gospel about the resurrection of Jesus is *euangelion*, good news, because it confirms the authenticity of Jesus' teaching and proclamation.

The problem with the Easter gospel is that it was often isolated from traditions about Jesus and degenerated into a metaphysical construct describing the "technology" of human salvation.

Surprisingly, the Gospel of Mark begins with the sentence "The beginning of the Gospel of Jesus Christ" (1:1). It does not mean that the Gospel of Mark begins here, since at that time "gospel" did not yet designate a book. The reader has to understand "gospel" in the original sense as the message about the resurrection of Jesus, as it is attested in the last verses of Mark (16:6–7),[37] and to realize that it is not possible to understand the import of the gospel as the message about the resurrection of Jesus without knowing Jesus' teaching and life—its "beginning." In the second generation of Jesus' followers and outside Palestine this step was necessary in order that the oral gospel not be isolated from Jesus tradition. In view of this fact, it is understandable that soon the term Gospel started to designate not only the Easter message but also the stories from Jesus' life (Justin) and, later, the individual canonical biographies of Jesus.

Problems with Prophetic Transmission of Jesus' Sayings

After the original post-Easter period of enthusiasm, when the adherents of Jesus enjoyed the new, spiritual yet real presence of their Lord, the problem of feedback moved to the foreground. The Christian prophets quoted the sayings of Jesus as the decisive authority in solving the problems of the group's adherents. As we have mentioned, Christian prophets and teachers apparently gathered the sayings from the tradition and proclaimed those that fitted the topical needs. So also did the apostle Paul, for example, in 1 Cor 7:10. The problem was that the tradition about Jesus did not contain sayings for every new problem arising among the Christians or in their surroundings. Paul was sincere and accurate when admitting that for certain problems he has not any command of the Lord (1 Cor 7:12, 25). But did John the Divine speak in accordance with the earthly Jesus in Rev 2:1–3:22 when he admonished in Jesus' name the Christian communities in Asia Minor? This may have been the case, but it is very difficult to judge, because he had to formulate Jesus' intention in a new situation and in his words. In the early church

---

37. According to Codex Sinaiticus (ℵ) and Vaticanus (B) and according to the witness of some early Christian authors (e.g., Clement of Alexandria and Origen), the Gospel of Mark ends with 16:8. For the problem of the longer ending, see Dormeyer 2002, 21–23.

the testing whether a prophetic reproduction of a dominical saying (a sentence of Jesus as the risen Lord) was authentic or not was one of the central problems. The gospel of Jesus' resurrection and his new presence gives authority to what Jesus proclaimed and what he did during his earthly life. But as to the content of the post-Easter proclamation, the earthly Jesus is its feedback. The Christian prophets had to respect the tradition about the earthly Jesus (the "memory" of him) as "feedback" of their proclamation. When in John 14:26 Jesus says that the Holy Spirit will remind (Greek: *hypomnēsei*) the community about all that Jesus said,[38] it is a clear hint about the way of testing the prophetic proclamations. It was the new decision anchored in what we known about Jesus' traditions as preserved in the memory (Greek: *mnemosynē, anamnēsis*) of the congregation. This rule has been expressed in a maxim: "Test the spirits to see whether they are from God, for many false prophets have gone out into the world. By this you know the spirit of God: every spirit that confesses that Jesus Christ has come in the flesh is from God" (1 John 4:1–2; 2 John 7; cf. Polycarp 7.a-b). A short survey of the *Gospel of Thomas* may illustrate how important such testing was: a substantial part of this large group of sayings bears visible signs of a spirituality of popular Platonism as it was common in the early second century. This means that many logia were developed, interpreted, and combined in a way that is different from the original tradition. This is an understandable process of adaptation, but without control it may cause the loss of group identity. This was a "spiritual deformation."

Admittedly, the pieces of tradition that have been embedded in the canonical Gospels are preserved in an interpreted form; but after they have been written and used in liturgy, they underwent only minor changes. By linking them with Jesus' deeds, with descriptions of his attitudes, and by placing them in the contingent past of Jesus' life, they have indeed been preserved. Papias of Hierapolis, who preferred the oral tradition, admitted that Mark had written down what he kept in memory (Greek: *emnēmoneusen*) and that he did not falsify (*pseusasthai*) anything (Eusebius, *Hist. Eccl.* 3.39.15). This is an important statement, revealing Papias's opinion about the superiority of the canonical Gospels. The struggle for the "earthen" shape of Jesus' proclamation, that is, the shape that included Jesus' deeds, prophetic symbols, healings and exorcisms, his attitude toward the poor, sick, women, children, and Samaritans, and especially his personal crisis and his death on the cross, is an important part of Christian piety, praxis, and theology. It was so consequential that from the many collections of Jesus' sayings only those that were included in texts of different genres survived.

---

38. Justin Martyr expressed one important dimension of the literary nature of Mark and the other canonical Gospels when calling them "memories of the apostles" (*apomnēmoneumata tōn apostolōn, Apol.* 1.66.3; 67.3), probably as a conscious allusion to the well-known *Memories of Socrates,* written in the fourth century B.C.

3. The Testimony and Jesus of History

The Gospels as Feedback of Christian Proclamation and Prophecy

In view of post-Easter spiritual enthusiasm, the decision to take into serious consideration the "memory" of Jesus was not self-evident. The books of the prophets in the Scriptures preserved the prophetic words in literary shape, and most of them have been put into a preserved or a reconstructed historical setting, for example, "At the beginning of the reign of King Jehoiakim . . . this word came from the Lord . . ." (Jer 26:1). In Jesus' case, his words conveyed a still higher authority, because they belonged to divine revelation in history.

Mark wrote his "gospel" as a book intended to be read in the liturgy of Christian communities as a counterpart to the Law and Prophets—the Jewish Bible, which in the Christian church was later called the Old Testament. The Greek *archē* ("beginning," in Mark 1:1 and John 1:1; cf. Luke 2—"from the beginning") or *genesis* (birth, genealogy, in Matt 1:1) remind the reader of the book of Genesis and claim an authority equal with it. Christian proclamation, which originally was considered to be a kind of sermon on biblical texts, became now liturgical text itself. The tradition about Jesus has been preserved and protected from falsification because it was framed by the life story of the earthly Jesus. The price paid for this preservation has been an increasing need to interpret the Gospels with their limited stock of Jesus' sayings by Christian sermons. The sermon became an additional metatext that served to apply the Jesus tradition in new situations, as it is still today. The decision of Mark to write a Gospel of this kind began the development of the Christian canon, including the Old and the New Testaments.

The Title of the Gospel of Thomas

It was necessary to discuss the character and function of the Gospel according to Mark in order to clarify the problem of the *Gospel of Thomas*. Now we see that by its literary shape the *Gospel of Thomas* seems to correspond with the earliest forms of transmitting Jesus tradition, especially the words of Jesus; but by the date of the origin of the version we have in Coptic translation, it is at least one generation later than the latest canonical Gospels (most probably John in its final redaction).

We have mentioned that according to its genre the *Gospel of Thomas* is similar to the sapiential literature. Nevertheless, unlike the sapiential literature, it includes some sayings that proclaim new rules of the kingdom of God and heralds its coming into human world (e.g., log. 9:1 or 73). Since it contains elements of a prophetic proclamation,[39] we can call the *Gospel of Thomas* sapiential literature only in the sense of Luke 11:49.[40] This is a saying of Jesus about the wisdom of God who sends

---

39. See De Conick 2002, 178f., 195ff., and pp. 20–25 below.
40. John S. Kloppenborg, *The Formation of Q* (Philadelphia: Fortress Press, 1987), 149.

prophets to Israel. In any case, the *Gospel of Thomas* is strikingly different from the canonical Gospels; and the formulation "The Gospel according to . . ." in the title (postscript) has been usurped from the canonical Gospels.[41] The intention of the editor of the preserved version was to obtain for this book an authority similar to that of the canonical Gospels. If the *Gospel of Thomas* or some of its parts originated earlier, which we consider probable, the *incipit* "The hidden words of the living Jesus" was the original title.

The Problem of Methodology

Modern historical criticism through critical analysis reconstructs the function of a text in a time that is distant from the present and is able to describe and interpret this ancient function in contemporary language.

The fact that in the second century the *Gospel of Thomas* tried to attain an authority similar to that of the canonical Gospels is important for our interpretation of its role in early Christianity, especially in Jesus research. We have to be aware of the fact that our interest in any text is motivated by the preliminary knowledge we have about it—by our expectation that the text may help us in our life. The positivist premise according to which we have to discuss every subject without partiality has been rejected by most of the philosophies in the second half of the twentieth century. Only when admitting our presuppositions and intentions can we control them. The positivism did not reflect such an important phenomenon as the choice of the subject of investigation, the research field. As for the *Gospel of Thomas*, it attracted the interest of scholars because it is linked with Jesus of Nazareth and may be considered the most important noncanonical source for Jesus research.

Methodologically we have to start with analyzing each text, including the *Gospel of Thomas*, as literature and discuss its inner text word. Richard Valantasis has written such a commentary. This does not mean that all subsequent commentaries should be of this kind. In our commentary, we start with analyzing the *Gospel of Thomas* as a literary unit as well. However, subsequently we discuss the origin of each saying. These two positions have to be distinguished, but they cannot be separated.

Gospel of Thomas—A Possible Source of Information about Jesus

It follows that we cannot avoid discussion about the teaching and proclamation of Jesus. Several American scholars from the "Jesus Seminar" undertook an experiment to rethink Jesus in his original categories. According to them, eschatological

---

41. Since the term "gospel" does not appear in the text of the *Gospel of Thomas*, it is practically certain that the title in the postscript is a later addition. See the comment on the title at the end in the running commentary.

enthusiasm is a post-Easter phenomenon influenced by Jewish apocalyptic. This could mean that the *Gospel of Thomas* not only as to its genre but also theologically may be nearer to Jesus than the Synoptics.[42] Jesus was considered to be a teacher of wisdom of a Stoic or Cynic kind, for whom the kingdom of God was the model of the ideal society; the apocalyptic orientation was introduced into his heritage after Easter and developed by Paul of Tarsus.[43]

Nevertheless, some of the findings of twentieth-century exegesis are irreversible. When we hear "The kingdom of God is at hand" (*eggizō, eggys eimi*), which is substantially linked with Jesus' proclamation (Mark 1:15; cf. Luke 10:9 par. [Q]; 21:31), it means a general transformation and fulfillment of our human history, which gives it its meaning (struggle against Satan and the last judgment).

And yet, in spite of its onesidedness, the attempt at a radical new understanding of Jesus as a prophet teaching wisdom, as, for example, the Cynic philosophers did, brought some new insights, namely, the observation about elements of Jesus' teaching that helped him and his followers to cope with the fact of the delayed coming of the kingdom of God on earth. Such insights inspired the thesis of Charles H. Dodd (1884–1973) about "realized (proleptic) eschatology" in Jesus traditions.[44] These were the anticipations of the kingdom in Jesus' activity (exorcisms—expelling unclean spirits: Luke 11:20 par. [Q]; cf. Luke 17:21) and the exhortation for seeking the kingdom of God (Luke 11:9 par. [Q]. Seeking supposes that the kingdom of heaven is accessible—a motif that occurs often in the *Gospel of Thomas*. Another important anticipation of the kingdom was table fellowship (later Eucharist—Mark 14:25; Luke 22:16). An additional pillar of the bridge between the earthly Jesus and post-Easter Christianity is his unique son–father relationship to God (Mark 14:36; cf. 15:35), which was mediated to other people in the Lord's Prayer (Luke 11:2–4 par. [Q]; *Didache*[45] 8:2). All of this does not exclude an apocalyptic horizon for Jesus' proclamation of the kingdom of God, as we have mentioned above, but it helped to transform Jesus' teaching into the proclamation of the post-Easter church.

Often the discussion about the validity of the *Gospel of Thomas* for Jesus research concentrates on the alternative: Is this an old collection, the roots of which reach to the apostolic generation, or is it an artificial product of the second century? If we answer that the latter is true, the conclusion is that the significance of the *Gospel of Thomas* for Jesus research will decrease. However, this is an inaccurate thesis.

Because the *Gospel of Thomas* originated at a time when some of the earlier Gospels had already attained canonical status, the author (editor) could have put his interpretation of Jesus' heritage in the frame that was common for the biblical Gospels. At about the same time, that is, the first part of the second century, this

---

42. For example, Crossan 1991, 260, 285; Borg 1994, 54ff.

43. The originator of this interpretation of Jesus was Downing (1988); his view is shared by Mack 1988, and Crossan 1991; for a critical analysis of their views, see Ebner 1998.

44. Dodd 1936,107.

45. An early Christian instruction on Christian piety from the beginning of the second century.

was the case with the *Gospel of Peter*. In these fragments of a Gospel[46] we find some spiritual ideas similar to those that can be found in the *Gospel of Thomas*, but their literary frame and setting, related to the passion story, are similar to that of the canonical Gospels. We can deduce that the last editor (author) of the *Gospel of Thomas* inherited the basic part of his Gospel as a collection of sayings and considered this shape so important that he dared a bold step: he called the collection "The Gospel according to Thomas" in the same way that the canonical Gospels have been called "The Gospel according to Mark, according to Matthew," and so on.[47] In this way he attempted to stress the import of the genre used in his Gospel. The simplest explanation of the authority that the genre of a collection of dominical sayings enjoyed in some parts of the church was its early status. We have already demonstrated that quotations of Jesus' sayings are attested as early as Paul.

The theory according to which the genre of the *Gospel of Thomas* is older than that of the canonical Gospels can be put in question by the fact that antiquity did know artificial collections of sayings from well-known texts (Greek: *kentōn*; Lat. *cento*).[48] Nevertheless, in most such collections the original texts are recognizable, and the collections were mostly parodies or popularizing extracts. This is not the case with the *Gospel of Thomas*. The theory of the late German scholar Hans-Martin Schenke that the *Gospel of Thomas* was a collection of logia from Papias's "Expositions of Dominical Sayings," which had been extracted from their context as parts of short exemplary stories (Greek: *chreia*),[49] is in fact not so far from a cento-hypothesis. Even if Schenke were right, our conclusion, which we have presented, remains the same: the *Gospel of Thomas* could be a witness to the authority and indirectly also to the antiquity of the collections of Jesus' sayings, even if in this case they are put into such a frame additionally. The value of individual sayings for a deeper knowledge of Jesus' teaching or self-understanding would in such a case decrease, but the text as whole would still serve as a document attesting the authority of a collection of sayings as the most ancient literary genre used by the followers of Jesus.

Nothing speaks in favor of the hypothesis about the *Gospel of Thomas* as a whole being a cento, even if some sayings may have been secondarily isolated from their original context before they were added to the *Gospel of Thomas*. An author of a cento would not put alongside each other sayings such as 12 and 13 (James or Thomas as leaders) or 12 and 14 (Jewish tradition and its rejection). The only

---

46. The *Gospel of the Savior* may have been inspired by the *Gospel of Peter* or be its lost part.

47. Matthew and Luke obviously intended to replace Mark. Matthew does not mention it, even though he incorporated it in his book. Luke mentioned Mark in a exprecative way as an attempt of one of his predecessors (Acts 1:1). John is intended to be a deep, spiritual interpretation of the material of the other Gospels. Providentially, the four Gospels survived in the liturgy and gradually spread in all directions. The local Christian communities had to create a designation that would distinguish these originally anonymous books (the supposed author was Jesus himself!) from each other, and at the same time express that they belong to the same genre: see M. Hengel 1984; and the commentary below on the last sentence of the *Gospel of Thomas*. The uniformity of the titles means that they originated as additions.

48. Haenchen 1961, 68ff.; Grant and Freedman 1960, 145.

49. Schenke 1998, 23.

explanation is that the sayings were grouped according to the catchwords in oral tradition.

Nevertheless, it is inaccurate to suppose that the *Gospel of Thomas* is one of the most ancient documents of Christian literature.[50] Not all sayings may have belonged to traditions that were independent from the canonical Gospels, even if the oral transmission was still going on at the end of the second century. However, the editor was convinced that his collection of Jesus' sayings was indeed the most authentic version.

John and Thomas

In the individual sayings we shall discover several features similar to the theology of the Gospel of John. This is understandable, because the Gospel of John and the whole of the Johannine tradition is linked with Syria. James H. Charlesworth with serious arguments maintains that Thomas was the "Beloved Disciple" of Jesus.[51] We may object that Thomas did not receive the divine mission (John 20:21).[52] Nevertheless, it is he whose solemn confession "My Lord and my God!" concludes the whole Gospel in its first version. It seems that there was a struggle about the heritage of Thomas. The Gospel of John, the author of which is unknown, may have originated in a group that was closely linked with pupils of Thomas. The opening logion of the *Gospel of Thomas* is a promise to those who discover the meaning of the following sayings: they will not taste[53] death. According to the Gospel of John 8:52, the one who keeps the words of Jesus will never taste[54] death.[55] Such parallels reveal the common features of the spiritual milieu in which the two streams, the Johannine and the Thomas, originated.

Princeton professor of religious studies Elaine Pagels has suggested that the *Gospel of Thomas* was excluded from the Christian canon by members of the Johannine group because it proclaimed that all people participate in the divine nature. According to Johannine theology, only Jesus was the divine Word (John 1:1); he was the revelation of God (1:18), whereas the *Gospel of Thomas* teaches about the divine substance hidden inside each human being (log. 84). For the Johannine group, which until the last decade of the first century was also situated in Syria, this denigrated the uniqueness of Jesus. The world was not capable of receiving the divine light unless Jesus has revealed it (John 1:1, 10). This, according to Pagels,

---

50. This is the case, e.g., with J. D. Crossan 1991, appendix I, and F. Vouga 1994, paragraph 2.2b; they build their views on their interpretation of the position of J. M. Robinson (see part 2 of this introduction); see also the criticism in Schröter 1997, 132ff.

51. Charlesworth 1995, 225, 242f., 388f.; on the Johannine school and the school of Thomas, see 360–89; for a synopsis of similar sayings in *Gospel of Thomas* and in the Gospel of John, see 372–73.

52. See Pagels 2003, 71.

53. Copt. *či tipe an.*

54. Greek *geuomai.*

55. For a synopsis of such parallels, see Charlesworth 1995, 372–73.

is the basic reason for the nonacceptance of the *Gospel of Thomas* into the canon[56] and against the theory of its dependence on John.[57]

We have to further specify the difference: The Gospel of John developed a paradoxical teaching about Jesus as Savior, that is, a christology that on the one hand declared Jesus to be God (John 20:28; cf. 10:30) and, on the other, stressed the humanity of Jesus, his full identity with Jesus of Nazareth (1:14, 18). The Johannine Jesus often speaks in the first person as God himself (cf. Exod 3:14, "I am who I am"), for example, "I am the way and the truth and the life" in John 14:6 (by way of answering the question of Thomas). However, all his "I am" sayings culminate in the thrice-repeated "I am" at the moment when the temple police came to arrest him and he confirms that he is identical to Jesus of Nazareth (18:5, 6, 8). These last "I am" words of Jesus confirm the declaration from the prologue about himself as Word incarnated (1:14). We do not know how thoroughly the Gospel of John was influenced by the pupils of Thomas and their theology and what was the relation between the Johannine and Thomas groups, but the Gospel of John, as well as the Johannine epistles (1 John 4:1–3; 2 John 7), clearly supports the paradoxical teaching about Jesus as God incarnated in a fully human being—one of the basic teachings of later Christian doctrine that is foreign to the *Gospel of Thomas*. The stress on Jesus' humanity means that God and his intentions are not hidden in some mysterious code but are as understandable and memorable as the life of a teacher and prophet can be.[58]

This means that the *Gospel of Thomas* and the Gospel of John represent two related but still different interpretations of Jesus' tradition. The Thomas group seems to have gained ground after the Johannine group left for Asia Minor at the end of the first or at the beginning of the second century.

The Gospel of Thomas and the Synoptics

As we have hinted in our discussion of the genre of the *Gospel of Thomas*, the opinions of the scholarly community are still divided in defining its relation to the Synoptic Gospels. A significant group maintains that the *Gospel of Thomas* is dependent on the Synoptic Gospels (Mark, Matthew, and Luke). In that case the *Gospel of Thomas* would not be valid as a source for Jesus research at all.[59] We have to mention the most important argument in favor of this opinion:

First, there are traces of the New Testament wording in the Coptic version of the *Gospel of Thomas*. This can be interpreted as an argument supporting the dependence of the *Gospel of Thomas* as a whole on the New Testament. Heinz

---

56. The elevation of Jesus to God obviously also caused the exclusion of the Johannine group from the synagogue (*aposynagōgos*, "excluded from the synagogue"); see J. Louis Martyn 1979, 31–34.

57. As assumed by R. E. Brown 1962–63, 176.

58. For a comparison of the theological intention of the Gospel of John and *Gospel of Thomas*, see Popkes 2006, 91ff.

59. Tuckett 1995, 200.

Schürmann, Wolfgang Schrage,[60] and especially Christopher M. Tuckett[61] demonstrated in their studies that the sayings that have parallels in the canonical Gospels originate in a combination of their biblical versions.[62]

Some similarities are indeed striking. For example, logion 6:6 corresponds to the parallel in the Coptic Sahidic version of Luke 8:17 in a significant way:

Thomas: And there is nothing covered that will remain undisclosed
Luke: And there is nothing[63] covered that will not become known (Coptic verb *eime*).

"And there is nothing" is a rare use of the Greek/Coptic *oude* (normally, "neither"); the *Gospel of Thomas* seems to have taken it over.[64] Unfortunately, in P.Oxy. 654 this part is destroyed. Likewise in log. 45 and Luke 6:45 there are apparent similarities in the whole structure of sentences.[65] In such cases it seems that the text of the *Gospel of Thomas* has been influenced by the canonical Gospels and was compiled after at least some of the canonical Gospels had spread among the communities of the original Christian church.[66] Principally we cannot exclude the possibility that the *Diatessaron* and the *Gospel of Thomas* may be dependent on a common source, probably the *Gospel of Hebrews,* which may be the fourth source for Tatian's *Harmony* (*Diatessaron*).[67]

Even in such case, it is possible that the *Gospel of Thomas* included other sayings from the independent tradition. In several Christian groups, oral tradition was cherished until the end of the second century. In his book against the heresies (written about 175–185), Irenaeus supposed the power of oral tradition in protecting Christians against heresies,[68] and Papias was able to interrogate the witnesses and personal observers of the teaching of the apostles.[69]

Nevertheless, the *Gospel of Thomas* could have been adapted to the Coptic Sahidic translation of the Gospels in the process of translating from Greek. Just as in the case that we discussed now, we may observe that the sentence from log. 6:6 is a relative clause corresponding to the second version of that saying from Luke and Matthew, and is derived from Q (not from Mark), so that the discussed sentence does not need to be dependent only on Luke.[70] The *Gospel of Thomas* also does not

---

60. Schrage 1964a, 15; Ménard 1981, 415, 426.

61. Tuckett 1995.

62. Fieger built his commentary on this assumption (1991).

63. In Coptic in both cases: *auo men laau.*

64. Schrage 1964a, 34–35; we mention this case since Schrage could rely on McArthur 1959–60, who presented the same observation as early as 1960, 287.

65. Schrage 1953a, 100–106.

66. See the detailed polemics against Schrage in Patterson 1993, 23f., and Uro 1998, e.g., 29–30.

67. Charlesworth 1974, 16; according to Baarda the *Diatessaron* may have influenced the Coptic translation of the *Gospel of Thomas*; however, he does not deny independent sources in the original text (Baarda 1983).

68. *Adv. haer.* 3.3.1.

69. *Hist. Eccl.* 3.39.4.

70. See Patterson 1993, 21f.

include the theme of knowledge (Greek: *ginosko*), which the Q version, with which the *Gospel of Thomas* has the relative clause in common, introduces in the same sentence. "Knowledge" was a key word not only in the Gnostic schools but also for most of the spiritual movements of late antiquity, and it helped to promote the ideas of the *Gospel of Thomas*. It was the knowledge of the things that are not visible.[71] And yet, the *Gospel of Thomas* does not mention it here, so that it is very probable that the author did not know the Synoptic text or at least the Synoptic context. Not every skeptical argument can be relativized in this way, but the search for close parallels with the Synoptics (or John) cannot present any decisive proof in favor of dependence of the *Gospel of Thomas* on the Synoptics.[72]

One valid argument in favor of the dependence of the *Gospel of Thomas* on the Synoptics is that of Christopher Tuckett, who mentions that in the *Gospel of Thomas* the beatitudes of the Sermon on the Mount/Plain[73] are scattered in various places (see sayings 54, 69:2, 68:1, and 69:1). Since this series of sayings is common to both Luke and Matthew, originating in the source Q and therefore more ancient than their redaction, according to Tuckett the sequence in the *Gospel of Thomas* must be secondary,[74] at least when compared with the meaningful sequence from the New Testament. Nevertheless, this is not a decisive argument for the dependence of the *Gospel of Thomas* on the canonical Gospels. Canonical Gospels do not represent the only set of traditions about Jesus. We have to suppose that from the very beginning fragments of memories circulated among Jesus' adherents, and the fact that from a speech of Jesus some of the hearers recalled only individual sayings that seemed to them memorable is understandable and probable. The narrative frame protected the sayings from transformation better than the genre of a collection of sentences, but the free circulation still did not stop immediately. In the newly published *Gospel of the Savior* (the Unknown Berlin Gospel) we find a parallel to logion 82,[75] which obviously was not taken over from a literary Gospel— either the *Gospel of Thomas* (no other trace of influence of the *Gospel of Thomas*) or from the Synoptics (different wording, Luke 12:49).

Most important is what Hugh Montefiore and Cuno H. Hunzinger demonstrated through analysis of the parables from the *Gospel of Thomas*: At least some of them are derived from nonbiblical sources. For example, the parable of the sower appears in a version that more accurately describes the growth of the seeds than Mark 4:1–9 and parallels.[76] And, what is more surprising, in *Gospel of Thomas,* the parable does not include the allegorical explanation from Mark 4:13–20 and parallels. This is unexpected indeed, because for the spiritual way of salvation that is being taught in the *Gospel of Thomas*, this would be a very suitable material.[77]

---

71. See *The Book of Thomas* (NHC II/7; 138,37ff.; cf. 145,1–3.

72. In principle, we cannot exclude the possibility that there is a reverse dependence and that the Sahidic translation was influenced by the *Gospel of Thomas*; see Vielhauer 1975, 627.

73. Luke 6:20–22 par. (Q).

74. Tuckett 1995, 195f.

75. See the commentary on log. 82.

76. Patterson 1993, 22f.

77. Montefiore 1960–61, 235–37, 248; and Hunzinger 1960, 845. This observation cannot be

The compiler of the *Gospel of Thomas* did not know the full text of the Synoptic Gospels. The thesis that the *Gospel of Thomas* may as whole be abstracted from the canonical Gospels resulted in negative conclusion.[78]

On the other hand, we can imagine that a collection of sayings constantly attracted new accruals from the oral tradition, because association with such a group gave authority to the sayings, and, for the collection of sayings, it meant a wider area of its application. A short glimpse at a synopsis confirms it. We meet such accruals very often. For example, in Luke 6:34 we find a saying added to the Q pattern of the sermon of Jesus, and in 6:38 also[79]— to give only two from many similiar accruals.[80]

With this in mind, we may sketch a model of transmission of Jesus traditions in the earliest period of the Jesus movement—in the origins of church.

The two improbable models are represented by the following statements: (1) the *Gospel of Thomas* is derived from Synoptics; (2) the *Gospel of Thomas* is an independent source, equivalent to the canonical Gospels.

The most probable model is more complex. The *Gospel of Thomas* originated later than Synoptics; and as a whole it represents a theological stream that appeared in the early second century. However, it included several sayings from traditions that were independent of the Synoptic Gospels and originated in oral tradition. Some pieces of authentic Jesus traditions are present here in a spiritual interpretation that depends on religious ideas of the early second century (see the comment on log. 22:6–7), and yet, others sayings typical of the ancient Jesus tradition are present in a shape similar to that found in the Synoptic Gospels: Jesus struggling (log. 35, 47, 58, 82); the kingdom of God as the eschatological future (log. 57, 63, 64, 76); or sayings typical of the social ethics of Jesus (log. 25, 39).

As for the intention of the collector, he obviously decided to gather all that characterized Jesus in a way that in his eyes was the only authentic one; he rejected the theology of those who derived their Easter faith from Jesus' resurrection (see the oral gospel as quoted in 1 Cor 15:3b–5). According to 1 Cor 15:11, such people (1 Cor 15:5–8) created a federation expressing the present impact of Jesus as a consequence of his being raised by God. This was the basis of the teaching of the mainstream church. For the group of Thomas and for other adherents of Jesus, probably also the group created by James the Just, the teaching of the federation was different from the teaching of Jesus, because Jesus did not expect a period in which the Messiah was well known and the messianic kingdom was not present. That is why

---

derogated by the fact that most of the parables in the *Gospel of Thomas* are interpreted in a Gnostic sense, as was stressed by A. Lindemann 1980, 216ff., 242f. For a summary of the discussion on the parables, see Fallon and Cameron 1988, 4210f.

78. This conclusion relativizes the thesis of Tuckett 1995, 200, according to which the *Gospel of Thomas* cannot be used as source in Jesus research; cf. Sieber 1990, 69.

79. We do not mention extant sayings that may originate from written sources.

80. In view of these arguments, it is premature to say that the *Gospel of Thomas* has no relation to older traditions, as Wood 2005, 584ff., maintained. He rightly observed that the eschatological sayings belong to the oldest traditions about Jesus, but as we shall demonstrate in the next section (The Language of the *Gospel of Thomas*), the compilers of the *Gospel of Thomas* may have known parts of these traditions from independent (oral) sources.

they transposed the kingdom of God into the spiritual realm. Their alternative liturgical reading—the individual sayings of Jesus gathered in a cluster—corresponds
to their theological position. Historically this may have been an alternative to a
resurrection christology from the very beginning.

4. The Genesis and Theology of the Gospel of Thomas

The Layers of the Gospel of Thomas

Reluctance is necessary when we reconstruct any phenomenon of history. Before
we try to sketch a tentative image of the development of the *Gospel of Thomas*, we
have to realize the nature of its development, in which periods ruled by tradition
are followed by a period in which individuals shaped the material according to their
spiritual inspiration.

What we have at our disposal as documents of the text are the Coptic translation from NHC II and fragments of the Greek version. These two documents represent two vertical cuts across the temporal dimension of the surviving text, and
we may use them to reconstruct at last its two versions (layers). We have to start
with the preserved Coptic version, which is the only material document of the text
as whole. Yet still we have a fragment of an obviously older version, at least as to
the theological or speculative development. It is the oldest attestation of this text,
as we have mentioned above in the paragraph on attestation (see Introduction, part
1). Hippolytus's quotation reads as follows: "The one who seeks me will find me in
children from seven years of age and onwards. For there, hiding in the fourteenth
aeon, I am revealed."[81] The speculation about aeons is typical for several Gnostic
groups. In the codex NHC II we find, for example, the tract on the *Hypostasis of the
Archons,* which summarizes the teachings of early Gnosticism. There, the aeons
are parts or dimensions of the Fullness (*plērōma*) of the spheres that divide the visible world from the celestial world of spiritual deities. In the preserved text of the
Gospel of Thomas we find only Platonizing ideas; no Gnostic theology.[82] Therefore
Hippolytus's quotation provides evidence of a gnosticizing reinterpretation of the
Gospel of Thomas. Though only a fragment, it reveals interpretative tendencies of
the *Gospel of Thomas* that led to its popularity among Gnostic groups and in Man-
ichaeism. We may call it layer *five.*

The available Coptic version of the *Gospel of Thomas* is not the original Coptic translation; nevertheless it could not have originated too many years later. It has
been copied by five various hands; the copying obviously took some time. Coptic as
a literary language written with an adapted Greek alphabet existed for only a few
decades at the time with which the preserved manuscript of the Gospel is associated by paleography,[83] that is, the mid-fourth century A.D.

---

81. Text and translation by Attridge 1989, 103f.
82. See below on the theology of the *Gospel of Thomas.*
83. A field of research dealing with ancient graphic signs and ways of writing.

The Coptic translation was based on one of the versions of the Greek original that was more similar to P.Oxy. 655 than to P.Oxy. 1. Papyrus 1 differs from the Coptic translation in the sequence of one saying. The translation circulated in several versions that were slightly different from each other, as can be demonstrated by comparison of the Coptic translation with the preserved Greek parts and partially also with the quotation from Hippolytus of Rome. We do not know the Greek text from which the Coptic translation has been made, but it is very probable that the sayings and phrases that have parallels in the canonical Gospels have been translated with regard to the text of the New Testament, which was then attaining canonical authority and under the influence of its Coptic translation. We may call the Coptic translation version number *four*.[84]

The translators of the *Gospel of Thomas* into Coptic obviously did know some ideas of the Gnostic teacher Valentinus, and they supposed that translating some sayings through Gnostic glasses meant rediscovering their original intention. This was not a Valentinian reinterpretation, however, and we have to be aware of the fact that the translators did not know that after a few years their translation of the *Gospel of Thomas* would be included in the same codex as the *Hypostasis of the Archons* (NHC II/4), *On the Origin of the World* (NHC II/5 and XIII/2), and with the Valentinian *Gospel of Philip* (NHC II/3)—typically Gnostic tractates.

When DeConick (2002) deduces that individual developments and reinterpretations of the *Gospel of Thomas* arose from problems (crises) in the community that used it, it is a sound idea; nevertheless, we have very little information about the history of the Thomas community and its social component. In any case, the idea of translating Greek texts into "barbarian" languages was not self-evident and has been developed in the Hellenistic period. When the Thomas group decided to translate into Coptic its main text on Jesus, it produced a document of its inner development. Translators, the equipment, and educated scribes—this all was accessible only for an advanced and influential group of religious communities.

The dating of the *third* version can be deduced from the date of the fragments of copies of its Greek text from Oxyrhynchus. It is the text from which the Coptic translation was made and which got the additional title "The Gospel according to Thomas."

As to the dating of P. Oxy. 1, it belongs to the beginning of the third century; P.Oxy. 654 and 655 are a few decades later.[85] A good deal of the adaptations to the text of the canonical Gospels in the parallel text segments may have originated already in that version, that is, in the period in which the canonical Gospels penetrated into the Thomas community (see log. 13 of our commentary). The fragments document the shape of the text after several decades of its passing on from one copy to another. They are most probably among the first manuscripts to reach Egypt or to be copied there. We have to assume that the *Gospel of Thomas* must have been

---

84. Valantasis 1997, 4f. has reconstructed seven layers. This may reflect the reality, but it is impossible to tell the layers from one another with regard to their theology or ideology; and with the increasing number of reconstructed layers, their hypothetical character is also increasing. See DeConick 2002, 186.

85. See Attridge 1989, 96–97.

known in Egypt about one generation earlier, that is, in the seventies or early eighties of the second century.

A portion of the readers of the *Gospel of Thomas* were Gnostics who left the
mainstream church; however, substantial numbers of them still lived inside the
Christian community and considered themselves to be the unappreciated spiritual
elite.[86] This was the situation of several Gnostic groups till about mid-fourth century.

In this period this collection of Jesus' sayings was already called the *Gospel of Thomas,* and it probably received a written title, "The Gospel according to
Thomas," at the end of the text as it is in the Coptic translation. This means that this
text claimed canonical authority. This, however, was not an authority that would
put it alongside the Gospels that we know as canonical. It rather means that for the
communities of its readers, the *Gospel of Thomas* got its own authority as a liturgical book in place of the canonical Gospels. We have already mentioned that the
genre was different. The elevation of such a text to the level of the canonical Gospels of mainstream Christianity meant the promotion of its genre and its theology.
It was a usurpation of the name Gospel for texts used among these groups.

There is a problem with the *second* layer, which was probably the first version
of the written Greek text that was linked with the name of Thomas. Those who
consider the *Gospel of Thomas* to be an anthology of reinterpreted texts from the
canonical Gospels doubt the existence of such a layer. What may justify our understanding of this earlier layer is first the fact that in the given version of the *Gospel
of Thomas* there is a visible tension between the sayings on the kingdom of God and
spiritual speculative wisdom. The beatitudes of those who are persecuted (logion
68:1) and of those who are persecuted in their heart (69:1) may serve as examples
of the secondary adaptation and interpretation of old apocalyptic sayings. Gilles
Quispel observed that several times one of the sayings that appears twice in the
Gospel of Thomas includes an "encratite" (ascetic, spiritualized) interpretation of
the basic saying: saying 106 of saying 48, 101 of 55, 69 of 68, and so forth.[87] The
second hint at a possible earlier version is the title of the book found at the end,
which is different from the opening title/summary. The opening sentence seems to
be older than the title at the end; the relation between them could be similar to the
relation between "The beginning of the Gospel" in Mark 1:1 and the additional title
"The Gospel according to Mark."

Clement of Alexandria has several times quoted sayings very similar to those
of the *Gospel of Thomas,*[88] but he never mentioned the source. Did he know them
from such an older version?

A possible date of origin of this second version may be achieved by chronologi-

86. In the *Apocalypse of Peter* from Nag Hammadi (VII/3), which originated after the *Gospel of
Thomas*, we still find criticism of those who called themselves bishops and deacons and who obviously
belonged to the same community (79,21–31; cf. Koschorke 1978, 64ff.).

87. Quispel 1967, 93.

88. See the commentary on log. 5, 8, 21, 27, 30, 45, and 99; J. Plátová, in his Czech study on
Clement and the *Gospel of Thomas* (*FS L. Tichý* [Olomouc: University Press, 2008], 164–71), supposes
that Clement may have known the *Gospel of Thomas* from the third or fourth version, since the text is

cal deduction: If the third layer dates back at least to the seventies of the second century, we have to suppose that it came to Egypt after it got a certain authority and spread in Hellenistic Christian communities in Syria, which may have taken at least another generation. Thereby we reach the mid-second century. The Greek version that we have in fragments originates at least one generation previous, but probably even earlier, in the twenties or thirties of the second century.

The difference between the supposed date of origin and the average date of the representative group of oldest manuscripts for the widespread and protected text of the canonical Gospels is at least one hundred years. According to this measure, the *Gospel of Thomas* should originate at the end of the first century,[89] unless it is, as we have mentioned, such a rare document as we have in the Papyrus Rylands, a mid-second-century fragment of the Gospel of John. It must have happened in the period in which this collection of Jesus' sayings were linked with the name of the apostle Thomas. The link is expressed by the opening sentence: "These are the secret sayings[90] which the living Jesus spoke. And Didymos Thomas wrote them down" (log. 1a). This means that Jesus is the very author and that Thomas is his witness, helper, and scribe. Jesus is the "Living One," obviously the eternally Living One, the teacher of divine wisdom and its content at the same time. The resurrection as a link with the earthly life of Jesus is mentioned in the *Gospel of Thomas* as well as in the "Q" source of Jesus' sayings.

The connection with the apostle Thomas is an indirect argument for the origin of this version in the postapostolic period. We have to be aware of the fact that most of Jesus' apostles appear as authors of early Christian writings—canonical as well as noncanonical—that were published (and probably also written) in the period beginning with the late second Christian generation, that is, when the apostles were no longer still living.[91] The reason for this boom was (1) the need to replace the leaders who were endowed with the highest authority as witnesses of Jesus' story by written documents containing their alleged spiritual heritage, and (2) the fact that the apostles were no longer able to protest against new interpretations of their message. This does not mean, for example, that Thomas would not be the apostle of Syria; it only means that the relation, if there is any, of the writings that circulated under his name to his own thoughts and witness would be indirect.[92] As we have noted, at that time the *Gospel of Thomas* circulated without the final title "The Gospel according to Thomas."

We cannot find any traces that the logia were translated from Aramaic, even if that were the case. Nevertheless, the *Gospel of Thomas* may possibly have been collected in a Greek-speaking setting from the very beginning or the most ancient

---

also quoting from Philo without indicating his name; cf. A. van den Hoek, "Techniques of Quotation in Clement of Alexandria," *Vigiliae Christianae* 50 (1996): 223–43.

89. This was the opinion about P.Oxy. 1 expressed by Grenfell and Hunt 1897, 2.

90. The Berliner Arbeitskreis für Koptisch-Gnostische Schriften (BAK) translates here "hidden words."

91. Koester 1980a, 435ff.

92. Walls 1980–81, 270.

layer may have consisted of Jesus' sayings spoken in Greek.[93] Anyhow, it is probable that there was a small collection of sayings that could be considered to be layer *one*. It served as the main source when the *Gospel of Thomas* was composed, but we cannot know anything of it.

To sum up: Some of the sayings that are developed and interpreted in the *Gospel of Thomas* were rooted in pre-Easter Jesus traditions. The Platonizing interpretation of Jesus' sayings reflects the spiritual tendencies of the early second century, so that the sayings from the most ancient layer would be those that are attested by the Synoptics and at the same time presented in the *Gospel of Thomas* without spiritualizing interpretation and mostly in a slightly different form, such as logion 25, the cluster in 32–36, 39, 47, 57–58, 63–64, 76, 82, and 95–96.[94] The words about outstanding representatives of apostolic generation in sayings 12 and 13 are of a later origin, and the Platonizing sayings are later developments (log. 7, 15, 18, 22, 42, 49, 50, 56, 60, 80, 84, 97, 105, and 111).[95] Only a few of them, such as log. 11, 21, 37, 51, 103, 111, and 113, developed from a collection of Jesus' sayings in which the eschatological expectation was still traceable.[96] The spiritualization, which must have started at the latest with the second version, was, according to DeConick, especially linked with hermeticism—the tractates ascribed to the Egyptian deity Hermes Trismegistos, which are attested in late antiquity but originated probably earlier, in the Hellenistic period.[97] Striking is the metaphor of drunkenness as the cause of ignorance.[98] Other motifs, such as spiritual enlightenment, are common to the *Gospel of Thomas* and other texts of its time (esp. Philo of Alexandria). On the other hand, speculation about the divine human being (*anthrōpos*) which is typical of Poimandres (*Corpus Hermeticum* I), is not apparent in the *Gospel of Thomas*.

This interpretation differs from the interpretation of Jesus in the "Jesus Seminar," as we have noted above. Since the discussion of the origins of the *Gospel of Thomas* was influenced by those who find the apocalyptic elements in Jesus traditions to be secondary, it is necessary to survey the mainstream in Jesus research in order that our thesis about the most ancient layer may be understandable: the transformation moved from eschatology to wisdom.

Logion 13 may reflect a conflict in one of the Jewish Christian groups about its leadership: Will the leader be James the Just, the representative of broader groups of Christian Jews, or Thomas in Syria?[99] In this case, the conflict must have taken place before A.D. 62. Thomas died A.D. 62. Nevertheless, it is more probable that the logion reflects a contest for the heritage of these personalities in a later period (about the time of the second version of the *Gospel of Thomas*). For the group using

---

93. With regard to Jesus speaking Greek, see Stanley E. Porter, *Criteria for Authenticity in Historical Jesus Research* (JSNTS 191; Sheffield, Sheffield Academic Press, 2000), 126–80, esp. 150ff.

94. See a similar reconstruction in DeConick 2002, 173.

95. I did not include the Platonizing sayings clearly developed from those belonging to the older layers; see the Gnostic mythological layer, as mentioned by Arnal 1995, 476–77.

96. It was Dunn 2003, 164, who correctly called them "de-eschatologized."

97. DeConick 2002, 192, 196.

98. Log. 28; cf. *Corp. herm.* VI,1ff.; cf. I,28ff.; NHC II/7 (*The Book of Thomas*), 143,22ff.

99. See Koester 1980, 435f.; cf. idem 1980a, 119.

this collection of Jesus' sayings it was Thomas who became the decisive figure. Unlike the groups that cherished the heritage of James the Just, the Thomas group separated from the synagogue about the same time as the mainstream church.

The Name of Thomas and the Thomas Writings

The *Gospel of Thomas* must not be mixed up with the *Infancy Gospel of Thomas*, which originated at the end of second century.

In the opening sentence of the *Gospel of Thomas* the author or mediator is called Didymos Judas Thomas—a name that in this form does not occur in the New Testament, another indirect hint in favor of the independent origin of some parts of the *Gospel of Thomas* from the canonical Gospels. Thomas, the added name, means "the Twin."[100] He obviously should be identical with Thomas Didymos, a disciple of Jesus (Mark 3:18 and parallels; John 11:16; 20:24; 21:2). Judas may have been his given name, which in the canonical Gospels was already forgotten.

According to the *Acts of Thomas* (ActTh 1 and 39) and the *Book of Thomas* (LibTh = NHC II/7, 138,5ff.) he was the twin of the Savior himself. The fact that the *Gospel of Thomas* does not explicitly mention this prominent family relation suggests that this was not a deeply rooted tradition. It may have been created by the author of the *Acts of Thomas* himself.

Before we discuss the origin and development of the *Gospel of Thomas,* we should mention all the books from the early Christian period ascribed to Thomas, the disciple of Jesus. The *Acts of Thomas* originate from the second part of the second or from the beginning of the third century, and the *Book of Thomas,* another text from the Nag Hammadi Codex II (NHC II/7), the first part of which is a dialogue of the Savior with Thomas and the second part, a revelatory monologue of the Savior, originated at least a generation after the third version of the *Gospel of Thomas.* Judas Thomas is the addressee of Jesus' revelations, but the writer who recorded them is, according to the prevalent understanding of the title (the last lines), a certain man who speaks about himself as Contender. This may be a symbolic title of the bearer of Jacobean parenetic traditions (see Jacob's struggle in Gen 32:23–33).[101]

The Thomas writings are all influenced by a spiritual piety molded by ideas of popular Platonism. This was one of the most influential spiritual streams of the early Roman period, which the writings mentioned above shared with many other texts, for example, with the *Dialogue of the Savior* (NHC III/5), a text that may help us to understand the *Gospel of Thomas.* Indirectly related to it are the *Odes of Solomon.*[102] The few instances of striking parallels to sayings 2, 22, 37, and 75 are found

---

100. "Twin" may be an inherited name, but it is more probable that the tradition supposed him to be a real twin brother.

101. The other understanding, represented by the older translations, was *The Book of Thomas the Contender;* see H.-M. Schenke, *Das Buch des Thomas* (NHC II/7, in idem, H.-G. Bethge, and U. U. Kaiser 2001, 279–91, here 281f.).

102. The *Odes of Solomon* originate in the same area as the *Gospel of Thomas* and share with it

in the *Acts of Thomas*.[103] Features that are common to all the writings ascribed to Thomas have not been identified, and the hypothesis of a school of Thomas cannot be substantiated.[104]

The first influential theologian of Syria was Tatian (ca. 120–180), whose *Diatessaron*, a harmonization of the four canonical Gospels, influenced liturgical life in Syria for almost two hundred years. Gilles Quispel has found some affinities between most of the sayings from the *Gospel of Thomas* that have parallels in the canonical Gospels and the *Diatessaron*,[105] which is however lost and can be reconstructed only from later translations and indirect sources.[106]

A lasting result of investigations in the Thomas literature is the confirmation of its appurtenance to the geographical and especially cultural and religious setting of Syria. In particular, Edessa, the capital of the kingdom of Osrhoéne, is the most ancient home of Christianity in that area. An indirect witness of the importance of Edessa for early Christianity is the apocryphal correspondence of Jesus with the ruler Abgar V from Edessa (4 B.C.–A.D. 7 and 13–50), which originated probably from the end of second century. Thomas has also been considered to be the missionary of Parthia and India. The *Acts of Thomas* from the beginning of the third century include the hymn called the Song of the Pearl (108–113), which expresses clearly the idea of the divine core of the human soul.[107] The hymn tells the story of a prince who came into a foreign country (material world) where he forgot about his origin and mission. Only the letter from the king, the Father, awoke him from his alienation. When reading the letter he realized "what was written concerned that which was engraved on my heart. And I immediately remembered that I was a son of kings . . ." (*Acts of Thomas* 111). The Hymn of the Pearl may be older than the rest of the *Acts of Thomas* and may have originated already in the second century.

The intellectual elements of the language of the *Gospel of Thomas* reveal that the intended readers belonged socially to the middle class, to urban Christians, not to monks from the countryside.[108]

The analysis of the structure of the *Gospel of Thomas*, in which Jesus, Thomas, and the witness who opens the book in the prologue speak to the reader, may suggest a reading in small conventicles of two or even one reader/hearer, as prompted in saying 30 and indirectly included in the theory of the pious person as the solitary one (log. 16:4 or 49). Such individual piety may eventually have led to the dissolution of the Thomas group as a social body.

Risto Uro summed up some of the typical features of Syriac Christianity of

---

the key role of the Word of God, but other teachings typical of the *Gospel of Thomas*, especially the divine core of humans, are not clearly present there.

103. See the commentary on the respective sayings.

104. Uro 1998, 5ff., 14, 16, 21.

105. Quispel 1967 and 1975; Klijn 1972; see the commentary below on log. 27.

106. Quispel 1959 and 1975; cf. the conclusions.

107. This was also one of the contemporary interpretations of mysteries, old religious festive activities expressing the mystery of life.

108. Khosroyev 1995, 241.

that time: a tendency toward asceticism and especially encratite[109] ideas (see log. 22; 27:1; 110; 114),[110] limited Hellenistic (European) influence, salvation understood as restitution rather than conversion, faith as mystical union with Christ, poetic language as the medium of theology.[111]

Nicholas Perrin (2002) presented a hypothesis according to which the original language of the *Gospel of Thomas* was Syriac. He supports this by citing numerous phrases and stylistic elements that are typical for Syriac and by noting the fact that the parts of the *Gospel of Thomas* that have parallels in the New Testament appear in a sequence corresponding to that of the *Diatessaron.*

The problem with this hypothesis is, first, its chronology. If the *Diatessaron* is ascribed to Tatian and originated about 170 A.D. in Syriac, and the Greek version of the *Gospel of Thomas* was translated from Syriac (as Perrin supposes), then we consequently have to suppose that it took some time for the Syriac text of the *Gospel of Thomas* or its Greek translation to come to Egypt and become widespread there. This signals trouble with the chronology, since Syriac literature started to develop not long before Tatian and the *Gospel of Thomas* in Syriac would have been one of the first texts written in Syriac. The second problem is that Semitic elements were present in the Greek of the eastern Mediterranean world, irrespective of the territory and the nature of the text.[112] The third problem with Perrin's hypothesis is the fact that we have no evidence for the existence of such a translation, such as fragments of the text, reports of ancient authors, and so forth.[113]

Since Syria was well Hellenized, as can be documented by the Gospel of John written in Greek, we have no reason to deny that the original language of the *Gospel of Thomas* was Greek and, as we have demonstrated, was much less pre-Gnostic than its Coptic translation.[114]

Between Gnosticism and Mainstream Christianity

The Gnostic[115] movement appears in the second century, even if its origins may reach as far back as the origins of Christianity. The *Gospel of Thomas*, even if it was undoubtedly popular in Gnostic groups, is not influenced by speculations from any Gnostic system. What we find in it is only a theology influenced by popular Platonic ideas that were accepted by the Gnostics. Nevertheless, it shares with Gnosticism the exhortation for a new self-understanding, liberation from the material world, and ascetic practices.[116]

---

109. Greek *enkrateia,* "restraint," mostly related to a Christian trajectory inspired by Tatian (ca. 120–173 A.D.) from Syria.

110. See DeConick 2002, 191f.

111. Uro 2003, 26–30; see also below on "The Theology of the Gospel of Thomas," 29–34.

112. M. Reiser, *Syntax und Stil des Markusevangeliums* (WUNT 2/11; Tübingen: Vandenhoeck & Ruprecht, 1984), 168.

113. See R. F. Schedinger's review of Perrin's book in *JBL* 122 (2003): 387–91, here 389.

114. DeConick 2002, 172.

115. For the terminology, see the note at the beginning of the introduction.

116. Valantasis 1999, 80.

Gnosis most probably originated in the first part of the second century A.D. at the fringes of Judaism. Its core was the teaching on the divine man, as may be deduced from Gen 1:26–27, which states that humans have been created "in the image" of God. A characteristic Gnostic idea is that humans have a divine substance but do not know it, because they are imprisoned in the material world. Most theories about the imprisonment of humans in matter consider the "fall" as a fatal error or even misunderstanding and not so much as guilt or sin. A rudimentary version of the Gnostic myth is seen in the words of the Son of Man in the tractate *The Dialogue of the Savior*, paragraph 135:[117]

> A seed of a power was deficient and it went down to (the) abyss of the earth. And the Greatness remembered (it) and he send the (Word to) it. It brought it up into (his presence) so that the First Word might not fail.

The Greatness is the highest God, the creator and omnipresent ruler of the spiritual world. The salvific act is the sending of his Word—the knowledge of the Divine. Salvation means, therefore, gaining the new knowledge, awakening from sleep. The motifs of repentance and conversion are not so crucial. Later, the Gnostics joined Christianity with the thought of some Gnostic thinkers, such as Valentinus in the mid-second century, combining Gnostic ideas with Christian teaching. Valentinus was in some respect an excellent interpreter of Paul's theology.

As to its origin, Gnosis is independent of Christianity,[118] but soon both of these streams penetrated each other, even if their roots were different and mostly antagonistic. We can imagine their relation as that of two bouquets of flowers. Each individual flower is kept together with its bouquet, but if we put the two bouquets next to each other we cannot tell to which some of the individual flowers belong. This is, however, a view influenced by Christian theology. The Gnostics would say that these were all flowers from the same spiritual meadow and that the bouquet is and can be kept together only by the spiritual secret teaching of Jesus. What the later church considered as the nicest flowers important for the proclamation of the Gospel and for the order of the common life was for the Gnostics, who considered themselves the spiritual core of the church, superfluous leaves trimming the bouquet.

The *Gospel of Thomas* is not Gnostic in the sense of Gnostic philosophy,[119] but its theology leads to a similar way of life as did Gnostic speculation. In many respects, the Christianity of *Thomas* could be considered a forerunner of the Gnostic distance from the world and focus on individual piety. That is why the *Gospel of Thomas* soon became popular among the Gnostics. The Thomas community joined

---

117. NHC III/5; 135,16–23.

118. In its substance, Gnosis is non-Christian and extra-Christian, even if we do not know whether it was pre-Christian. Arguments about a heterodox Jewish origin of one type of Gnostic teaching, in which the heavenly man (*anthrōpos*) was the redeemer, has been proposed by Schenke 1962. Gnostic systems, including one with a female protagonist (Wisdom, *sophia*), seem to be secondary developments.

119. A different view can be found in Popkes 2005, 111 or 142. The *Gospel of Thomas* can be understood in terms of the Gnostic paradigm of argument.

with Christianity and practiced an ascetic way of life. In theology they accepted Thomas's rejection of the ecclesiastical teaching about the sacrificial death of Jesus.

> Excursus: The statement about Jesus' death as sacrifice was difficult to understand, because after 70 A.D. many people did not know the meaning of the cult in the temple of Jerusalem. Already in the New Testament period, statements about the sacrificial death of Jesus were not understandable for non-Jews. The authors of New Testament texts re-interpreted it in new ways: the apostle Paul, by his teaching on justification; Mark, by his narration of the passion story as Jesus' existential crisis answered by God through the resurrection, and so forth. The Thomas group left this pivotal confession of the Christian majority undeveloped.

The piety of the Thomas community proved to be influential up to the present. In many Christian groups, a skeptical view of the world, the oppression of sexuality, and a spiritual interpretation of all biblical traditions are implicitly or even explicitly considered to be the very core of Christian piety. Practice and mostly also pastoral counseling are different, but silently the values of the *Gospel of Thomas* are accepted as an ideal by more Christians than we might imagine. What can be stressed as a counterbalance is the fact that the Jesus of history remains the norm ("feedback") of all Christian teaching, ethics, and piety. Through their canonization, the Gospels kept their position in Christian liturgy, and reading them helped to keep alive Jesus' vision of the kingdom of God as the inspiration for social renewal and as a promise for human history. These dimensions of life are not reflected in the *Gospel of Thomas*. I grew up in a country that was dominated by communists, and I started to study Gnosticism, because it was the Gnostic thinking that the Marxist ideology imposed on Christians. For the communists, it appeared to be more innocent than Christianity linked with the memory of the earthly Jesus.

Since the *Gospel of Thomas* displays some features of pre-Gnostic reflection, we occasionally may use the Gnostic model for interpretation of some of its ideas. But on the whole, the *Gospel of Thomas* is as Gnostic as was, for example, Philo of Alexandria, the great Jewish thinker, about one generation older than Jesus.[120] Historically, the *Gospel of Thomas* represents a piece of Jesus tradition developed and interpreted in the first part of the second century according to the theology of the Thomas community. Only some individual sayings preserve the oldest Jesus traditions. To explain the *Gospel of Thomas* by means of Gnosticism would be an anachronism.

The Theology of the Gospel of Thomas[121]

As we have mentioned, the ancient structuring of Jesus traditions in the *Gospel of Thomas* represents a literary and theological alternative to the canonical Gospels.

---

120. According to Jonas 1954, 70ff., Philo can also be considered a Gnostic. Jonas, however, uses a typological, not a historical, definition of Gnosticism.

121. See esp. Koester et al. 1989, 3–45.

Psychologically, the title "Gospel" supported its authority. The editor of the third version, who added the title "The Gospel according to Thomas," considered "Gospel" to be a short expression of Jesus' new presence in his community through his spiritually effective words.

In the *Gospel of Thomas, salvation* is not linked with Jesus' death as it was in the tradition of Lord's Supper (eucharist) (1 Cor 11:24; Mark 14:24; cf. 10:45); nor is it connected with his resurrection, as proclaimed in the earliest church (1 Cor 15:12; 1 Thess 1:10); rather, it is derived from Jesus' salvific teaching. This is the reason why the *Gospel of Thomas* does not need to narrate the passion story or report Jesus' resurrection as an act directly related to the earthly Jesus. Resurrection is the presence of the "living" Jesus in the hearts of his initiated followers, the liberation of the soul from the flesh of material body (log. 29, 87, 112). If we would like to know the spiritual background of this idea, we find in Philo of Alexandria a general consideration about individual souls as extensions of the one eternal divine soul.[122] God penetrates the visible world but transcends it at the same time.[123] The soul is the very image of God given to the humans, as it is written in Gen 1:27.[124] This is the inner reason for humans to live according to God.[125] It is a theology and anthropology different from Gnosticism, but not so distant from the intention of *Thomas.*

We have to suppose that these ideas were not just Philo's invention. Similar ideas associated with divine wisdom appear in the sapiential literature (Wis 9:9; Sir 24:9) and with the *logos* as the universal principle found in Greek thinking from Heraclitus to Philo.[126] Against this background it is understandable that one's true orientation in life is not derived from the memory of Jesus, as in the canonical Gospels, but rather from prophetic initiation into these spiritual instructions. In the mind of the editor, the text of the *Gospel of Thomas* is important not because it expresses the intention of Jesus of Nazareth himself but because it represents the wisdom and prophecy of the omnipresent and living (God) Father (log. 3:4). The exhortations (admonitions, paraenetic sentences) concentrate on seeking the spiritual kingdom, eternal life, the quiet center of the changing world (log. 50), a center of security (Latin, *centrum securitatis*) as the later mystics used to say.

In Thomas's *christology,* Jesus demonstrates and reveals God's will, and he lives in close relationship to God. Speculation about his divine nature as developed in the postbiblical period is not present here. We know that in history Jesus experienced a shattering of his own expectations, and the reader of the Synoptic Gospels learns that it was only his unique relation to God that remained valid and that God "raised [him] from the dead." In the *Gospel of Thomas,* this is not mentioned; the "living Jesus" teaches there an eternal wisdom; like a mystagogue, he initiates others into it (log. 17). From eternity he is one with God, the living Father, who in the world made visible through him his image and his will. This tendency helped to resolve the problems created by the delayed parousia (second coming of Jesus).

---

122. *Leg. alleg.* 1.39f.
123. *Quod deterius potiori insidiari soleat* 86.
124. *Leg. alleg.* 1.38; see Popkes 2006, 287f.
125. *De opif. mundi* 144; see Jervell 1960, 63ff.
126. E.g., *De somn.* II.242.

However, we cannot exclude that in fact it is a remnant of the ecstatic Easter experience (cf. 1 Cor 12:1–9) before the followers of Jesus formulated the confession of Jesus' resurrection.

The horizon of the kingdom of God moves to the background, and the reform concentrates on reshaping human personality. Its spiritual awakening is a fundamental fact, much as his own process of thinking was fundamental for Descartes. The fact that Jesus now leads to the sphere of eternal life and rest (Greek *anapausis,* log. 50, 60, 90) is more important than what he has done on earth. That is why the *Gospel of Thomas* does not use the title Messiah (Christ). Jesus is one with God (see log. 30); he is the one who offers unity with God to all humans and gives them to drink from the spring of life. This is more important than messianic titles.

Recently, Richard Valantasis stressed the pragmatics of encratite *piety* and *morals* as interpreted in the *Gospel of Thomas:* it was not ascetic in principle (see log. 6); the ascetic elements served as a means of self-formation and for developing a new identity for the believer.[127] Active charity is not rejected; rejected are only institutionalized deeds of piety (log. 14 and 6; cf. the commentary on log. 62:2). We can even find a compact layer of social ethics. The motivation is unusual: it is the other side of the distance from the world. Inside the group and its neighborhood, social solidarity is not neglected. We may call it *layer S* (social): Heal the sick in any country (log. 14:4); love your brother as you would your life (25:1–2); blessed are those who suffer from hunger to satisfy the belly of one who wishes it (69:2); give to them what is in your hands (88:2); do not lend at interest (95:1–2).

We have discussed the characteristics of salvation in the *Gospel of Thomas* as individual salvation from spiritual sleep, drunkenness, forgetfulness, and death. The concept is handicapped by the practical absence of statements about the meaning of history and the world as God's creation. The collector of the sayings most probably would not deny the identity of God as Savior and as Creator, but practically his soteriology (teaching on salvation) concentrates on individual human life. The problem is the human way of life: where we originate, who we are, and what are we going to became.[128] In most of the canonical traditions and texts, both projects are kept together through the apocalyptic horizon of the last judgment. At the end of history, God's truth will prevail. The kingdom of God was expected as a social and cosmic reality, and individual humans looked forward to their own resurrection and appearance before the judgment seat of God—the Son of Man or Jesus as his agent. In this way, social and personal hopes were integrated. The *Gospel of Thomas,* together with a wide range of spiritual traditions, narrowed the horizon of hope toward a personal union with God in the divine milieu.

The striking feature of the proper theology (*teaching on creation*) of the *Gospel of Thomas,* namely, the distance from the world in its present shape, is the other side of the present spiritual activity of the living Jesus. The ideal hearer of Jesus' instructions is called *monachos* ("a solitary one")[129] (log. 16, 49, and 75). Later it

---

127. Valantasis 1999, 71, 77.

128. A popular Gnostic theme, e.g., in *Excerpta ex Theodoto* 36 (preserved by Clement of Alexandria); NHC II/7 (*The Book of Thomas*), 138,8–10.

129. It is a Greek expression. Coptic took over many Greek words; more than 10 percent of its

became a term for hermits and then for monks. In the *Gospel of Thomas* it refers to people who disassociate themselves from alienated society and even family (log. 16; cf. 55) and who are deeply rooted (log. 40) in the image of the Divine (log. 84).[130] Such a person is wise and strives for the knowledge of God, the inner light (log. 33), for the treasure, which is so near and still hidden to most worldly people (log. 76). A radical expression of the distance from the world is the labeling of it as a carcass or "body" in logion 56 and logion 80.[131] But even this does not need to be interpreted as a document of Gnostic teaching that the world was the creation of a lower deity. In logion 12:2, we read very positively about the creation of the earth and the heavens. The visible world is probably supposed to be a corrupted part of God's creation. These ideas do not yet represent Gnostic theories as such, even if the Gnostics liked to read them.[132]

The spirituality and *pneumatology* (teaching on the Spirit) of the *Gospel of Thomas* is indirectly related to the post-Easter enthusiasm of Jesus' followers. The apostle Paul is also a theologian of the Spirit (the Lord is the Spirit [2 Cor 3:17]), and he put Jesus into a new context of a cosmic myth (Gal 4:4–7; 1 Cor 8:6).[133] Nevertheless, Paul's version of the mythic story is still linked with Jesus' death on the cross, which is a part of the human world and of history. The myth does not put Jesus in the shade; it even expressed his impact in the human world.[134] We have already mentioned that the *Gospel of Thomas* rejects Jewish cultic duties; it relativizes them, as do Jesus and Paul: logion 53 says that if circumcision were beneficial, then fathers would beget the children circumcised. "But the circumcision in the spirit has prevailed over everything." So the Spirit is the power linking humans with the Living One. This means that the *Gospel of Thomas* presupposes a Jewish setting but offers a radically new interpretation of its heritage, rejecting its traditional shape.[135] Reading the sayings of Jesus is not an intellectual bridge toward the truth of salvation. It calls for a mystic conversion.

Teaching about the church, in theological language called *ecclesiology*, is not developed as such. It is present in the portrait of Jesus' disciples, because in the Thomas group all members considered themselves to be disciples of the Son of the Living One. Nevertheless, the portrait of the disciples is negative. They do not understand Jesus' preaching. This motif occasionally appears in the canonical Gospels, especially in the Gospel of John (e.g., 4:31–36), but here it is a consequential image: Jesus has to teach them about piety, rebirth, resurrection, the Hebrew Bible, and its commandments.[136] The reader may identify them with the leaders of the mainstream church (they are entrusted with a field . . . , log. 21:2). When disciples

---

vocabulary. On *monachos*, see esp. Popkes 2006, 147ff.; but also see below, commentary on log. 16.

130. Some of these sayings have parallels in the Synoptic Gospels (log. 16, 55, 99, 101, 109, and 110), but the context or adaptation of the wording suggests a different interpretation (Uro 1998, 143ff.).

131. See the commentary on log. 60.

132. Doran 1987; see literature on log. 96; Lelyveld 1987, 150ff. (according to her, the *Gospel of Thomas* contains pantheistic features).

133. Mack 1988, 98ff.; this is what the Gnostics appreciated.

134. Pokorný 1987, 198ff.

135. Schröter (1997, 126–29) placed more stress on the Jewish background.

136. See log. 6 (12), 13 (14), 18, 37, 43, 51–53, 99.

question Jesus, he always ironizes their assumptions.[137] They are almost identical with the people of the world (log. 28), who may change their minds, become thirsty, and drink truth from Jesus' mouth (log. 28:2). The model of an ideal disciple is sketched in 19:2; he listens to the words of Jesus.

Some people have the way toward true discipleship open: Salome (log. 61:1–4) and, as we shall see, Mary Magdalene herself (log. 114:1–3). Peter, who tried to exclude Mary Magdalene from the group of disciples, is ridiculed. Mary will enter the kingdom of heaven. And, there are two men who already became true disciples: James the Just (log. 12) and above all Thomas himself (log. 13), who transcended even the position of a disciple: Jesus declared that he is not longer Thomas's teacher. Thomas is drinking (directly) from his mouth (13:5; cf. log. 108). Peter stands in his shadow (log. 13:2). This is the foundation of a reborn group of disciples, a true fellowship of Jesus.[138]

As for the *themes* of the sayings of the *Gospel of Thomas*, they can be thematically divided into those that concentrate on problems similar to those in the source of the Q sayings: sayings on the kingdom of God, apocalyptic sayings, and those (exhortations, proverbs, and others) that concentrate on the interpretation of apocalyptic traditions in a spiritualizing way. It does not mean that all the sayings from the second group were simply added from traditions that cannot be traced to Jesus, but only that some sayings were extended in a spiritual way. We have to take seriously the image of Jesus that the *Gospel of Thomas* is offering to us, but our critical knowledge about the dating and the structure of the *Gospel of Thomas* have to be preserved in order that we may define the relation of the Thomas portrait of Jesus to the Jesus of history.

The *eschatology* of the *Gospel of Thomas*, the spiritualizing interpretation of the ancient apocalyptical traditions of Jesus, is a remarkable achievement of the editors of the *Gospel of Thomas*; in its boldness it is similar to that of the authors of the Synoptic Gospels, who put Jesus traditions into the framework of Easter confessions. In the *Gospel of Thomas,* the stress shifted toward inner communication with God, seeking the kingdom of God and striving for it in the present time. Paul's teaching on justification by faith has at least one common dimension with this attitude: the present conversion and rebuilding of human personality.

The *Gospel of Thomas* with its spiritual interpretation of the kingdom of God can be understood as a development of some of the elements of Synoptic theology: the idea of the kingdom of God, as anticipated in the present by table fellowship (Mark 14:25 and parallels), cannot be derived only from the post-Easter development of Christian faith. Even the future expectation of the kingdom, so typical for Jesus in the Synoptic Gospels (Mark 1:14–15 and parallels), is not fully absent in the *Gospel of Thomas*. Its traces are preserved in logion 46:2 or 103, where the kingdom of God in its unexpected coming is compared with an attack of robbers: "Blessed the person who knows at which point (of the house) the robbers are going

---

137. See Brankaer 2004, 29. The idea of a Thomas ecclesiology is taken from J. Brankaer; cf. also the literature on log. 114:

138. See log. 19 and the commentary.

to enter. . . ."[139] But on the whole, the *Gospel of Thomas* avoids some of the themes so typical for the Jesus traditions and later ecclesiastical teaching on sin, *hamartology*. The *Gospel of Thomas* avoids some of its key terms, such as faith (*pistis*), sin (*hamartia*), and forgiveness (*aphesis*). Since faith means confidence in the kingdom of God as the victorious horizon of history, its absence from the *Gospel of Thomas* may be a symptom of an escapist piety.

Ideas typical of the *Gospel of Thomas* are grouped around the theme of *revelation*: it brings the mystery revealed to the group of the elect (log. 38), and revelation happens when people understand Jesus' sayings (log. 1), experience a conversion, and rebuild their scale of values (log. 110). The nearest analogy in the Synoptics is Mark 4:10–12 and parallels. In Mark, however, the mystery does not relate to a hidden and forgotten truth, but rather to something that is mysterious because of its inexhaustible depth.[140]

A final note: in spite of all that we have said, how difficult is it to express the difference between the *Gospel of Thomas* and the canonical Gospels! When reading the *Gospel of Thomas* we often feel sympathy for the Thomas group. Fascinating was its courage to proclaim the gospel about the Savior who taught them the way of inner renewal in the astonishing discovery of their own divine substance. It is a gospel full of joy in liberation from the alienated world and its values.

And yet, those who know the canonical Gospels may miss in the *Gospel of Thomas* the story of Jesus, his vision of the kingdom of God as a restoration of the Creator's intention, the relief of forgiveness, the atmosphere of social communication in anticipation of the kingdom, and faith as the experience of God's presence in human life, including real, physical death with its unique importance.

---

139. See the motif of the coming of the kingdom in other early Christian writings such as 1 Thess 4:13–18; the widespread presence of this motif confirms that it cannot originate in a later layer of Jesus traditions; see Allison 1998, 46ff.

140. Haufe 1972, 420.

II. Commentary

Opening sentence
and logion **1**
32,10–14a
page / lines

These are the hidden words
which the living Jesus spoke.
And Didymos Judas Thomas
wrote them down.
And he said:
"Whoever finds the meaning
of these words
will not taste death."

This saying has its Greek parallel in P.Oxy. 654,1–5; The text there is damaged but obviously corresponds to the Coptic version, with only the cognomen Didymos missing.

A

The reader of the first lines in fact hears three voices and the witness of three persons: Jesus, Thomas, and the narrator. Jesus is proclaiming the words of life, while the two others make the reader aware that it is Jesus who is speaking. All three invite the reader to become their fellow.[1]

The *hidden words* relate to a mystery that is proclaimed by Jesus and can thereby become manifest (log. 5, 6:5–6). The problem is that people are alienated. They "live in drunkenness"; they do not know that the most precious value ("pearl") is in their possession (log. 76); they do not seek it (log. 92); and they ignore God as the Father: they have not "ears to hear" (see log. 8:4 and 96:3).

The proclaimer is the *living* Jesus, which means that his words mark out the way of life and are themselves the light (log. 50). To hear and follow them means the resurrection of that which has already come (log. 51). Jesus participates in the power of God.

The words are the individual sayings. Each of them is like a call awakening the reader from his sleep ("the word is very near to you; it is in your mouth and in your heart for you to observe"),[2] but at the same time the words as a whole constitute a wisdom that offers a true orientation in life and may lead the awakened people on the true path. The living Jesus *spoke* to them: the past tense makes the reader aware of the fact that divine revelation has entered our temporal dimension. It has been comprehended in human words and *written* in letters and ink at a certain time, with which the proper names *Jesus* and *Thomas Didymos* are bound together. Nevertheless, this was not an aspect that the author of the *Gospel of Thomas* intended to

---

1. Valantasis 1997.
2. Deut 30:14, quoted by Paul in Rom 10:8.

stress. For him, Jesus—who is permanently bound together with God as the Living One—is an ever-present mediator of salvific wisdom. As we noted in the introduction, this author's christology is different in principle from the christology of death and resurrection, because in his view Jesus is the ever-present mediator between human beings and God. The incarnation has simply made people aware of him as a dimension of God's being. This is an idea that has its analogy in canonical texts such as 1 Cor 8:6 and hymns such as Col 1:15–20; Heb 1:1–2; or the prologue of the Gospel of John. In the mainstream church, however, the time of Jesus' temporal life "on earth" is clearly the normative period.

In the canonical Gospels Jesus declared that the time of his presence on earth would be limited by his death (Mark 2:20 and parallels), but here it is instead the spiritual death (the "not seeking") of individual human beings that limits or disrupts communication with God as mediated by Jesus: "Look for the Living One while *you* are alive" (log. 59).[3]

The sayings are eternally valid, since their source is the *living Jesus* who participates in eternal life. He "has" it (Rev 1:18), because he is the origin of the All; he is omnipresent and practically identical with the All, and still he transcends it (log. 77; cf. John 1:10).

"And he said" may grammatically refer to Thomas, but it is Jesus who speaks here—the Living One. Only the Living One can proclaim the overcoming of death (*will not taste death*). In the Gospel of John we read the words of Jesus: "I tell you, whoever keeps my word will never see death" (8:51; cf 5:24). Here this means anyone who finds the *meaning* or interpretation[4] (Gr. *hermeneia*[5]). To *find the meaning* means to realize that what the living Jesus says is a matter of life and death—the beginning and the end in the eternal sense and at the same time the beginning and end of the *Gospel of Thomas*: ". . . he sought the one" (log. 107) and "whoever has found himself" (log. 111:3).[6]

This interpretation presupposes a certain amount of information (teaching), but at the same time it is a matter of inner harmony with the divine truth. In the introduction we noted that in the Hymn of the Pearl from the *Acts of Thomas* the prince who lived alienated in a foreign country awoke from sleep and recognized the voice of his father, the king, only when he saw his father's letter. Reading it, he declared, "What was written concerned that which was engraved on my heart" (*Acts of Thomas* 111)[7]; this later narrative may nonetheless be used as a metaphor for the discovery of the meaning of the written words of the *Gospel of Thomas*. To find orientation in the alienated world means (1) to know the sayings of Jesus and (2) to achieve an inner resonance with their content, to understand that they medi-

---

3. A trace of the experience reflected in the Synoptics can be found log. 38:2. Cf. the comment on log. 60.

4. Attridge 1989.

5. The Greek expression is taken over in the Coptic translation. Coptic has taken over many Greek expressions.

6. Hedrick 1994, 117ff.

7. Translation by Elliott 1999.

ate the way to God himself, to the Father (see sayings 18 and 19, which also close with the promise of not tasting death).

B

The *Gospel of Thomas* concentrates more on the teaching of Jesus than on his person, because his teaching is the revelation of eternal wisdom. This reflects the pre-Easter mode of tradition, even if the individual sayings may have been reinterpreted or even formulated in the post-Easter period.

In Mark 4:10–12 we also find some elements of the concept of mystery as expressed in the sentences of the *Gospel of Thomas*. That the sayings have been written down is in fact a hint that they have been selected from a much broader tradition (cf. John 21:25). Thomas is already an interpreter who offers what in his opinion are the most important elements of the tradition.

Literature

Meyer 1991.
Hedrick 1994: 117–18.

2	(1) Jesus says:[8] "The one who seeks
32,14b–19a	should not cease seeking until he finds
	(2) and when he finds, he will be dismayed.
	(3) And when he is dismayed he will be astonished.
	(4) And he will be king over All."

This saying has its Greek parallel in P.Oxy. 654,5–9; the differences: ". . . will be [dismayed. When] he will be dismayed, he will be king. [And being king, he will attain re]st."

A

The general exhortation to *seek* linked to the promise of *finding* is repeated in log. 92 (second sentence in 94) and is explicated by parables: seeking the largest sheep (log. 107), finding a big fish (8), finding a pearl (76:1–2), or seeking (76:3) and finding a treasure (109). The concept of seeking implies the notion that it is not the result of human activity and creativity but that passivity is not a proper attitude either. Seeking is the proper activity in relation to a precious subject, which is in this case identical with God and eternal life. Real life is sometimes compared to a path, but the concept of search is an even more precise expression of this deep movement.

---

8. Where the saying is not put into any narrative frame, the grammatical form *peče* can be translated in the present tense.

Finding is the counterpart of seeking,[9] but it is surprising that it is described as a shock: "When he finds, he will be *dismayed, astonished*." This is the result of the encounter of a human being who has grown up in the alienated world with the holiness of God (*mysterium tremendum*). In the Greek version, the reaction is expressed by the verb *thambeuomai*, which can mean both admiration (Acts 3:11) and fear (Mark 10:24). The fact that in Coptic we find two verbs (to dismay = *šterter* and to be astonished = *ᶜr špēre*) may be explained as an attempt to express both dimensions of the Greek expression.[10] A parallel expression of astonishment from the mouth of Thomas appears in log. 13:4: "Teacher, my mouth cannot bear at all to say who you are like." The *Gospel of Philip* promises that even the name Christian will evoke a similar reaction: "If you say, 'I am a Christian,' the [world] will tremble" (NHC II, 62,26–35[esp. 32–33]).[11] This indirect reference to Jesus can clarify our understanding of astonishment as a response to an encounter with God: it is an astonishment at the fact that God can be encountered by humans at all: "Jesus says: If the flesh came into being because of the spirit, it is a wonder. But if the spirit (came into being) because of the body, it is a wonder of wonders" (log. 29).

The person who is astonished is called "the ruler." The translator decided on the expression "be king" as equivalent, since this has to be understood as a signal that the divine kingdom is being realized in the inner encounter with God. According to Luke 22:29–30, the disciples of Jesus will inherit the kingdom of God and become rulers and judges. They "*will attain rest*" (Greek, *anapauomai*). This is the passive dimension of becoming king. The rest is the counterpart of any activity; it is the content of the seventh day, of the Jewish Sabbath (Exod 20:8–11). In the Letter to the Hebrews 3:11, 18 (cf. *2 Clement* 5:5) heavenly rest is identical with the kingdom of God. It is the fulfillment of human life (log. 51; cf. 90). Death is the end of life, while "rest" is its fulfillment and salvation (log. 60:6).

In the Coptic version the final step is the ruling *over All*. Since God is the Lord over All, to participate in his rule means to be king over All. The All clearly means the visible and invisible world (Eph 1:22).

B

The second sentence of the saying has a parallel in the *Gospel of Hebrews* (fragment I: Clem. Alex. *Stromata* II.9.45.5, cf. V.14.96.3). The compiler of the *Gospel of Thomas* may have been dependent on the *Gospel of Hebrews* or else may have shared a common source with it.

Compared with the parallel to the first part of this logion in Luke 11:9–13 and parallels (Q) and in log. 94, the version in the *Gospel of Thomas* is enlarged by other elements, just as it is in log. 92.

The search for the kingdom of God, as represented in Luke 12:31 par (Q),

---

9. See a parallel in *Dialogue of the Savior* (NHC III/5; 129,14f.).

10. Another explanation of the difference: *Thaumazein* and *thambein* are the equivalents of the two Coptic verbs in Greek. One of them may be omitted by the scribe because of their similarity (Kasser 1961).

11. It is interesting to note that in the philosophy of the nineteenth and twentieth century, astonishment is the beginning of fruitful self-reflection.

assumes that the kingdom is a reality with an immediate influence on the present, but in its fullness is the absolute future of All. In the *Gospel of Thomas* the present dimension of the kingdom is dominant. This concept is explicated in the next logion (3) and in log. 113. In 1 Cor 4:8[12] Paul criticized a group in the Corinthian Christian community whose members "were already filled," "became rich," and were already "kings." They had obviously experienced the fulfillment of the beatitudes of Luke 6:20–21: "blessed are you the poor, since yours is the kingdom of God." Paul ridiculed them ("so that we might be kings with you") and sought to convince them that God's judgment was not something that human beings could take into their own hands. Possibly they were shaken and astonished, in the sense of the inner ecstatic experience of spiritual elevation. In that case the second logion would express the piety criticized by Paul—the piety of those who boasted among their fellow Christians (1 Cor 4:7) and judged them (1 Cor 4:5); in short, the piety of the Thomas group.

3

32,18b–33,5a

(1) Jesus says:
"If those who lead you say to you:
'Look, the kingdom is in the sky!,'
then the birds of the sky will precede you.
(2) If they say to you: 'It is in the sea,'
then the fish (pl.) will precede you.
(3) Rather: The kingdom is inside of you
and outside of you."
(4) "When you come to know yourselves,
then you will be known, and you will realize
that you are the children of the living Father.
(5) But if you do not come to know yourselves,
then you exist in poverty and you are poverty."

There are many gaps in the Greek version in P.Oxy. 654, 9–21, and it is most probable that instead of "The kingdom is inside you" it reads "The kingdom of God is inside you."[13] There is a similar omission of the word "God" in log. 27. The Coptic translator shortened the text.

A

The third saying demonstrates by parables that salvation means an inner transformation and that the kingdom of God cannot be bound to a certain space. *Lead* may carry a pejorative meaning such as "drag" or even "mislead." *Look . . .* often introduces an important statement, as in Luke 17:20–21, and the semantic axis *sky*

---

12. Cf. Luke 17:21.
13. See Attridge 1989, 100, 114.

and *sea*[14] is well known in the Bible in connection with the theme of the nearness of God: according to Rom 10:6–8 it is not necessary to look for the word of God in the heavens or in the abyss, since it is (through faith) in our heart. The imagery of this passage is influenced by Deut 30:11–14, where a similar nearness is characteristic of God's commandment. The elementary expression of this promise and experience is the Lord's Prayer: the praying person can immediately communicate with God and address him as father (Matt 6:9–13; Gal 4:6–7). Human beings have *to know themselves*, which means conversion and overcoming alienation from God.[15]

"Inside you and outside you" is most probably an expression of the idea that the divine kingdom is spiritually present inside the spiritually reborn person, but at the same time it is present everywhere in the divine area:[16] see logia 2, 51, 96, or 113.

On the *living God,* see the comment on the opening sentence.

Poverty, according to saying 29:3, means the "fleshly" world, which in its sinful existence is far removed from God's fullness of life and knowledge.

The meaning of the saying is: do not be lead astray, concentrate on what is essential for salvation.

B

A similar theme (the warning not to turn away from what is essential for salvation) can be found in Mark 13:21–23: "And if anyone says to you at that time. 'Look! Here is the Messiah' or 'Look: There he is'—do not believe it." The difference is that in Mark 13 the saying relates to the expectation of a Messiah and warns not against a nonspiritual concept of the Messiah but against false identification of him.

Logion 3, by contrast, contains instruction on how to interpret the expectation of the fulfillment of the eschatological promises; it is similar to log. 51 or 113.

Those who stress the eschatology of the present in Jesus' teaching see this saying as one of the pillars of their theory that Jesus was a teacher of the cynic kind, as discussed above in the introduction.[17] In some respects it reminds us of the interpretation of Jesus' teaching suggested by the famous biblical scholar Charles H. Dodd[18] even before the Nag Hammadi texts were published. We cannot interpret this as a mutilation of Jesus' teaching a priori, for although Jesus admittedly expected the imminent coming of the kingdom as an eschatological and cosmic event of absolute validity, he also mentioned the present impact of the coming kingdom. For example, in the parable of the sower (Mark 4:1–9; log. 9) we find the eschatological future as the time of harvest, but the present sowing as the moment of decision.

All the same, the shift in the *Gospel of Thomas* is clear. The social dimension

---

14. See Deut 30:11–14; Glasson 1976–77, 153.

15. Crossan 1991, 287–91.

16. According to Hippolytus, *Philos.* 5.7.20f., the Gnostic Naassenes spoke about the kingdom of God in the same way.

17. See above, in the section on Theology.

18. C. H. Dodd, *The Interpretation of the Fourth Gospel* (Cambridge: Cambridge University Press, 1953), 147f. [in commentary on John 11:23ff.].

is pushed into the background and the kingdom of God is conceived more as a kind of spiritual refuge or shelter.

The kingdom in the *sky* and in the *sea* may be a satirical transformation of the concept of kingdom of God. In the Gospel of Matthew the kingdom of God is called the "kingdom of the heavens" (a strictly Jewish formulation used to avoid pronouncing the word God), and here it is ironically called "the kingdom in the sky" and put on the same level as a "kingdom in the sea."

Literature

Glasson, T. F. 1976–77. "The *Gospel of Thomas*, Saying 3 and Deuteronomy 30:11–14," *Expository Times* 78:151–53.

4	(1) Jesus says:
33,4b–10a	"The person old in his days will not hesitate
	to ask a child seven days old
	about the place of life,
	and he will live.
	(2) For many who are first in place
	will become last,
	(3) and they will become a single one."

The Greek text in P.Oxy. 654, 21–27 is damaged and contains grammatical errors. The second sentence concerns the positive reversal of the positions: ". . . will become last, and those who are last in place will become first."

A

The saying reverses the conventions of this world. The norm is that the child has to ask the adults, but here it is the other way round. The aim is to reach the original unity that recognizes no difference between teacher and student, old and young, great and small. An analogical proposal about overcoming differences appears in log. 22; cf. *Corp. Herm.* IV,8.

In the Jewish context, a *seven-day-old child*, if a boy, was circumcised (see Gen 17:12; Lev 12:3; Phil 3:5).[19] Newly baptized Christians were compared to children (1 Pet 2:2). The baptized child belonged to God's people, like an adult. In Luke 2:46 we have the scene from the obviously old legend about the teachers listening to the twelve-year-old Jesus. The advantage of the child is that it is aware of its weakness and is thereby nearer to God: "I thank you, Father, Lord of heaven and earth, because you have hidden these things from the wise . . . and revealed them to children," says Jesus in Luke 10:21 par (Q).

---

19. An observation elaborated by Zuzana Vítková in her seminar work at the Centre for Biblical Studies in Prague.

The place of life is the divine kingdom as the area in which God is immediately present. Such an area is spiritual and may extend into the human soul or mind (cf. log. 3 and 24:3).

The exchange of the roles of the *first and the last* (cf. Mark 10:31 parr.) does not mean that the rich will be poor in the kingdom of God and vice versa. It is more an illustration of the different values that are valid in the face of God. For many, the coming of his kingdom means hope, but for others it means judgment.

The single one (Copt. *oua ouōt*) in this case has a negative meaning, different from the "single ones" as the translation of *monos* or *monachos,* which denotes those who are concentrated on God alone (log. 16, and elsewhere).

B

The saying has its parallel in Hippolytus's report on the Naassene Gnostics:[20] "The one who seeks me shall find me in children of seven years and older, since there I reveal myself in the fourteenth eon." The first sentence could be considered a variation on this logion, but the second is clearly a secondary development in line with Gnostic teaching.

Literature

Kee, Howard. 1963. "'Becoming a Child' in the *Gospel of Thomas*," *Journal of Biblical Literature* 82:307–14.

Klijn, A. F. J. 1962. "The 'Single One' in the *Gospel of Thomas*," *Journal of Biblical Literature* 81:271–78.

5	Jesus says:
33,10b–14a	(1) "Come to know what is in front of you and that which is hidden from you will become clear to you. (2) For there is nothing hidden that will not become manifest."

P.Oxy. 654, 27–31 has an addition at the end, namely, ". . . not be manifest, and (nothing) buried that [will not be raised]." This reconstruction is supported by a discovery described by Henri Ch. Puech. A linen funeral band from Christian Egypt bears the inscription, "Jesus says: There is nothing buried that will not be raised."

The Coptic version has a parallel in the Manichean book of *Kefalaia* (Chapters of a teacher) 163,28f., also preserved in Coptic translation—one of the few traces of the *Gospel of Thomas* in Manicheism.

---

20. See above in the introduction, in the section on attestation.

A

Logion 5 is connected with the following saying by the one common sentence of central significance: "For there is nothing hidden that will not become revealed (manifest)"; but the two sayings set this in different contexts. To interpret logion 5 we have to understand its first sentence, that is, how can the sensual perception of "*what is in front of you*"[21] make manifest "*what is hidden*"? This may be a short (elliptic) expression of an analogy: in the same way as we recognize the world in front of us, so it is possible to recognize the hidden truth by inner intuition.[22] The other interpretation would be that a realistic recognition of the consequences of Jesus' appearance in the life of Christian communities motivates us to search for the truth that will soon be manifest—for the kingdom of God (cf. 2 Cor 10:7).

The second sentence, about the *hidden that will become manifest* (the biblical analogy is in Mark 4:22 parr. and Luke 12:2; Luke 8:17 par. [Q]), means that what Jesus proclaimed, limited in space and time, has a universal future in the face of God.

B

The apparent Synoptic parallels might be considered an argument for the dependence of the *Gospel of Thomas* on the Synoptics. Nevertheless, the fact that the two sentences of the saying are linked together by words about the *hidden* (Gr. *kalyptō, kryptō*; Copt. *hōp*) and *revealed* (Gr. *phaneron eimi/ginomai*; Copt. *ōnh ebol/ qōlp*), might equally plausibly suggest that the two original sayings had already been combined (conflated) in the pre-Synoptic tradition.[23]

In Matt 10:26 the saying on the hidden and the revealed appears in the context of an exhortation to the disciples not to fear detractors, while it appears in the more spiritual sense in the later Christian-Gnostic literature[24] and in the Manichean texts.

The saying is one of the small group of logia that explicitly contains an exhortation and a view into the future. In the most ancient Jesus traditions the eschatology of the future ("... *will become clear, manifest*") meant the coming of the kingdom of God. Since the author (collector) of the *Gospel of Thomas* was not explicitly oriented to an apocalyptic expectation of the kingdom, he would not have produced such a saying himself. The addition about *resurrection* in the Greek version may, however, be a post-Easter accrual expressing the hope of general resurrection, based on the resurrection of Jesus (cf. 1 Cor 15:20ff.), and it formally corresponds to additions such as those we we find in Matt 12:40 (Jonah in the belly of the sea monster as an image of Jesus's death and resurrection; compare with the Lukan parallel in Luke 11:30 [Q]—the story of Jonah was a prophetic sign).

In the New Testament we find the metaphor "image of God" for the Savior in Col 1:15 (cf. 3:10; 2 Cor 4:4). In Gnostic interpretation the "image" was a mirror of

---

21. Hedrick 1994, 244: a semiticism.
22. Valantasis 1997.
23. Patterson 1993, 21.
24. E.g., NHC II/5; 125,17–19.

the divine nature in the human soul. Human beings could recognize themselves in the Savior. (*Corp. Herm.* XI, 20).

Literature

Puech, H.-C. 1978b. "Un logion de Jesus sur bandelette funéraire (1955)," in idem 1978a, 59–62.

6
33,14b–23a

(1) His disciples questioned him, (and) they said to him: "Do you want us to fast? And in which way should we pray and give alms. And what diet should we observe?"
(2) Jesus says: "Do not lie.
(3) And do not do what you hate.
(4) For everything is disclosed in view of <the truth>.[25]
(5) For there is nothing hidden that will not become revealed.
(6) And there is nothing covered that will remain undisclosed."

P.Oxy. 654, 32–40 does not include sentence 6 and has a different reading in sentence 4; see below note 25. The question about fasting is also posed less fundamentally: "How should we fast?"

A

In Jewish piety, *prayers*, fasting (diet), and, above all, *almsgiving* were considered the basic good deeds (Tobit 12:8). According to Matt 6:1–18, Jesus offered a new interpretation of this praxis but he did not reject it. Sentences 2, 3 and 4 of this saying bear witness to the same tradition with a strong stress on inner acceptance of God's will and a new orientation in human social relations.

The sayings on the *lie* and *truth* relate to each other. Truth is the opposite of the lie as un-truth. The lie denoted all perverted and deviant human relations: Col 3:9; cf. Eph 4:25; *Did* 3:5; Matt 5:37.

Inside this chiastic literary structure we find the Golden Rule in a shortened version: *And do not do what you hate.* As a principle it expresses one of the main dimensions of justice as it was experienced in antiquity; in the Bible we find it in Matt 7:12 and Luke 6:31 (Q). It is in fact a rational rule, even if people in their blindness do not realize it, but here it is also a hint in the direction of the future in history and in interhuman relations. In the Bible, the validity of this rule is based

---

25. The Coptic text reads "in view of heaven." It may be a scribal error (the Copt. *pe* instead of *me*).

supraethically on God's love for humankind. This is the reason why the exhortation to love, as we read it in logion 25, is likewise not merely an ethical imperative but has deeply based pragmatics.

Love can intervene as the prospect of new foundations for relations originally defined in another way.[26]

B

In the most reliable traditions about Jesus, the *revelation of the (now) hidden* meant the coming of the kingdom of God. In the *Gospel of Thomas* its meaning is more that of a revelation identical with inner self-understanding, as in logion 3:3. Nevertheless, the presence of such traces of the apocalyptic dimension of the kingdom is a supporting argument in favor of the authenticity of the eschatological proclamation of Jesus. At the same time, it confirms the reliability of the tradition that precisely this proclamation was a point of issue between Jesus and his disciples. The solution offered by the *Gospel of Thomas* is one of the possible reactions to the demanding complexity and social impact of Jesus's proclamation of the kingdom.

Our interpretation of the preserved text would be modified if we considered logion 14 to be Jesus's original answer to the question of the disciples. It is an answer that unlike Matt 6:1–18 simply implies abandonment of the Jewish acts of piety.

This might, however, be explained in terms of a scribal error in copying the Greek text. The scribe may have jumped by mistake to a saying that discusses the Golden Rule, then added the end of the preceding saying and finally, having reread a larger part of the text and discovered that he had neglected to copy Jesus' answer to the question of the disciples from the beginning of the saying, added it as logion 14.

The original wording of the Greek text from which P.Oxy. 654 or some of its predecessors were copied would consequently read: "'Do you want us to fast? And in which way should we pray and give alms? And what diet should we observe?' Jesus said to them: 'If you fast you will bring sin for yourselves, etc. . . .'" (follows the rest of logion 14:1–3).

For the possible dependence of log. 6:6 on the Synoptics or any other common source, see the paragraph on the relation between the *Gospel of Thomas* and the Synoptics in the introduction.

The tradition of criticism of ritual piety is also documented in *Didache* 8:1–3 (about A.D. 110).

7	(1) Jesus says: "Blessed is the lion,
33,23b–28a	that a person will eat
	and the lion will become human.
	(2) And anathema is the person

---

26. Ricoeur 1990, 62ff.

whom a lion will eat
and the lion will become human."[27]

The Greek version from P.Oxy. 654,40–42 is so damaged (only fragments of five words) that it can be only partially reconstructed by means of analogy with the Coptic version and cannot be used as evidence of the Greek text.

A

The saying speaks of how a *lion,* who in the hierarchy of creatures has a lower position than *human beings,* can profit from contact with humans, even if he becomes their food.

In antiquity, to *eat* meant to transform the eaten subject into the eating person, as it still does in some primitive totemic societies today. Thus, the first sentence of the saying expresses the value of the humanity (*Blessed . . .*) that absorbs and so elevates animal elements, while conversely the second sentence warns (on pain of *anathema = to be cursed*) against the lion—the animal power itself overcoming and swallowing the human soul.

B

The main textual problem is the concluding sentence. It may be that a scribal error produced it instead of the more logical conclusion: "and the person will became a lion."[28] We have positively identified several scribal errors in the preserved Coptic copy, and this makes it more likely that there are other errors. Admittedly, recent scholarship has preferred to keep to the preserved version, because in the anthropology of the *Gospel of Thomas* the human soul is eternal, even if hidden and imprisoned in a lion's body. In fact, however, sayings 87 and 112 support the hypothesis of scribal error: "Woe to the soul that depends on the flesh" (log. 112:2;[29] cf. 87:2).

For later Gnostic readers this saying was obviously quite attractive. In the tractate *On the Origin of the World* from the second codex (NHC II/5) we find a drawing shaped as a *gemma* and presenting the god Jaldabaoth with a lion's head, and other similar Gnostic ideas can be found elsewhere.[30] This may have been inspired by the metaphor of God as lion from Job 10:16 or Hos 5:14. The lion's face symbolizes the arrogance of the power of alienation and darkness.

In the *Gospel of Thomas* the image of the lion was most probably inspired by Plato's *Politeia* (588B–589B), copied in Coptic translation in NHC VI, 48,16–51,23. There the lion represents the animal part of human nature. A more detailed discus-

---

27. Most probably a copyist's error; "and the person will be the lion" would be the original text.

28. So Ménard 1975; and Kasser 1961.

29. See the survey in the commentary on log. 112.

30. E.g., NHC II/1, 11,35–12,4; *Pistis Sophia* (a Gnostic text from Codex Askew, third century), 31; cf. Vítková 2; Jackson 1988.

sion of the idea that the spirit always dominates the animal part as soon as it is realized as spirit appears in the *Gospel of Philip* (NHC II/3; 54,18–55,5).

Literature

Jackson, H. 1988. *The Lion Becomes Man*. Atlanta, GA: Society of Biblical Literature.

Vítková, Zuzana. 2003. "The Lion in the Gospel of Thomas," Czech manuscript. Prague: Center of Biblical Studies.

8
33,28b–34, 3a

And he says:
(1) "The person is like a sensible fisherman,
who cast his net into the sea
and drew it from the sea filled with little fish.
(2) Among them the sensible fisherman
found a large, fine fish.
(3) He threw all the little fish
back into the sea, (and) he chose the large fish effortlessly.
(4) Whoever has ears to hear should hear."

A

The parable has its analogy in Matt 13:47–50:

> Again the kingdom of heaven is like a net that was thrown into the sea and caught fish of every kind; when it was full they drew it ashore, sat down, and put the good into the baskets but threw out the bad. So it will be at the end of the age. The angels will come out and separate the evil from the righteous and throw them into the furnace of fire, where there will weeping and gnashing of teeth.

In the *Gospel of Thomas* we find several divergences from this version: The *sensible* (wise) *fisherman* seems to act illogically. He throws his catch back to the sea and keeps only one *large fish*.[31] It is because the large fish, like the large branch in logion 20:4, the largest sheep in logion 107:2, and the pearl in logion 76:1, represents the revealed mystery of the divine core of humanity—the human soul. The wise fisherman is an archetypal figure, like the vigilant master of the house (log. 21:5) or the prudent merchant from logion 76:2. Everyday experience, re-formed and transformed, helps the reader find orientation in human life.

The concluding exhortation, *"Whoever has ears to hear should hear,"* leads

---

31. This may already have been influenced by the notion of fish as an acrostic of the words of Christian confession and symbol of Christians; see Plisch 2007, 56.

the reader to deeper self-understanding in the face of the proclamation of God's kingdom. It does not hint at any coded meaning hidden under the surface of the text, as has often been thought.

B

The well-known parable is presented in a form stressing the value of the human soul. This is most probably a secondary development in comparison with the Matthean version, which stresses the last judgment. The Coptic translator or probably the reviewer of the Greek version (we have no surviving Greek version of this saying) must have known the biblical version. Secondary developments of fishing traditions in a different direction include transformations of memories of fishing with Jesus into models of mission: see Luke 5:1–11 and John 21:1–14.

In relation to our saying, the Matthean version is the older one. Thomas has developed a version that is slightly different from that of Matthew. Instead of the kingdom of heaven, the subject of the developed metaphor is a *person*. And it is the *soil* that gives the fruit, not the *seed*.[32] The kingdom is interpreted individually; it is "personalized." And the fruit does not come from the seed but from the power inside the soil. The theme of judgment and the coming of the kingdom as social or even cosmic phenomenon are absent or at least not mentioned.[33]

This is a version independent of the Synoptics, but not older than the short version.[34]

A similar transformation from eschatology to a new self-understanding is evident in the concluding exhortation, which originally belonged to an apocalyptic tradition (Mark 4:9; Rev 2:7; cf. log. 21:5–11).

Literature

Baarda, Tjitze. 1991. "'Chose' or 'Collected': Concerning an Aramaism in the *Gospel of Thomas* and the Question of Independence," *Harvard Theological Review* 84:373–97.

Morrice, William G. 1983–84. "The Parable of the Dragnet and the *Gospel of Thomas*," *Expository Times* 95:200–272.

9	(1) Jesus says:
34,3b–13	"Look a sower went out.
	He filled his hand (with seeds),
	(and) he scattered (them).
	(2) Some fell on the path

---

32. Schrage 1964a, 46–47.

33. Morrice 1983–84, 272.

34. Baarda 1991 argues from the textual signs common to log. 8 and the *Diatessaron* traditions in favor of the priority of the version from the *Gospel of Thomas*.

and the birds came and pecked them up.
(3) Others fell on the rock,
and did not take root in the soil,
and they did not put forth ears.
(4) And others fell among the thorns,
they choked the seeds, and the worm ate them.
(5) And others fell on good soil,
and it produced good fruit.
It yielded sixty per measure
and one hundred and twenty per measure."

A

A *sower* who *went out* is Jesus as the revealer who came from the divine area to the world to bring the *seeds* of knowledge. Many people failed to accept the seeds because they were blinded by earthly preoccupations and care (*path, rock, thorns*), but those who accept them bring an unexpected spiritual yield, much larger than a real yield. The third sentence poetically expresses the relationship between the depth of faith (*root*) and its growth (*put forth ears*).[35]

B

The parable, known from Mark 4:3–9 parr., from the very beginning assumed an apocalyptical horizon (harvest), which is well expressed in the Synoptic version. The ecclesiastical interpretation, preserved in a special explanation (Mark 4:13–20 parr.), concentrates on the allegorical explication of the dangers and obstacles preventing the hearers from accepting the proclaimed gospel. The *seed* is able to receive new life from the *soil*. In antiquity this was a widespread religious idea.[36] The allegorical explication would have fitted well into the development of this idea to express inward conversion in the *Gospel of Thomas*, but the compiler was evidently unfamiliar with it. For several influential scholars this has been an argument for the origin of Thomas sayings in a tradition independent of the Synoptics.[37] Their argument is valid. In the groups influenced by Platonism, as propounded, for example, by the learned Jew Philo of Alexandria, allegory was widely used as a means of spiritual interpretation of texts. The parable was definitely taken over from a tradition independent of the Synoptics.

Literature

Crossan, J. Dominic. 1973. "The Seed Parables of Jesus," *Journal of Biblical Literature* 92:244–66.

---

35. Plisch 2007.
36. See the description of the Eleusinian mysteries in Hippolytus, *Philos.* 5.8.29f.
37. Cullmann 1966, 585; Hunzinger 1960; Patterson 1993); 22f.; or Crossan 1973, 250f.

10	Jesus says:
34,14–16a	"I have cast fire upon the world,
	and see, I am guarding it until it blazes."

A

Fire meant God's judgment on human sins (Matt 3:10 par.; 1 Cor 3:15; cf. log. 13:8) or the testing of the believers (1 Pet 1:7; Rev 3:18); but here the fire is obviously Jesus' potent proclamation of the kingdom and its inner power, which even changes human minds.

B

The problems start with the translation of this saying. Unlike in Luke 12:49 (Q),[38] where the saying ends with "and how I wish it were already kindled!" (Gr. *anaptomai*), in this logion we read *"and see, I am guarding it until it blazes."*[39] Another possible translation is: "I am protecting it (the world) until it blazes"[40] or even "until it burns." Less probable, even if grammatically possible, is the rendering "until (the world) burns." The Coptic version may simply be a free translation, but it might also be a conscious adaptation reminding readers/hearers that the legacy of their small community will become a light for all the world.

The interpretation of this saying has been a problem since its earliest attestation. The *fire* was originally the power of apocalyptic transformation—a transformation "as through the fire"[41]—a new beginning. The next parallel in Thomas is logion 82, about Jesus acting as a fire, and logion 16 about the apocalyptic fire and struggle. A parallel is also preserved in the *Gospel of the Savior* (Unknown Berlin Gospel) 107,42–47, which introduces the Savior's call for his disciples (readers) to gather around him. A parallel is mentioned by Origen.[42]

The problems with its interpretation indirectly support its authenticity. Since it was already not quite comprehensible in meaning in the third generation, its survival in the transmitted text was most probably due to a consciousness of its age.

11	(1) Jesus says:
34,16b–25a	"This heaven will pass away,
	and the (heaven) above it will pass away.
	(2) And the dead are not alive,
	and the living will not die.

---

38. See Schürmann 1968.
39. This is the NHD translation.
40. This is the alternative translation suggested by the authors of NHD.
41. See 1 Cor 3:15 on salvation through God's judgment.
42. *Homil. Lat. in Jerem.* 3,3.

(3) In the days when you consumed
what was dead, you made it alive.
When you are in the light, what will you do?
(4) On the day when you were one,
you became two. But when you become two,
What will you do?"

A

The logion is, in fact, a small collection of sayings. All of them are aphoristic in style and provoke the reader to reevaluate his or her thinking.

The first two sentences are linked by the eschatological prospect. The opening phrase has its parallel in Mark 13:31 parr. (*This heaven will pass away*) and develops strange eschatological ideas. The meaning of the first sentence seems to be self-evident; it proclaims the temporary nature of the visible and invisible creation. In log. 111:1 we find another parallel.

The second sentence, which speaks of the *dead* and the *living,* demands a metaphoric interpretation. There are people in the world who live without contact with the true spiritual life. They are spiritually dead and will not be *alive* in the kingdom. They are as dead, that is, without any future prospect, just as this world (cf. log. 56 and 80; the world as carcass), in which people forget their origin in God. The living are those who still possess the knowledge about God and who will find the fulfillment of their life.

In our comment on the seventh saying we mentioned that to *consume* (sentence 3) means to transform the food into our inner self. Here the idea is explicitly proclaimed. The basic idea is expressed in a short statement and followed by two rhetorical questions. The first states that the one who is *in light* (enlightened) should share his light with others, as expressed in sayings 24 and 50. This may be a short expression of a logical chain: dead—alive—light.[43]

The second question (sentence 4) is a unit that developed its special meaning (semantics) from the biblical story of the creation of woman from Adam's rib (Gen 2:21–24).[44] *You were one, you became two* means Adam = Adam + Eve. This is related to real human beings in their sexual polarity (see log. 114) but also serves as an image of the inner split in human beings. The question is an exhortation to those who have *become two* to return to inner unity. It may apply explicitly to those who were married as man and wife. Marriage is obviously rejected on principle: the "solitary" are the elect, as is expressed in log. 23 and 75.

To do (Copt. *eire*) does not relate to everyday human activity but rather to misdirected steps toward salvation, since two persons (a pair) are split and unable to attain unity with God. Salvation is rest, the eternal Sabbath (log. 50, 51, 60, 90), and the activity that it requires is the inner, intuitive unity of a single person with God.

---

43. Reconstruction in Plisch 2007.
44. Valantasis 1997.

B

The short sayings and rhetorical questions are typical of the Jesus traditions. The apocalyptic horizon relates to Jesus, as well as the view of the eschatological future as the space for a new life. What is different here, however, is the understanding of the unity of human personality. In the Synoptic tradition, the exhortation for unity is rooted in the validity of marriage as a unity of man and woman blessed by God himself (as we find in Mark 10:9ff. parr.; cf. Luke 16:18 par. [Q]). The intention of logion 11 is a reinterpretation of Jesus' teaching in a way that stresses the ascetic repression of sexuality. The Gnostics developed this idea into the theory of the creation of woman as the beginning of human catastrophe: In the *Gospel of Philip* (NHC II, 68,22–26) we read: "When Eve was still in Adam, death did not exist. When she was separated from him, death came into being. If he enters again and attains his former self, death will be no more." This is a Gnostic teaching that involves the belief that the Creator of this world was a lower deity. The latter still found an indirect argument for celibacy in Matt 19:12 (eunuchs for the sake of the kingdom of heaven), [45] yet this was not considered to be a model for the life of Jesus' followers in general, but just one of the possible ways of preparing for the apocalyptic change.

Later, the Gnostic teaching that sexuality was a lower part of life was to influence the church, and the idea has afflicted Christianity up to the present time.

12
34,25b–30a

(1) The disciples said to Jesus:
"We know that you will depart from us.
Who (then) will rule over us?"
Jesus said to them:
"Wherever you have come from,[46]
you should go to James the Just,
for whose sake heaven and earth
came into being."

A

James is Jesus' brother. According to Gal 2:9, 12; and Acts 21:18, he was the leader of the Christian community in Jerusalem,[47] and according to the *Gospel of Hebrews* was the first to be addressed by Jesus when he shared a table with his disciples after his resurrection.[48] From the second century, James was called "*the Just*," because of his martyrdom.[49]

---

45. Cf. 1 Cor 7:8.
46. The text may have been corrupted. It could also be translated as "Wherever you will have come to ..." (NHD).
47. See also their testimony in Eusebius, *Hist. Eccl.* 2.23.4–18.
48. Jerome *De viris illustribus* II (r. 362).
49. See the second *Revelation of James* (NHC V/4; 44,14–15); on the martyrdom, see the testi-

Wherever you have came from: The obvious meaning is that the place of origin of the followers of Jesus, or of the hearers or readers of this saying is not important.

The concluding praise of James (*for whose sake heaven and earth came into being*)[50] shows the links between the *Gospel of Thomas* and the group of James's disciples. If we read it together with the previous saying according to which the heavens would pass away, the significance of James acquires a cosmic dimension.[51]

B

A dispute about priority among Jesus' disciples is mentioned in Mark 9:34ff. parr., in which Jesus forbids discussion of the matter. Both in Mark and the *Gospel of Thomas* the question is provoked by the imminence of Jesus' death. In the *Gospel of Thomas,* the passion of Jesus is not mentioned, but it is presupposed here and in sayings 38, 55, 58, 68, and 69.[52] The praise of James in the *Gospel of Thomas* may express the solidarity of the groups of James and Thomas when they were criticized by the mainstream church, which looked to the apostle Peter as its heraldic figure (Matt 16:16f.). In the declaration from 1 Cor 15:3b–5 (its supporters are enumerated in 1 Cor 15:5–8), the leading role of Peter is justified by the priority of his encounter with the risen Lord even if the model of collegial leadership (Gr. *ekklēsia*) is still attested in Matt 18:16–17. Here, in the combination of sayings 12 and 13, we observe an attempt to create another group, whose teaching was supposed to be the tradition of Jesus as it was expressed in the *Gospel of Thomas* (see Introduction: Theology). The Thomas group also acknowledged the authority of James and evidently accepted his disciples in its communities. Later Jewish Christianity coexisted with Gnosticism.

These were problems that arose at the end of the first century, when Christians experienced the absence of the apostolic generation as a problem of personal leadership. They compensated for the absence of the apostles, the eyewitnesses of Jesus, by reading and commenting on their books. As we have mentioned in the introduction, almost all of the texts that circulated under the name of the apostles are pseudepigrapha, texts that are linked with the name of an apostle on a secondary basis.

13
34,30b–35, 14a

(1) Jesus said to his disciples:
"Compare me and tell me whom I am like."
(2) Simon Peter said to him:
"You are like a just messenger."

---

mony of Hegesippus (second century) preserved by Eusebius (*Hist. Eccl.* 2.23.4–18); for other evidence see Plisch 2007, 64.

50. It originates in a Jewish Christian setting; on the parallels with the Talmud, see Leipoldt 1967.

51. Brankaer 2004, 12.

52. See Voorgang 1991, 145–46.

(3) Matthew said to him:
"You are like an (especially) wise philosopher."
(4) Thomas said to him:
"Teacher, my mouth <can> not bear at all
to say whom you are like."
(5) Jesus said: "I am not your teacher.
For you have drunk, you become intoxicated
at the bubbling spring that I have measured out."
(6) And he took him (and) withdrew,
(and) he said three words to him.
(7) But when Thomas came back to his companions,
they asked him: "What did Jesus say to you?"
(8) Thomas said to them: "If I tell you
one of the words he said to me,
you will pick up stones and throw them at me,
and fire will come out of the stones
(and) burn you up."

A

This is again a discussion of Jesus' true identity, as in Mark 8:27–30 parr. *Peter* is the first to answer the question of Jesus. He compares Jesus to a *messenger*. It must, nevertheless, be noted that the term *angelos,* taken over from Greek, may be used here in the specific sense of angel as a celestial being, a meaning quite common in the Hellenistic period (cf. Luke 2:9). In 1 John 1:5 Jesus is bearer of the message (Gr. *angelia*) that God is Light, but in Christian doctrine Jesus was clearly more than a messenger or angel. Unlike in Matt 16:16, here Peter's answer is evidently inadequate and serves to point up the superior answers of the other disciples.

According to *Matthew* Jesus is an (especially) *wise philosopher*. This may be considered a higher degree of comprehension of Jesus. According to Luke 7:35 par. (Q), Jesus is wisdom itself. Philosophy may mean simply a teaching, but the notion of philosophy as discussion of the deepest problems of the world and mankind may already be present here. In the *Tripartite Tractate* from NHC I it is declared that neither music, nor rhetoric, nor medicine and philosophy can express the ineffable character of God (110,14). Here philosophy is (a) a wise teaching,[53] and it may already be (b) a special kind of scholarly dispute. But even Matthew's answer is insufficient.

It is *Thomas* with whom the series of answers culminates. He says that his *mouth cannot say who Jesus is like*. This is not flattery; it means that Jesus is like God himself. This is what Thomas has expressed in an apophatic (negative) way: God as ineffable, invisible, imperishable, and so forth. And so too is Jesus. This is

---

53. See the characteristics of Jesus as legislator in the pseudepigraphic letter of Mara bar Serapion (page 46) originating from about the beginning of second century.

the language of mystical movements throughout human history. It supposes that sinful human beings can bear God's presence only when that presence is revealed indirectly. Otherwise they would be killed by his holiness.[54]

The title "Christ" ("the Anointed One"; Gr. *christos,* Hebr. *māšīah*) is avoided, and the Thomas group did not use it. Effectively this meant that Thomas had reached the goal of any discipleship; that is, he had transcended it (*I am not your teacher* [log. 13:5]) and achieved a still closer, celestial, relation to Jesus and God as the Living One.

Drinking from a spring means obtaining true knowledge (log. 108; cf. John 4:10–14). In *Acts of Thomas* 147 the sober *drunk*enness (Lat. *sobria ebrietas*) mentioned is evidently mystical knowledge (Acts 2:13, 15f.).[55] What Jesus says about Thomas in sentence 5 means that he has already reached the presence of God. Therefore, Jesus can say, "*I am not your teacher.*"

The *three words* from the sixth sentence remain a mystery. The opinions of scholars differ,[56] although they agree that it was evidently an extremely significant revelation bringing Thomas near God.[57] That it was a mystery from the very beginning and not only for us in the twenty-first century is confirmed by an allusion in the *Acts of Thomas* 47: "You told me three words with which I am inflamed, but which I cannot communicate to others," says Thomas in a prayer praising Jesus as man and as God.

The *spring* is a metaphor for the source of life, at least according to the *Discourse on the Eighth and Ninth* (NHC VI/6, 58,13–17).

Stoning was an old Jewish punishment for blasphemy; it is mentioned in early Christian literature and evidently illegally practiced in Jesus' time (see John 8:5 [the woman caught in adultery]; Acts 7:54, 58f. [Stephen]).

On *fire.* see the comment on logion 10.

B

This extended saying is analogical to the story about Jesus' identity in Mark 8:27–30 parr. The disciples, at Jesus' instigation, try to express his identity and dignity in words, and in the end one of them hints at his real meaning. Yet the saying here contradicts the story, in which Peter played the central role, since it is *Thomas* who is starring this time. The scene culminates with Jesus offering instruction on how to enter God's presence (sentence 5).

The basic plot is the search for the true identity of the hero (in the literary sense), which in the theory of literature is called the *anagnōrisis*, recognition or discernment. The other people in the story learn the true identity of Jesus, and the

---

54. On the ineffability of God, see NHC I/5, 52,6–54,1.

55. Cf. Philo *De Ebrietate* 148; on spiritual ecstasy, see Hippolytus *Philos.* 5.8.6f.; cf. Eph 5:18.

56. Arai 1992: "I am equal to God"; Grant and Freedman 1960: "Kaulakau, Daulasau, Zéesar" [from the Naassene tractate, according to Hippolytus *Philos.* 5.8]; Puech 1978: the names of Trinity; Schenke 1986: "You shall not die until I come"; in Coptic all these suggestions can be expressed in three words.

57. Leipoldt 1967.

reader/hearer learns through the story the precious nature of the revelation given to him and the value of his own confession.

Here Thomas, whose role we discussed in our comments on the beginning of the *Gospel,* plays the part of the ideal disciple of Jesus and prototypical Christian.[58]

Literature

Arai, Sasagu. 1992. "Zu 'Drei Worte' Jesu im Logion 13 des EvTh," *Annual of the Japanese Biblical Institute* 18:62–66.

Lewy, Hans. 1929. *Sobria Ebrietas.* Giessen: Töpelmann.

Pokorný, Petr. 1965. *Der Epheserbrief und die Gnosis.* Berlin: EVA, 92f.

Schenke, Hans-Martin. 1986. "The Function and Background of the Beloved Disciple in the Gospel of John," in Ch. W. Hedrick, and R. Hodgson, Jr., eds., *Nag Hammadi, Gnosticism and Early Christianity.* Peabody, MA: Hendrickson, 127–55.

14
35,14b–27a

(1) Jesus said to them,
"If you fast, you will bring forth sin for yourselves.
(2) And if you pray, you will be condemned.
(3) And if you give alms,
you will do harm to your spirits.
(4) And if you go into any land
and wander from place to place,
(and) if they take you in,
(then) eat what they will set before you.
Heal the sick among them!
(5) For what goes into your mouth
will not defile you.
Rather, what comes out
of your mouth, will defile you."

A

The fourteenth saying consists of three main units: the first concerns the Jewish deeds of piety (*alms, prayer, and fasting;* sentences 1–3); the second is about the sending and mission of the disciples; and the third deals with problems of ritual purity.

In the sixth logion the Jewish pious acts are replaced by the Golden Rule. Here they are proclaimed as harmful (*you will be condemned . . . you will do harm to your*

---

58. Uro 1998, 77f.

spirits) and simply rejected. *Spirits* (souls) are the spirits of each of the members of the community. The provocative rejection was understood as a protest against the form of piety practiced in the great church as described, for example, in the *Didache* (beginning of the second century). Sentence 5 presents a similar radically critical attitude toward cultic purity. The reason is obviously that institutionalized piety (Lat. *praxis pietatis*) may obscure the necessity of inner conversion. In log. 27 we read an exhortation to fasting in the sense of a general abstinence from the world.

The fourth sentence, dealing with the Christian mission, clearly transcends the Galilean setting and is formulated as a general rule for Christian missionaries, or Christians as strangers: "... *any land ... from place to place.*"[59]

The saying about *eating* what is, in cultic terms, impure food is logically linked with the preceding exhortation to eat all that is offered. To do so is not only not a transgression of God's will, but it is even suggested that the impure meals may be made pure and "humanized," as suggested in logion 7.[60] *Eat what they will set before you* is also an allusion to Gen 1:29, in which God gives human beings all the fruits of paradise to eat. The disciple of Jesus anticipates life in paradise, where all that is eaten is the food of life (cf. the *Gospel of Philip* 121,22).[61]

The logic of the combination of the three units may be that the problem of the authority of Jewish Law was especially acute in the missionary areas where Jewish Law was unknown.

B

The proper relationship to the Law and Jewish traditions was an urgent question in early Christianity. Unlike in Matt 6:1–18, where Jesus radicalized the traditional duties and put them in a new frame, here they are rejected. We do not know whether this was meant as polemic against Judaism but only that it was intended to express a distance from all human institutions. What is most shocking is the rejection of *prayer*. This openly contradicts the teaching and practice of Jesus himself. The social consequences of such an attitude were reduced by the one-sided stress on individual conversion, even if, for example, the rejection of *alms* did not mean rejection of charity so much as emphasis on its noninstitutional and spontaneous performance (see log. 62:2).

The difference between the Matthean discussion of the theme of the acts of piety and the Thomas approach may reflect the fact that Jesus used two different strategies when expressing his ideas about the reform of Judaism: rejection and transformation.

Unlike the treatment of the deeds of piety, the criticism of the purity laws (sentence 5 and log. 89) does not differ from the Synoptic tradition in Mark 7:15 parr.

---

59. Literally, "countryside" (Gr. *chōra*).

60. See the *Gospel of Philip* (NHC II, 77,2–8), where the priest—the holy one—by consecrating purifies the bread and all that he touches.

61. Schrage 1964a, 54.

It may even depend on the version in Matt 15:11, most probably only in the Coptic translation.[62]

The tradition about the sending out of the disciples has its parallel in Mark 6:10f. and Luke 10:8f. (Q). *Healing* in the sense of unexpected or miraculous healings is attested only in the canonical Gospels and the Acts of the Apostles and in a part of the corresponding apocryphal literature. In the later church it was considered part of the period of revelation and God's incarnation in Jesus. Nonetheless, next to the proclamation of the Gospel, healing and care for the sick remained important functions of a sound church. We do not know how far healing was a distinctive feature of the Thomas group. In the *Gospel of Thomas* it is mentioned only here and in logion 31, where it appears only in a proverb.

We have suggested a possible inner structure for this composite logion (end of part A of our commentary), but the hypothesis we mentioned in our commentary on saying 6 is more probable, that is, the first sentence of this saying may originally have been the answer given by Jesus to the question posed by his disciples in logion 6:1.

The original wording would have been:

His disciples questioned him, (and) they said to him: "Do you want us to fast? And in which way should we pray and give alms? And which diet should we observe?" Jesus said to them: "If you fast, you will bring forth sin for yourselves. And if you pray, you will be condemned. And if you give alms, you will do harm to your spirits."

The sequence of the deeds of piety in the question of the disciples and in the answer of Jesus differs from the sequence in Matthew. This is one of the arguments for the passage's independence of the text of the Synoptics, even if the wording of sentences 4 and 5 may have been affected specifically in the Coptic version by the Coptic translation of the Synoptics.[63]

---

15   Jesus says:
35,27b–31a   "When you see one who was not born from woman,
               fall on your face (and) worship him.
               That one is your Father."

A

The *one who was not born from a woman* is God himself, entering into human beings as a spiritual person. The believers are his children (log. 50:1–2; *Acts of Thomas* 30 and 67). Jesus is the revealer of this close relation to God: "The father

---

62. Uro 1998, 29–30.
63. See Schröter 1997, 232; cf. 134.

and I are one," he says in John 10:30. For the view of the *Gospel of Thomas* on *women,* see log. 11:4 and log. 114.

We do not know what it means *to see* God himself. Obviously it relates to a mystic vision.

Since it is God himself who is mentioned here, the response to his presence has to be adoration: *Fall on your face and worship him* is *proskynēsis,* adoration in a deep bow. The same Coptic terminology is used in Matt 4:9 for the Devil's demand for adoration when he tempts Jesus.[64] It promises Jesus dominion over the kingdoms of the earth if he bows down to the Devil.

B

In the Gospel according to Matthew Jesus refused the Devil, and ultimately, after his resurrection, he was worshiped in the same way by his disciples, and "All authority in heaven and on earth was given to him" (28:17–18).

16
35,31b–36,5a

(1) Jesus says:
"Perhaps the people think that
I have come to cast peace upon the earth.
(2) But they do not know that
I have come to cast dissension
upon the earth: fire, sword, war.
(3) For they will be five in one house:
There will be three against two
and two against three,
the father against the son and
the son against the father.
(4) And they will stand as solitary ones."

A

The point is that following Jesus is very demanding. Distancing oneself from the world provokes resistance from the other side.[65] It causes divisions affecting even the closest relationships in the family (see log. 55, 61, and 101). *Fire, sword,* and *war* do not imply any militant or expansionist attitude on the side of Jesus' followers, but rather the risks run by those who follow the living Jesus on the way toward the heavenly Father. Division in the family (*three against two in one house*) is a phenomenon that has accompanied persecution and critical situations right through human history.

I have come is a metaphor for the whole of Jesus' earthly life (see, for example, John 5:43), or—expressed in the vocabulary of later Christian dogmatic—his incarnation.

---

64. See Plisch 2007, 72.

65. A similar saying appears in the late Gnostic tractate *Pistis Sophia* 119.

Here we find a sentence about the *solitary ones* (Gr. and Copt. *monachoi*), which is not present in the Synoptic parallels. A solitary is a person who has come close to God and become aware of his/her own divine substance (see log. 4 and 23 and commentary). These form a group of individuals, every one of whom is directly linked with God, as expressed by Jesus' revelatory speech about the branch and trees in John 15:1–10. The solitary ones take their direct responsibility before God seriously.

B

The "I-came" saying has its parallel in Q (Luke 12:49, 52f.), where these words stress the momentousness of the expected apocalyptic judgment. Since the saying on the fire is mysterious (see log. 10 and comment) and must already have puzzled the readers of the Gospels, it obviously survived in the Jesus tradition because it was well known as a part of the most ancient tradition about Jesus.

17
36,5b–9a

Jesus says:
"I will give you what no eye has seen,
and what no ear has heard,
and what no hand has touched,
and what has not occurred
to human mind."

A

We can understand these words as an attempt at an apophatic expression of astonishment (see the comment on log. 13) before the glory of the new age, as referred to in logion 13. *What no hand has touched* may be understood as a polemic against 1 John 1:1, where we read about the apostles touching Jesus with their hands. According to John 20:27, the risen Jesus told doubting Thomas that he could touch his wounds. It seems that Thomas did not do so, for he immediately reacted by confessing his faith (v. 28). Touching Jesus was considered witness to his real humanity (see John 1:14). In the *Gospel of Thomas* all this is a secondary phenomenon, given the belief that the living Jesus is present in spiritual form in the community of his disciples. It is therefore more probable that saying 17 is simply an attempt to express the otherness of the promised salvation—its difference from all human hopes.

B

The saying is one of the many versions of a phrase referring to a hidden reality of great import.[66] In the Prophets, Isa 64:3f. uses a similar word in a saying on the punishment of the enemies of Israel and God's protection of his people. Paul quoted it in 1 Cor 2:9, Jesus' later followers in *2 Clem* 11:7.[67]

---

66. There is an indirect quotation in Manichean fragment 789 from Turfan (Onuki 1991, 407.)
67. For a survey of the various versions see Plisch 2007.

Literature

Onuki, Takashi. 1991. "Traditionsgeschichte von Th.Ev. 17 und ihre christologische Relevanz," in *Anfänge der Christologie* (FS F. Hahn). Göttingen: Vandenhoeck & Ruprecht, 399–415.

18
36,9b - 17a
	(1) The disciples said to Jesus:
	"Tell us what our end will be."
	(2) Jesus said:
	"Have you already discovered the beginning
	  that you are now asking about the end?
	  For where the beginning is,
	  there the end will be too.
	(3) Blessed is he who will stand at the beginning.
	And he will know the end,
	and he will not taste death."

A

The saying has two parts: a wise statement (*gnōmon*) and a beatitude. In the first part Jesus answers the disciples' question about hope in death, and does so ironically, telling them that the question is not well posed. The disciples have asked about hope in their future death. Jesus changed the question: it is not about time but about place. The end and the beginning are one, because the Living One is perpetually present.[68] There is only one source of life from its beginning to its end.[69]

The changes are visible on the periphery. In the center, in the very presence of God, *the beginning* and *the end* are identical. That is why the one who stands at the beginning also *knows* the end, and those who are reborn know the mystery of the beginning and of the end. God with his creative power stands at the beginning and at the end. "It is for thy sake that everything has come into being and everything will return to you," is said about the Invisible Spirit in the *Apocryphon of John* (NHC II/1; 9,7f.).[70] The beginning of the next saying (19:1) presupposes the same idea: The beginning of human life is a beginning after the end, so that the end may turn into a new beginning.

---

68. Valantasis 1997, 86.

69. "The circle has the same beginning and end" is a saying from the Heraclitus tradition: Hermann Diels, *Doxographi Graeci,* trans. R. D. Hicks (Berlin: de Gruyter, 1929), V.6.

70. Translation by Frederik Wisse.

B

The saying might be taken to be a confession of the unity of God as Creator and God as Savior. It is more probable, however, that here we have a text reflecting the inner piety of Thomas Christians—a model of a true Christian whose life is spiritually integrated because he identifies himself with God but is not dissolved in him. By contrast, the eschatology and personal hope of Christians from the mainstream church developed more toward the model of communion with God.

Literature

Puech, Henri Ch. 1978. "La gnose et le temps," in idem, *En quête de la gnose.* Bibliothèque des sciences religieuses. Paris, 215–70.

19	(1) Jesus says:
36,17b–25	"Blessed is he who was before he came into being.
	(2) If you become disciples of mine (and)
	listen to my words, these stones will serve you.
	(3) For you have five trees in Paradise
	which do not change during summer (and) winter.
	And their leaves do not fall.
	(4) Whoever will come to know them
	will not taste death."

A

The theme of the preceding saying is continued here in the first part: through Jesus, the true and initiated reader discovers the ideal image of the disciple and the human being in general, the very Adam (see log. 15 and 85). This means awareness of his or her own preexistence, that is, the fact that his/her life is anchored before he/she was born (*before he came into being*). The source of life is in God's creative power, in which the beginning and the end meet.

The words, mentioned in the second sentence, are all the sayings typical for the *Gospel of Thomas*.[71] Here it is clearly suggested that not all hearers are automatically disciples. Only those who truly listen to the words of Jesus are disciples. *These stones will serve you* is an allusion to the traditional metaphor of the divine power that can change stones into human beings or into bread, as is mentioned in Luke 3:8 par.; 4:3 (Q), and here it expresses the wonder of spiritual rebirth. The rest of creation exists for the sake of such reborn people.

The *five trees* from *Paradise* (the third part) represent a developed image of Paradise with the tree of life (Gen 2:9). According to early Christian apocalyptic expectations, the tree of life will reappear at the end of the ages (Rev 2:7; 22:2). *Their leaves do not fall*—they are unchanging. In the Manichean *Psalm Book* 161,

---

71. See the commentary on the prologue.

17–29 this motif was further elaborated: the leaves of these trees do not move; they are absolutely quiet, as a true Christian is (see sayings 50:3 and 90 [end]).

The concluding part (sentence four: *Whoever will come to know them*) has a parallel in Irenaeus (*Epideixis* 43) and relates to the saying on the trees. To *know the trees* means, however, to take seriously all the sayings of Jesus. *Will not taste death*: in the *Gospel of Philip* we find a saying about those who are nourished by truth and will not die (NHC II/3; 73,22–23).

B

This is a composite saying that has been put together from four smaller units. In the first we meet the idea of the preexistence of human beings. The literature of mainstream Christianity, of the church, knows only the preexistence of Jesus Christ. The notion that Jesus was with God before his "earthly birth" (see Phil 2:6–11) and even when God created the world (1 Cor 8:6) expresses the idea that Jesus as the revelation of God represents a constant, unchangeable feature of God's character and that therefore his disciples in all places and in all ages can rely on the validity of what he proclaimed. The idea of the preexistence of individual Christians does not appear in Christian dogmatics. We read of eternal election (Eph 1:4); but essentially human beings are regarded as temporary, and their eternity means that their temporary lives are kept in God's memory and achieve communion with him. This is a Christian teaching with origins in the New Testament. The *Gospel of Thomas* presents a different idea: to discover eternity means to get rid of temporality.

What was expressed in the preceding saying through theological interpretation of a philosophical rule is now narrated in two metaphorical sayings on stones as servants and quiet trees as models of the end and fulfillment. Perhaps the editor intended to provoke the reader into pondering his or her own life.[72] The Christian Gnostics took over the idea of individual preexistence.[73]

20
36,26–33a

(1) The disciples said to Jesus:
"Tell us whom the kingdom of heaven is like!"
(2) He said to them: It is like a mustard seed.
(3) <It> is the smallest of all seeds.
(4) But when it falls on cultivated soil,
it produces a large branch (and)
it (the branch) becomes shelter
for the birds of the sky."

A

The hearers, who in the preceding saying were exhorted to become *disciples,* are now addressed as already being disciples. A parable known earlier only from

---

72. Valantasis 1997.
73. *The Gospel of Philip* (NHC II/3, 64,10–12).

Mark 4:30–32 par. is presented here with one significant change: a *large branch* is mentioned. Like the large, fine fish from logion 8 and great pearl from logion 79, this image stresses the special ability and mission of those who are great because they know their inner divine core, because they are true disciples.

The parable concentrates on the contrast between the present small and seemingly insignificant status of the kingdom of heaven (a Jewish term for the kingdom of God also used in the Gospel of Matthew) and its future (eschatological) full reality as home for human beings (*shelter of the birds of sky*—literally "of heavens," as also in Mark 4:32). According to Matt 6:26 par. (Q) the birds of heaven serve as one of the models of the life of Jesus' followers.

In addition, the contrast between the present hidden character of the mustard seed serves here as a metaphor for the immateriality of the invisible soul.[74]

Recently commentators have become aware of connotations of danger in this metaphor of the expanding kingdom of God. Mustard was considered an aggressive weed.[75] Yet it is the theme of home that is crucial.

B

The renarrated version in *Gospel of Thomas* is the first step toward the later Gnostic interpretation. The text is similar to Matt 13:31f., and it has a few features in common with Luke 13:18–21.[76]

21
36,33b–37, 19

(1) Mary said to Jesus:
"Whom are your disciples like?"
(2) He said: "They are like servants[77]
who are entrusted with a field
that is not theirs.
(3) When the owners of the field arrive,
They will say: 'Let us have our field.'
(4) (But) they are naked[78] in their presence
so as to let them have it,
(and thus) to give them their field."
(5) "That is why I say:
When the master of the house learns
that the thief is about to come,
he will be on guard before he comes
(and) will not let him break into his house,
his domain, to carry out his possessions.

---

74. This is also the tendency of the later Gnostic understanding of this parable in the Naassene treatise: Hippolytus *Philos.* 5.9.6 or in the *Dialogue of the Savior*, where the mustard seed is of earthly and heavenly origin (NHC III/5; 144,5–7).

75. Crossan 1991, 276–79.

76. Schrage 1964.

77. Literally "small children"; *pais* may have been used in the Greek original in the sense of "boy" or "servant."

78. Probably a scribal omission.

(6) (But) you, be on guard against the world!

(7) Gird your loins with great strength,

so that the robbers will not find a way to get to you."

(8) "For the necessities for which you are waiting

(with longing) will be found.[79]

(9) There ought to be a wise person among you!

(10) When the fruit was ripe, he came quickly

with his sickle in his hand,

(and) he harvested it.

(11) Whoever has ears to hear should hear." ·

A

A collection of sayings about the disciples of Jesus, who should be prepared for transition from earthly to eternal life.

The *Mary* who addressed Jesus is obviously Mary Magdalene, not his mother Mary. Mary Magdalene appears in several branches of the Jesus tradition as a disciple of Jesus.[80]

Her question helps to concentrate the reader's attention on Jesus' words and to prepare him for leaving this world. The *field* as an image of the world appears in Jesus' parables in the Synoptics. Being *entrusted with a field* means the missionary task in the world (Matt 13:38). The *owners* of the field are God and his angels. The *naked*ness of the *disciples* as *servants* (literally "children")[81] means that their souls will (after death)[82] put off the body, as the apostle Paul says in 2 Cor 5:1–5.[83] The *Gospel of Thomas* interprets the hope in death as liberation from all that is represented by the human body and as return to the One, to the Solitary One, as referred to in logion 16:4 and 49. Nakedness is a kind of liberation. If we read "children" instead of "servants,"[84] which is a very probable reading, the scene would belong to a series of images from tradition about Jesus in which children play a positive role, as in Matt 11:16 par. (Q).

The *house* in the second short story is obviously the divine kingdom and is not the same as the field in the first sentence. This is a slightly different version of the eschatological exhortation in Matt 24:43 (cf. Mark 3:27). The disciples of Jesus have to be on guard against the *world* (sentence 6), or against the *thief* (sentence 5), or the *robbers* (sentence 7). Unlike the house (the home), the world is a temporary phenomenon. Those who cling to the material dimension of the world will be sur-

---

79. An alternative translation is offered by the translators of NHD: "For the possession you are watching out for they will find."

80. Esp. in the *Gospel of Mary* from the *Papyrus Berolinensis Gnosticus* = the Gnostic papyrus from Berlin.

81. Copt. *šēre šēm*; since "babies" does not fit the context, it is possible to understand the children as "boys" or *Burschen* in German; see Plisch 2007, 86; cf. note 77 above.

82. See Leipoldt 1967.

83. Kee 1963 suggests that nakedness means the overcoming of sexuality.

84. See note 77.

prised by the thief or by robbers—that is, by the destruction of the world and of the body, but the wise *master of the house*, who knows God's mysteries (see log. 8 and 76:2) is prepared (*Gird your loins*)[85] *to protect his domain* and his spiritual *possessions* (cf. log. 103), obviously his spiritual body.

The words on the harvest (*ripe fruit*) are an exhortation to a prompt and good decision (Mark 4:29—Joel 3[4]:13).

For the concluding exhortation, see saying 8.

B

The different themes and changes in the addressed persons (Mary, "you" [sentence 6], "whoever" [sentence 11]) suggest that here we have a collection of sayings that are linked by the theme of the transience of human life and the fleeting character of this world. From sentence 5 onward, we read text units that have parallels in the Synoptics, that speak about the unexpected end of the world and coming of the kingdom of God, and that warn against self-confidence. The first part is a more spiritual interpretation of some traditions of Jesus' sayings.

Some later texts developed speculations about Mary Magdalene. The earliest information is preserved in Luke 8:1–3, which speaks of a group of women who supported Jesus and his disciples. This group was obviously considered equal to the Twelve. Mary belonged to it and in Luke 8:3 is even mentioned as the first. In the *Gospel of Thomas* she appears once more in the mysterious saying 114.[86]

Paul was afraid of the situation between death and new life—the "unclothing" of the mortal body. He wished to live until the end of this age, to avoid an interim status of this kind and to put on his new body directly over his mortal body. He spoke of a heavenly (1 Cor 15:40; 2 Cor 5:2f.) or spiritual (1 Cor 15:44) body. This did not mean any immateriality, but a body governed by the Spirit of God. Since the body is a bearer of identity (face, voice, bodily contact), Paul's eschatology and anthropology were social in the deep sense of this word.

Literature

Kee, Howard. 1963. "'Becoming a Child' in the *Gospel of Thomas*," *Journal of Biblical Studies* 82:307–14.

Ricci, Carla. 1994. *Mary Magdalene and Many Others*. Minneapolis: Fortress Press (transl. from Italian).

Toyoshima, K. 1983. "Neue Vorschläge zur Lesung und Übersetzung von ThEv. Log. 21. 103 und 68b," *Annual of Japanese Biblical Institute* 9:230–41.

---

85. Cf. Luke 12:35, 37. "Girding the loins" is probably identical to acquiring the Great Power (cf. Acts 8:10) given by God to Adam (log. 85).

86. According to later Gnostic speculation from the *Gospel of Philip*, Jesus and Mary were a spiritual couple—a syzygy (NHC II/2; 59,8).

22 37,20–35	(1) Jesus saw infants being suckled. (2) He said to his disciples: "These little ones being suckled are like those who enter the kingdom." (3) They said to him: "Then will we enter the kingdom as little ones?" (4) Jesus said to them: "When you make the two into one and when you make the inside like the outside and the outside like the inside and the above like the below, — (5) that is to make the male and the female into a single one, so that the male will not be male and the female will not be female — (6) and when you make eyes instead of an eye and a hand instead of a hand and a foot instead of a foot, an image instead of an image, (7) then you will enter [the kingdom]."

A

The theme of the *child* may be a connecting link with the preceding saying (21:2 and note 77). The scene is similar to that of Mark 10:13–15 parr: the child represents the newborn (John 3:4f.; 1 Pet 2:2) baptized and integrated person (see log. 4!). The literal translation of *suckled*—"receiving milk" is an analogy to 1 Pet 2:2, where the reborn (neophytes) demand pure, spiritual milk.

The second section (from sentence 4 on) exhorts the reader/hearer to overcome the opposites that are typical of the corrupted world (*two into one, inside—outside,* and so on; cf. Gal 3:28 and Eph 2:14–16);[87] it speaks in a seemingly meaningless way (tautologically) about replacing one part of the body by the same part—*hand instead of a hand,* and so on. In fact, it means the replacement of the mortal body by the spiritual body, as Paul had mentioned it and as we have discussed in the comment on the preceding saying. Here we have a description of an overall rebirth and conversion. Its crucial element was the suppression of sexuality (see also log. 114:2f.). *An image instead of an image* (or a face instead of a face[88]) is consequently the full transformation and restoration of human personality—the exchange of the mortal parts (*eye, foot*) and mortal scheme of the body (*image*) for immortal parts (see log. 83 and 84).

---

87. These are explicitly social and cultural opposites. In the Gnostic milieu, the theory of overcoming of opposites developed into a teaching on the spiritual transformation of human personality. The best description is in the *Gospel of Philip* (NHC II/2; 67,10ff.).

88. Gr. *eikōn* is used in this way in the *Acts of Peter and Twelve Apostles* from NHC VI/1; 2,24.

To enter the kingdom is a construction known from the Synoptic Gospels and typical of the ancient Jesus traditions (Mark 9:47; 10:15, 23; Matt 23:13 [Q]; Matt 5:20; 7:21; 21:36).[89] It is derived from the biblical words about entering the Promised Land (Josh 19:49, 51; cf. the Pauline phrase "to inherit the kingdom of God" [Gal 5:21; 1 Cor 6:9, 10; 15:50; Eph 5:5]).

B

This logion is, in fact, a dialogue in which the disciples of Jesus do not understand his way of speaking—a theme well known from the Gospel of John.[90]

The idea of a new (individual) body is attested in 2 Macc 6–7, the story of the martyrdom of seven brothers. When tortured by having limb after limb cut off, the third brother "put out his tongue and courageously stretched forth his hands and said nobly, 'I got these from Heaven . . . and from him I hope to get them back again'" (7:10). This may be the original context of the formulation about the exchange of limbs.

Literature

Schwanz, Peter. 1970. *Imago Dei als christologisch-anthropologisches Problem der Alten Kirche*. Halle: Max Niemeyer.

For other secondary literature on the theme of the suppression of sexuality, see log. 114—Literature.

23
38,1–3a

(1) Jesus says:
"I will choose you, one from a thousand
and two from ten thousand.
(2) And they will stand as one individual."

A

This saying has indirect parallels in Jewish literature [91] (*4 Esra* 7:47) and in the New Testament: "For many are called, but few are chosen" (Matt 22:14). It expresses the fact that in each religion the number of those who really practice piety is lower than the number of members of the group or society. The real representatives of such a group are those who are members by choice.

Individual or "single one" (log. 4:3 and here Copt. *oua ouōt*; log. 16:4 and 49:1 Gr. *monachos*) is a reference to those who are united with God as the branches are joined with the vine (see John 15:1–11).

---

89. The last two occurrences originate from the special Matthean sources.

90. See, e.g., John 3:4.

91. *4 Esra* 7:47 is included only in the Old Slavonic version.

B

The true representatives of a group or even a movement are a minority among those whom they represent and lead. Minorities of this kind reflect on the identity and mission of the groups concerned and become their leaders. There are also minorities of a different kind, who use consciousness of elite status as a means of survival. The readers of the *Gospel of Thomas* together with its author/collector were obviously just on the boundary between the two alternatives. Similar maxims (wise rules) about *one from thousand* can be found in Eccles 6:6 and Irenaeus (*Adv. haer.* 1.24.6).[92]

24 38,3b–10a	(1) His disciples said: "Show us the place where you are, because it is necessary for us to seek it." (2) He said to them: "Whoever has ears, should hear! (3) Light exists inside a person of light, and he[93] shines on the whole world. If he does not shine, there is darkness."

The Greek version from P.Oxy. 655 (fragment d) contains only eighteen letters from five words, each of them at the end of a line (see Attridge 1989). For the reconstruction, see part B of this comment.

A

The problem for the disciples of Jesus was that of lasting communication with Jesus: "Lord we do not know where you are going," says Thomas to Jesus according to John 14:5.

The *place* of Jesus is the divine kingdom as the realm of eternal life.[94] Nevertheless, from Jesus' answer we may deduce that he is present inside *each* of his disciples as his inner *light*, as the source of his inner enlightenment. *Light* makes orientation on the way of life possible, and he who discovers Jesus inside himself *shines on the whole world* (see Matt 5:14–16). *If he does not shine*: the one who does not shine is not light, is not linked with Jesus. And on the other hand: knowledge of Jesus as source of light is a stabilizing power of the universe. The inner *darkness* is the very source of social darkness in the world (see Matt 6:22f.).[95]

This can be considered the answer to Jesus' rhetorical question in logion 11: "When you are in the light, what will you do?" (cf. log. 50:1).

---

92. See Ménard 1975.
93. Another possible translation is "it shines."
94. Franzmann 1996, 79.
95. This part of the *Gospel of Thomas* is reflected in the *Dialogue of the Savior* (NHC III/5; 125,18–126,8).

B

Here the *Gospel of Thomas* reflects an important step in the development of the Synoptic version of this logion: "Is a lamp brought in to be put under a bushel, or under a bed, and not on a stand?" (Mark 4:21; Luke 8:16f.). Originally, it was a promise, an assurance, pragmatic information about the character of the kingdom as God's light. The Matthean exhortation "Let your light shine before others, so that they may see your good works and give glory to your Father who is in heaven" (Matt 5:16) is then a transformation of a promise held out to members of the group into an instruction for the disciples of Jesus in their mission. The *Gospel of Thomas* has preserved the indicative version of the sentence on light, even if it also alludes to the exhortation.

Paul-Hubert Poirier has attempted to reconstruct Greek remnants of the Greek version that seems to be the text translated into Coptic: "Inside a person of light is light and it shines on the whole world. If it does not shine, he is darkness." A similar saying is attested in the (Ethiopian) book *1 Enoch* 5:7.[96] In John 12:35 we read a similar argument, but there the light is not so inherent in individual persons: "Walk while you have the light, so that the darkness may not overtake you. . . . While you have the light, believe in the light, so that you may become children of light."

Literature

Poirier, Paul-Hubert. 2002. "Un parallèle grec partiel au logion 24 de l'Évangile selon Thomas," in *For the Children: Perfect Instruction* (FS H.-M. Schenke). Leiden/Boston: Brill, 95–100.

25
38,10b–12a

(1) Jesus says:
"Love your brother like your life!
(2) Protect him like the apple of your eye!"

A

Jesus' commandment to love is expressed here in two parallel sentences. This is a solemn formulation (Lat. *parallelismus membrorum*), common in Semitic languages.[97] Unlike the well-known version in Mark 12:32 par. and already attested in Lev 19:18,[98] the commandment is here related to brother, not to neighbor. This is a semantic shift that took place when the saying was used predominantly as an inner rule in the common life of Jesus' followers. Parallels such as 1 John 2:10; 3:10; 4:21; or John 15:13 (friend) have a similar function. This was not a limitation of love but rather its concrete embodiment in the daily life of the community.

---

96. See Poirier 2002, 97.
97. This is a sign of authenticity, Grobel 1961–62.
98. Other New Testament instances are in Rom 13:9; Gal 5:14; and James 2:8.

B

The metaphor of *the apple of the eye* is a new feature. It is a metaphor well known in many cultures; in Israel, for example, in Psalm 17:8 (LXX Psalm 16:8) or in the *Letter of Barnabas* 19:9 (related to those who proclaim the Word of God). Since the parallelism is a Semitic phenomenon, this saying may have been part of the ancient Jesus tradition.

Literature

Grobel, Kendrick. 1961–62. "How Gnostic Is the *Gospel of Thomas*," *New Testament Studies* 9:367–73.
Popkes 2005: 45ff.

26	(1) Jesus said:
38,12b–17a	"You see the splinter
	that is in your brother's eye,
	but you do not see the beam
	that is in your (own) eye.
	(2) When you remove the beam from your eye,
	then you will see clearly (enough)
	to remove the splinter from your brother's eye."

In the Greek version from P.Oxy. 1, 1–4 only fragments from the second sentence are legible.

A

This is a well-attested saying from ancient Jesus tradition. The term *brother* links it with the preceding saying. The intention is clear and valid in all human communities across the centuries, but the reference to brother as member of the religious group hints at a specific function in the congregation of Thomas Christians.

B

The text is almost identical with Matt 7:3, 5: Luke 6:41 (Q).

27	(1) "If you do not abstain from the world,[99]
38,17b–20a	you will not find the kingdom.
	(2) If you do not make the (whole) week
	into a Sabbath, you will not see the Father."

---

99. The other possible translation offered by NHD is "If you do not fast against the world."

The Greek text in P. Oxy. 1,4–11 is practically identical with the Coptic translation, but in the former instead of "kingdom" we read "kingdom of God."

A

The logion is once again a parallelism: the same thing is expressed in two ways. *Abstain*—fast is not abandoned here as in saying 14, but is instead reinterpreted in a radical way. It is no longer an expression of piety but rather of distance from the visible world as such.[100] Now we see what was meant by Jesus' rejection of Jewish deeds of piety in sayings 6 and 14: fasting means to keep a distance from the world; to keep *Sabbath* (as the seventh day) holy means to live the whole *week* (Sabbath as seven days) before God. In the practice of the Thomas group this meant a life full of meditation.[101]

In the *Gospel of Thomas*, to *see* means the same as to discover and know the very substance of a phenomenon or a person. The concept of seeing is a link connecting this saying with the preceding one.

For the concept of the *kingdom of God* in the *Gospel of Thomas*, see the comment on log. 49.

B

The first sentence is also attested by Clement of Alexandria (*Strom.* 3.15.99).

Literature

Brown, Peter. 1992. "The Sabbath and the Week in Thomas 27," *Novum Testamentum* 34:123.

28	(1) Jesus says:
38,20b–31a	"I stood in the middle of the world,
	and in flesh I appeared to them.
	(2) I found all of them drunk.
	None of them did I find thirsty.
	(3) And my soul ached
	for the children of humanity,
	because they are blind in their heart,
	and they cannot see;
	for they came into the world empty,
	(and) they also seek to depart

---

100. Brankaer 2004, 10.

101. It was not an ascetic's or a hermit's life, but rather an inner transformation, a life in a spiritual light; see Brown 1992 and Valantasis 1999.

from the world empty.
(4) But now they are drunk.
(But) when they shake off their (intoxication
from) wine, then they will change their mind."

In the Greek P.Oxy. 1, 11–21 the end of the third sentence and the sentence 4 are illegible or entirely missing (torn out).

A

This saying is, in fact, a short hymn. *In flesh I appeared to them* is a statement similar to the words in 1 Tim 3:16 ("He was revealed in flesh"). It expresses the alienation of the world but does not imply any rejection of the world as such. Now the people of the world are *blind* or *drunk*, but they may repent and change their mind.[102] We can almost say that they are not yet *thirsty* and are therefore still *empty*. According to saying 74, they are empty because they have not found access to the source of the water of life. The other people who are mentioned in part 4 are the same persons after they have found the spring of water, as described in saying 13:5.[103] In the *Odes of Solomon* (probably first century A.D.) this hope is expressed in a joyous tone:

"And so I drank and became intoxicated
 from the living water that does not die.
 And my intoxication was not with ignorance;
 but I abandoned vanity;
 and turned toward the Most High, my God,
 and was enriched by his favors."[104]

The consequence of awakening from spiritual sleep is repentance (*they will change their mind*). In Coptic, the Greek word *metanoeō* is used, which in the Septuagint corresponds to the Hebrew expression *shūb*, which means repentance or conversion as a turning point in life and as a change of the direction of the journey of life.

B

The short hymn with its poetic language has no parallel in the Synoptic Gospels.[105]

Unlike in John 1:14, where the Word became flesh (Gr. *egeneto sarx*), here Jesus appeared in flesh (*sarx* is clearly legible in the Greek version), but as we can see from a comparison of the hymn with 1 Tim 3:16, this cannot be considered to

---

102. Uro 1998, 47f.
103. Cf. the image of the source of life in John 7:37 or Rev 22:17.
104. *Od. Sol.* 11:7–9 (trans. James H. Charlesworth 1985).
105. The scene of Jesus among blind souls reappears later in *Pist. Soph.* 141.

be a heretical (docetic) statement[106] that denies the full reality of Jesus' appearance. With this saying, the *Gospel of Thomas* became acceptable for the readers of the Gospel of John, and here we may recognize the common basis of the specific Syriac piety and theology.

In the Gnostic (Valentinian) *Gospel of Truth* (NHC I/3; 31,4–9) the idea of the incarnation of Jesus has also been maintained, but it is now understood as a means of rescuing the divine particles hidden in each human individual. The *Gospel of Thomas* was later claimed by the Gnostics, and this was the reason why the church rejected it. Obviously the church's decision was wise, given the many ambiguous statements in the *Gospel of Thomas*; but although the latter sees the material *world* as corrupted and generally lower than the spiritual world, it does not substantially reject it. The next saying (log. 29) even praises God's incarnation.

*Blind*ness means the same as *drunken*ness[107]—loss of orientation in life and a life without prospects.[108]

Emptiness is clearly a negative property and is in no way an analogy to naked-ness, which we met in log. 21.

As concerns repentance (*change* of *mind*), it is important to know that it is present in the *Gospel of Thomas* as a biblical concept, also represented by John the Baptist and by Jesus himself. Nevertheless, it is only here that it appears.

Literature

Charlesworth, James H. 1985. "The Odes of Solomon," in idem, ed., *Old Testament Pseudepigrapha I*. New York: Doubleday, 725–71.

29
38,31b–39,2a

(1) Jesus says:
"If the flesh came into being because of the spirit,
it is a wonder;
(2) but if the spirit (came into being),
because of the body,
it is a wonder of wonders."
(3) Yet I marvel at
how this great wealth
has taken up residence in this poverty.

P.Oxy. 1, 22 contains only one legible word: poverty.

---

106. So Gärtner 1961 or Ménard 1975.

107. For the later Gnostic theories, see *Gospel of Truth* (NHC I/3); 28,28ff.; Matt 23:16, 24).

108. On spiritual drunkenness, see Philo *De Ebrietate* (On sobriety) and the Hermetic ideas on drunkenness as alienation in *Corp. Herm.* VII,1; and *Gospel of Truth* 22,16–21.

A

If the flesh: this relates once again to the incarnation rather than to creation. God revealed himself in the world in the human shape of Jesus to save lost humankind. This is characterized as a *wonder*. Still more marvelous (*wonder of wonders*), however, are the workings of God's spirit, which is responsible for the effect of the incarnation, that is, the spiritual conversion of human beings.

Sentence 3 is probably a comment written from the point of view of the school of Thomas (see the prologue).[109] He is astounded at how the ray of God's love has reached into the realm of spiritual darkness and *poverty* of ignorance (see saying 3:5).

B

The comparison of marvels is apparently intended to mean that spiritual enlightenment is higher than incarnation—the bodily presence of Jesus as representative (Son) of God on earth. Yet the symmetrical shape of log. 29:1 and 2 still suggests that the activity of the Spirit is mutually related to incarnation.

30	(1) Jesus says:
39,2–5a	"Where there are three gods,
	they are gods.[110]
	(2) Where there are two or one,
	I am with him."

P.Oxy. 1, 23–30 is damaged, but a probable reconstruction is still possible: J(esu)s [say]s: "Where there are [three], they are without God, and where there is but [a single one], I say that I am with [him]. Lift up the stone, and you will find me there. Split a piece of wood, and I am there."[111]

"Without God" is in Greek *atheioi*. Even if the *a* (Lat. *alpha privativum—* god*less*) is not clearly legible, *a* is the only possible prefix before *theioi* (Attridge 1981). "Three" obviously refers to human beings, and the Coptic scribe simply wrote "gods" by mistake.[112]

In the Coptic version, lines 27b–30 of the Greek original have their parallel in log. 77:2–3 (in reversed order).

109. See Plisch 2007, 102.
110. Most probably a scribal error; see the Greek version and the discussion here in section B.
111. Translation by Attridge 1989.
112. See Plisch 2007.

A

We have just indicated that *gods* is most probably a secondary version that originated by mutilation of the Greek text, and the sentence relates to human beings. If not, it must have meant lower deities. Whatever the case, the saying makes the reader aware of the decisive level of religious experience as proclaimed by Thomas.[113] A gathering of more than two (divine) members cannot participate in the unity of the true God as represented by (the living) Jesus and mediated by Jesus to human beings (*I am with him*). The ideal disciples of Jesus are the solitary ones (log. 16:4; 49 and 75).

The second sentence of the Greek version describes how Jesus is present to everybody and everywhere. This sounds like pantheism, but Jesus is not identical with the universe; he is simply everywhere present.[114] The idea reflects the experience of Jesus's accessibility by prayer and through benediction in every place, but here this original intention is reinterpreted in accordance with the theory of a God who penetrates the whole and yet still transcends it.[115]

B

A saying concerning different numbers of people and Jesus' presence among them is first attested in Matt 18:20, which already states that God's presence as mediated by Jesus is not bound to the Temple, and God is present even in the smallest group gathered in his name. There, however, the stress is on the fact of the gathering, whose members are able to agree in their prayers. This was Matthew's understanding (Matt 18:19), but here it is the individual dimension of piety that is stressed.[116]

Given that in Matthew 18 and in several other later echoes of this saying the gods are not mentioned in connection with the gathering of three, the first word *gods* in the Coptic text must be a secondary element. It may have been written by mistake or as a conscious innovation of one of the traditional versions of this saying—an alteration by which the community expressed distrust for the theology of the mainstream church with its tendency toward a Trinitarian concept of God, as can be seen in Matt 28:19–20. It is even possible that the Coptic translator consciously omitted the particle that would have made the saying a denial of the divine character of the three (Three?) in order to avoid a direct conflict with the mainstream church, and adopted a different strategy, that is, the statement that compared with the direct presence of Jesus, the existence of three gods represents a lower religious experience.

The second sentence of the Greek version is identical to saying 77:2–3. This means that (for unclear reasons) the Coptic translator changed the sequence of sayings or may have wanted to avoid a doubling.

---

113. So de Suarez 1974, 191.

114. In the theory of religion this would be called panentheism.

115. In the introduction we discussed this concept in connection with the ideas of Philo of Alexandria.

116. Cf. *Corp. Herm.* I,2; Clement of Alexandria, *Strom.* 3.69.4.

Literature

Attridge, Harold W. 1981. "The Original Text of Gos. Thom., Saying 30," *Bulletin of the American Society of Papyrologists* 18:27–32.

Pokorný, Petr. 1999. "Wo zwei oder drei versammelt sind in meinem Namen . . . (Mt 18,20)," in *Gemeinde ohne Tempel—Community without Temple. Zur Substituierung und Transformation des Jerusalemer Tempels* (Konferenz Greifswald 1998; WUNT 116; Tübingen: Mohr Siebeck), 477–88.

31
39,5b–7a

(1) Jesus says:
"No prophet is accepted in his (own) village.
(2) A physician does not heal those who
know him."

P.Oxy. 1, 30–35 corresponds to the Coptic version.

A

The experience expressed in the two parallel sentences of this saying is universal. It is in fact a proverb. Those who serve others through their skills and authority are better accepted by people who do not know them in their daily life. The problem is its function in the *Gospel of Thomas*. It is puzzling, since in Thomas theology to *know* (Gr. version *ginōskein*) is a positive value, perhaps *the* positive dimension of human being. The difficulty is with the character of the knowledge. To know somebody as a human person may obscure our interest in his/her teaching and the message they are mediating to us. Since Jesus proclaimed the kingdom of God and healed the sick (Matt 9:35), he was prophet and healer at the same time.

B

The proverb is deeply anchored in the Jesus tradition. The first sentence concerning the prophet has its parallel in Mark 6:4 and John 4:44, but only in Luke 4:23–24 are both parts (physician—prophet) mentioned together (in reverse order). Schürmann[117] has found analogies between the Thomas and Lukan version and therefore argued for the dependence of *Gospel of Thomas* 31 on Luke. In fact the Lukan version as well as Mark 6:4 seem secondary developments of a common source, and log. 31 may in fact be the most ancient version adapted to the frame of the *Gospel of Thomas*.[118]

Later the Gnostics were to understand this saying as an expression of the difference between the heavens and the earthly home.

---

117. Schürmann 1968, 229F.
118. Koester 1980a, 123.

32	Jesus says:
39,7b–10a	"A city built upon a high mountain (and)
	fortified cannot fall, nor can it be hidden."

P.Oxy. 1, 36–41 has practically the same wording (. . . on the top of high mountains . . .).

A

This is a saying proclaiming that the community of Jesus's followers (*city*) is their home, their (*fortified*) shelter, and the center of their mission (*nor can it be hidden*). It supposes a centripetal, attractive mission that is concentrated on the inner enlightenment of the individual: "Light exists inside a person of light, and he shines on the whole world" (log. 24:3).

B

This has a parallel in Matt 5:14 and Isa 2:2, where the project of a centripetal mission is well attested. The two attributes of the city (*built on mountain* plus *fortified*) and the doubled predicate (*cannot fall* plus *cannot be hidden*) are a kind of parallelism typical of Hebrew and Aramaic and well attested in the Jesus tradition. The saying may have originated in pre-Synoptic tradition, even if the meaning implied in the *Gospel of Thomas* is related to personal spiritual enlightenment.

The combination of the motifs of security and visibility is not common in Hebrew maxims (*māšāl*),[119] and in the most ancient Jesus tradition it was introduced to express the interrelated dimensions of God's kingdom. It is the series of sayings (log. 32 to 36) with clear parallels in the Synoptic Gospels, and together with log. 33 it is one of the few sayings relating to the mission of the community of Jesus' people.

33	(1) Jesus says:
39,10b–18a	"What you will hear with your ear
	{with the other ear}[120]
	Proclaim from your rooftops.
	(2) For no one lights a lamp
	(and) puts it under a bushel,
	nor does he put it in a hidden place.
	(3) Rather, he puts it on a lampstand,
	so that every one who comes in and goes out
	will see its light,"

---

119. See Beardslee 1972, 87.
120. See the commentary here in part B.

P.Oxy. is damaged here. Only the first part of the first sentence is more or less legible, and seems to correspond with the Coptic version.

A

The preceding saying about the centripetal mission is supplemented here by an exhortation to share the light as an element of the expansive, centrifugal mission. The exhortation is based on an assurance that has its analogy in saying 24: "Light exists in a person of light and he shines on the whole world." This is the inner reason why here, in logion 33:2–3, the proclamation is compared to light. *Hear* means to hear the spirit of God bringing the knowledge of the divine core of every human being as God's creation.

The second sentence of saying 24 indicates that the sharing of the *light* is inherent in its nature as light: "If he does not shine, there is darkness." The most ancient meaning of this saying is an assurance about the light intended to shine for human beings. If it is light, then it must become visible as light (Mark 4:21). A *hidden* light is nonsense. This is intended as an exhortation to mission.

B

The closest parallel to the first sentence is Matt 10:27: Luke 12:3 (Q); and to the second, Mark 4:21; Luke 8:16 (most similar wording); and Matt 5:15–16; Luke 11:33 (Q?). The mysterious first sentence is probably the result of a scribal error. According to the translators of the NHD there are two further possible ways of reading the text in a way that makes sense. These are either: ". . . with your *ear*, proclaim from your *rooftops* into someone else's ear,"[121] or: ". . . with your (one) ear (and) with (your) other ear proclaim from . . ." (as an idiomatic play paraphrasing "with both ears"). *Rooftop*—the flat roof over the highest part of the house was used as a living place, and since the houses mostly had no windows onto the street, it was also the place from which it was possible to see the "world."

The similarity between Matt 10:27 and the *Gospel of Thomas* 33:1 may have been stressed by the Coptic translator.

34	Jesus says:
39,18b–20a	"If a blind (person) leads a blind (person),
	both will fall into a pit."

A

The general meaning is clear. Here it functions as the reverse formulation of the preceding saying on the light that enables human beings to see their way on

---

121. This is how Kasser understood it (1961).

the path toward the goal and fulfillment of their lives. *Blind*ness is the opposite of spiritual enlightenment [cf. log. 28:3]).[122]

B

A proverb, also quoted in an almost literally identical version in Matt 15:14. In Luke 6:39 it is rhetorically expanded.

35
39,20b–24a

(1) Jesus says:
"It is not possible for someone
to enter the house of a strong (person)
(and) take it by force unless he binds his hands.
(2) Then he will loot his house."

A

Jesus appears here in the role of a robber who takes over a house by force. The meaning is that Jesus overcame the Devil—the emancipated embodiment of alienation and even rebellion against God. He is the *strong* one who seeks to govern the world, as he appears in Mark 3:27 par.; and, according to Mark 1:17, Jesus or God himself is the stronger one: stronger than John the Baptist, who is announcing his coming, and stronger than the strong one. In saying 98, the strong one is called "a powerful person" (Gr. *megistanos*). The terrorist who prepared to attack him, became strong enough and successfully overcame him, metaphorically represents the victorious kingdom. It is Jesus again. *Take it:* this relates to the strong man as well as to his house. Both understandings of the text are possible.

This is the active counterpart to the defense against the attack of Evil as expressed in logion 21.

B

The series of sayings with parallels in the Synoptics (in this case Mark 3:27: Matt 12:29) interprets the appearance and activities of Jesus in terms of a cosmic conflict between God's agents headed by Jesus and the Evil one and the powers he is misusing to further his destructive activity. This is most clearly visible in the stories about Jesus casting out unclean spirits (the exorcisms), such as in Mark 1:23–26 or 5:1–13. All the moral exhortations are simply a consequence of this proclamation of Jesus's victory in the apocalyptic conflict. The unclean spirits still struggle against God, but in the heavens, the key area for future hope, they are already defeated: Luke 10:18; Rev 12:9. In the *Gospel of Thomas,* it is all interpreted in a more spiritual way.

The ancient layer of the Jesus tradition, from which sayings 31 to 36 are taken, assumes Satan to be a real subject who has dominion over various powers (Eph 2:2). This may be interpreted as the accumulated sin that has turned against sinful

---

122. Cf. from a later period NHC II/2 (*GosPhil*); 645ff.

human beings, and misuses the spiritual, social, cultural, political, or economic powers, originally the good creation of God (Col 1:16), for destructive purposes (Eph 6:12).

The basic interpretation of the Christian faith was that Jesus was the victor in the universal cosmic struggle against the powers of evil.[123] This awareness has been weakened by spiritual interpretation in the sense of individual salvation, but even in the *Gospel of Thomas* we can identify the basic attitude: not moralism but proclamation of a changed situation for humankind.

The image of a robber binding a strong man is an image quite different from that of spiritual light, inner conversion, awakening from sleep, or obtaining true knowledge, yet the power and authority of the ancient Jesus tradition were so strong that the editor of *Gospel of Thomas* did not dare to leave these sayings out.

36
39,24b–27a

Jesus says:
"Do not worry from morning to evening
and from evening to morning
about what you will wear."

The damaged P.Oxy. 655, 1,1–17 contains a version with more parallels to the text from Q: ". . . from morning . . . from evening . . . morning, neither . . . what . . . eat . . . clothing . . . what you . . . wear. Of . . . more value are you than . . . which . . . card nor spin . . . cloth . . . you also. Who might add to your stature (or: the span of your life), he will give you also your cloth."

A

The *Gospel of Thomas* stresses the freedom of the disciple of Jesus, which can be gained by liberation from family ties (log. 55), social setting (log. 42), religious traditions (log. 14), and here from clothing (*what you will wear*).

Valantasis (1997) rightly points out the inner tension between the stress on the carefree and unworried (*do not worry*) life of the disciple of Jesus and the strategically minded care of those who protect their house from the influence of the world, which comes like a thief (log. 21:5–10), or of those who are training their bodies to be capable of binding the strong man (log. 35 and 98). Wisdom is to find a true balance between pious freedom from care and wise vigilance and planning of life with respect to eternity.

B

In the collection Q, this saying belongs to a set of sayings commenting on the Lord's Prayer (Matt 6:25, 28; Luke 12:22, 27). As a consequence of the coming of

---

123. In systematic theology this was stressed by Gustaf Aulén, *Christus Victor* (London: SPCK, 1931).

the kingdom of God it proclaims liberation from the inner stress caused by daily care for life and livelihood.

The Greek version is more similar to the version from Q, with only the sentence "For life is more than food, and the body more than clothing" (Luke 12:23 [Q]) missing. From this, James M. Robinson (2000) has argued that the *Gospel of Thomas* quoted an independent tradition and that Luke 12:23 is an addition.

The fact that only the warning against care over clothes remained (*what you will wear*) may be connected to the idea of nakedness as liberation from body (log. 21:4 and the neighboring log. 37:2).

Literature

Robinson 1999: 61–77.

Robinson, James, and Christoph Heil. 2000. "The Lilies of the Field: Saying 36 of the *Gospel of Thomas* and Secondary Accretions in Q 12,22b–31," *New Testament Studies* 47:1–25.

37
39,27b–40,2a

(1) His disciples said:
"When you will appear to us
and when will we see you?"
(2) Jesus said:
"When you undress without being ashamed
and take your clothes (and)
put them under your feet like little children
(and) trample on them,
(3) then [you] will come to the
Son of the Living One,
and you will not be afraid."

In P.Oxy. 655, 1,17–2,1 only sentence 1 and 2a are legible; the text seems to correspond to the Coptic version.

A

The question asked by the disciples is strange. Jesus, with whom they can speak, is exhorted to *appear* to them. This obviously relates to the appearance of Jesus in his celestial glory, as when he was transfigured (Mark 9:2–3).[124] Saying 24 represents a spiritualized version of this pious demand. Jesus' answer corrects the question itself, a strategy that is an old feature of Jesus traditions.[125] He says

---

124. It may have related to Jesus' baptism (Mark 1:9–11) and be internally experienced in Christian baptism as well (Smith 1978).

125. See, e.g., Mark 12:13–17.

that he will not appear at the end of history (as many Christians expected and still expect), but that his followers will discover his spiritual presence in the experience of spiritual ripening. The hallmark of this ripening toward the fulfillment of life is the overcoming of shame. The fact that the *appear*ance (revelation) of Jesus is not yet visible is explained in saying 28: human beings are drunk and have to shake off their drunkenness. The overcoming of sexuality and of *shame* as its counterpart is another expression of the process of becoming spiritually sober. In *Acts of Thomas* 14 we read: "I shall no longer remain covered, since the garment of shame has been taken away from me."[126] The garment may have been the body itself, which for some pious people became irrelevant.

All this is illustrated by a parable of little children who *trample on their clothes*. It is an image of those who distance themselves from their material existence. In practical terms, it means to suppress sexuality, as can be deduced from saying 22:5, where little children (22:1–2) are described as nonsexual beings. In this sense the disciples of Jesus have to *undress*.[127]

Put under your feet may be an allusion to Ps 110:1 ("until I make your enemies your footstool") and may be proclaiming the material body to be an enemy of the human soul.[128]

The Living One is God himself, as is the "living Father" in saying 50:2; the *Son of the Living One* is Jesus.

B

The understanding of naked children as the model of nonsexual beings is confirmed by a saying quoted in Clement of Alexandria (*Strom.* 3.13.92): "When you trample on the cloth of shame and two become one and the male will become female, there will be neither man nor woman."

In all such proclamations about overcoming the difference between the sexes and liberation from the body, the attractiveness of sexuality is, in fact, not so much suppressed as, to some extent, psychologically promoted.

Literature

Smith, Jonathan Z. 1978. "The Garments of Shame (1966)," in idem, *Map Is Not Territory: Studies in History of Religions* (SJLA 23). Leiden: Brill, 1–23.

38	(1) Jesus says:
40,2b–7a	"Many times you have desired
	to hear these words,
	these, that I am speaking to you,

---

126. See Uro 2003, 15–16, 65f.
127. On children who are models of spiritually living humans, see on log. 4, 21, 22, 46.
128. On material body as cloth, see *Dialogue of the Savior* (NHC III/5), 143,11–22..

> and you have no one else
> from whom to hear them.
> (2) There will be days
> when you will seek me,
> (and) you will not find me."

P.Oxy. 655, 2,2–11 evidently contains the same text, but only a few letters are legible.

A

What is discussed is the preliminary understanding with which the Thomas readers decided (*desired*) to read (hear) the *Gospel of Thomas*: the search for the wisdom (*these words*) of the living Jesus, and the love of the kingdom of God.[129] This is a twofold logion, the first sentence of which stresses the unique character of Jesus' message as God's revelation; the second is an exhortation not to miss the proper occasion for inner conversion ("now I am willing to tell you" = log. 92:2). The now is clearly identical with the time of reading the *Gospel of Thomas*.

B

The second sentence originally related to the end of Jesus's earthly life—"the days will come, when the bridegroom is taken away from them . . ." (Mark 2:20 parr.).[130] The version from John 7:34, "You will search for me, but you will not find me; and where I am, you cannot come," is a bridge between the Synoptic version and the *Gospel of Thomas*.

The saying is quoted by Irenaeus in *Adv. haer.* 1.20.2.

39	(1) Jesus says:
40,7b–13a	"The Pharisees and the scribes
	have received the keys of knowledge,
	(but) they have hidden them.
	(2) Neither have they entered,
	nor have they allowed
	to enter those who wished to.
	(3) You, however, be as shrewd as serpents
	and as innocent as doves."

In P.Oxy. 655, 2,11–23 only some syllables have survived. The Greek version is unlikely to have differed from the Coptic one, except that instead of *those who wished to* (enter) it has a participle (*entering*).

---

129. Log. 1 and 59; cf. Matt 13:17.
130. Cf. John 7:33–36; 8:21; Luke 17:22.

A

The Pharisees and the scribes represent a group whose activities have a close reference to the community of the readers of the *Gospel of Thomas*, but who are nonetheless dangerous. They have *hidden the keys of knowledge,* which are in their possession. The same motif appears in log. 102: "Woe to them, Pharisees, for they are like a dog sleeping in a cattle trough, for it neither eats nor [lets] the cattle eat." This is a reproach addressed to all who offer an interpretation of the authoritative text (the Jewish Bible, sayings of Jesus) that does not correspond to the unique inner experience of the Thomas group.

The second sentence, with a parallel in Matt 10:16, exhorts the readers cautious and vigilant (*shrewd as serpents*) and at the same time sincere and friendly (*innocent as doves*) proclamation of the kingdom of God.

B

Another composite saying. The first sentence has its parallel in Luke 11:52 and Matt 23:13 (Q) and may have been influenced by the Synoptic wording.[131] The only difference is that instead of the warning "Woe!," the whole sentence is indicative. The polemic against Pharisees is taken out of the original context and transformed into an attack on the organized mainstream church.

---

40   (1) Jesus says:
40,13b–16a   "A grapevine was planted outside
              (the vineyard) of the Father.
               (2) And since it is not supported,
              it will be pulled up by its root (and) will perish."

It is possible that P.Oxy. 655 included at least a part of this saying at its end (fragments *f* and *g*), but not a single letter is identifiable.

A

The image of a *grapevine* and *vineyard* is quite common in early Christian literature (e.g., John 15:1–10). This saying introduces the new motif of grapevines that are not *supported.* In connection with the preceding logion, it may mean that even in Christian communities there are people who do not recognize that their souls can and should be linked with God.[132] They are described as blind (log. 28) or drunk (log. 34).[133] Their prospect is death (*will perish*). The image of an unsupported grapevine has its analogy in the biblical image of the house build on sand (Matt 7:24–27; Luke 6:47–49 [Q]).

---

131. Schröter 1997, 139.
132. Haenchen 1961, 62.
133. Valantasis 1997.

B

Originally this was a warning against a piety shaped by the Law but lacking inner relationship to God. A life lived in this way would end in the adverse judgment of God. Here the original apocalyptic background is present in a quite indirect way.

41
40,16b–18

(1) Jesus says:
"Whoever has (something) in his hand,
(something more) will be given to him.
(2) And whoever has nothing,
even the little he has will be taken from him."

A

This is a proverb expressing the sad fact that the possessions of the rich man who *has* something *in his hand* tend to increase, while the poor man who *has nothing* is exploited and becomes even poorer. In the Jesus tradition, however, the proverb has been set in the context of the kingdom of God. Jesus explains that the kingdom of God is increasing and that those who accept its promise and participate in its inner power will find more than they expected. Those who refuse it, however, will lose their great chance of life: "For to him who has will more be given; and from him who has not, even what he has will be taken away" (Mark 4:25). The interpretation offered here understands the possession *in the hand* of the rich as the divine substance of every human being. Those who are not aware of it lose their prospect of life, while those who realize it and cherish their divine substance increase in their inner power (*will be given*) and missionary influence (see log. 33). Such people are "supported" in the sense of the preceding saying. According to log. 70 they may be saved by what they have "within themselves." This is the mystery of the divine kingdom, as mentioned in the prologue (hidden words, Gr. *logoi apokry-phoi*) and in log. 62 (Gr. *mystērion*); see Mark 4:11.

B

The *Gospel of Thomas* took this saying from a tradition independent of the Synoptics and interpreted it on the basis of the idea that salvation means to become aware of one's own divine substance.

42
40,19

Jesus says: "Become passersby."

A

An expression of the distance from the world that is frequent in Christian literature: "Let those who . . . deal with the world [be] as though they had no dealings with it" (1 Cor 7:31); ". . . the world passes away" (1 John 2:17). In the *Gospel of Thomas* the *passersby* are those who have liberated themselves from care for "worldly" matters—the solitary ones, as they are identified in log. 16, 49, and 75.

B

Formulated as a sapiential maxim, the saying expresses one dimension of Christian ethics. The mainstream Christian strategy is a rather different ("Rejoice with those who rejoice, weep with those who weep"; Rom 12:15) and pragmatic explication of Jesus's compassion for those who suffer (Mark 6:34; Gr. *splagchnizō*).

Joachim Jeremias quoted one noncanonical saying of Jesus written in Arabic on a bridge in India: "This world is a bridge. Pass it, but do not build your house on it." Plisch found a better parallel in Philo of Alexandria, who was about one generation older than Jesus: "On the royal way should we pass by earthly issues" (*Imm.* 159).

Literature

Jeremias, Joachim. 1948. *Unbekannte Jesusworte* (AANT 16). Zürich: Zwingli, 84f.

---

43 40,20–26a	(1) His disciples said to him: "Who are you to say this to us?" (2) "Do you not realize from what I say to you who I am? (3) But you have become like the Jews: They love the tree, (but) they hate its fruit. Or they love the fruit, (but) they hate the tree."

A

This is a warning introduced as a question about Jesus' identity, as in saying 91.[134] *To say this* may relate to the preceding saying,[135] so that here we may have a unique case of an explicit connection between two sayings. The strange feature of Jesus' authority (*who I am*) would then be his proclamation of the transitory

---

134. The parallels are in Mark 6:14–16 parr.; 8:27–30 parr.
135. Kasser 1961.

character of this world. His authority to say it means that he is linked with God, the Creator of the world.

In its third sentence the saying characterizes two alternative attitudes attributed to the "Jews." They represent the immediate neighbors of the readers, but have become an obstacle on their way toward salvation.[136]

The image of a tree and its fruits is well known in the Synoptic Gospels (Matt 12:33 par.; 7:16–20 par.) and appears in saying 45. God is the *tree*, while Jesus, his Son and his wisdom, is his *fruit*. The Jews and other religious people like them love God but do not accept the Son, or they amicably tolerate the messianic people but do not understand the character of God as revealer of authentic wisdom.

B

The Thomas Christians understood the saying criticizing the Jewish opponents of Jesus as criticism of the mainstream church. The situation of the tolerated spiritualistic groups in the early church can be illustrated by examples from later writings from Nag Hammadi, where the "we" represents the spiritually ripe "elect" who still live inside the mainstream church but consider its representatives (bishops and deacons), who seeing themselves as the real spiritual core of the church, to be incapable of leading others to the source of truth.[137]

44	(1) Jesus says:
40,26b–31a	"Whoever blasphemes against the Father,
	it will be forgiven him;
	(2) and whoever blasphemes against the son,
	it will be forgiven him.
	(3) But whoever blasphemes against the Holy Spirit,
	it will not be forgiven him,
	neither on earth nor in heaven."

A

The *blasphemy against the Holy Spirit is unforgivable* because the Holy Spirit is the mediator of Jesus' sayings.

The sin against God the Father can be forgiven because the Spirit can lead to repentance, but to blaspheme the Spirit means to deny the divine spark in one's own soul and therefore means to lose communion with the Father and the Son. The addition in 3, ". . . *will not be forgiven . . . neither on earth nor in heaven,*" presupposes the omnipresence of the Holy Spirit (see the *Gospel of Philip*—NHC II/2; 59,12–18).

---

136. Lambdin 1989.
137. See also the introduction, the section on the layers of the *Gospel of Thomas*.

B

Originally, these were the words of Jesus in response to those who charged him with acting in the name of the Evil One (a "Faustian" accusation). This was a sin in the deepest sense: a perversion of values, not just the simple transgression of a commandment. In its most ancient form, it is recorded in the Gospel of Mark 3:28–30 par. The Gospel of Luke 12:10 offers a later version, the meaning of which is that to have denied Jesus as the "Son of Man" during his earthly life was a forgivable sin, but it was unforgivable to deny him as the Living One (as the Risen Lord) in the post-Easter time. Matthew 12:31f. combines both versions. The *Gospel of Thomas* has a wording similar to that taken from Q (Luke 12:10) and develops it into a Trinitarian structure. In the preserved form it is a secondary version.

The individual versions:

Matt 12:31–32	Mark 3:28–29	Luke 12:10	GosThom 44
Every sin	All sins		Whoever
and blasphemy			blasphemes
			the Father
will be forgiven men	will be forgiven		will be forgiven
	to the sons of men		
whoever blasphemes	whoever blasphemes	who blasphemes	whoever blasphemes
against the H. S.	against the H. S.	against the H. S.	against the H. S.
will not be forgiven	will never have forgiveness	will not be forgiven	will not be forgiven
whoever		every one who	whoever
says a word		speaks a word	blasphemes
against the Son of Man		against the Son of Man	against the Son
will be forgiven		will be forgiven	will be forgiven

Original sequence
Matthew: every sin, Holy Spirit, Son of Man
Mark: all sins (to the sons of men), Holy Spirit
Luke: Son of Man, Holy Spirit
Thomas: Father, Son, Holy Spirit

The Gospel of Mark was one of the two sources for Matthew and Luke, their second source being Q. Luke must have known Mark, but decided for Q. The *Gospel of Thomas*'s version is similar to the version from Q, but it adds the words about God the Father and instead of the sin against the Son of Man mentions only the blasphemy against the son.

Literature
Kloppenborg et al. 1990:58.

45	(1) Jesus says:
40,31b–41,6a	"Grapes are not harvested from thorns,
	nor are figs picked from thistles,
	for they do not produce fruit.
	(2) A good person brings forth,
	good from his treasure.
	(3) A bad person brings (forth) evil
	from the bad treasure
	that is in his heart,
	and (in fact) he speaks evil.
	(4) For out of the abundance of the heart
	he brings forth evil."

A

The first sentence is a parable expressing the idea that human behavior and activities are dependent on basic attitude or character and can be considered its consequences (*not grapes from thorns, nor figs from thistles*). In the ancient Jesus tradition the basic attitude was faith in God. Sentences 2 to 4 tell us that basic orientation in life also influences the expressions of faith presented by language (*heart—speaking*). The two sentences interpret each other. Both kinds of outer consequences (activity and speaking) indicate the real character of the individual human being. In this saying Jesus was stressing the practical application of the commandment of love.

B

The first sentence is almost identical with Luke 6:44b–45; Matt 7:16 (Sermon on the Plain/Sermon on the Mount). The structure corresponds more to the Lukan version (7:45). The Matthean version reveals that the whole developed from several individual sayings. The last sentence has its analogy in Matt 12:34b–35.

Literature

Schürmann, Heinz. 1969. *Das Lukasevangelium I* (Herders Komm. III/1). Freiburg i. Br.: Herder, on Luke 6:44–45.

46	(1) Jesus says:
41,6b–12a	"From Adam to John the Baptist,
	among those born from of women

> there is no one who surpasses John the Baptist
> so that his [that is John's] eyes need not be downcast."[138]
> (2) But I have (also) said:
> "Whoever among you becomes little
> will know the kingdom and will surpass John."

A

After the sayings about James the Just and Thomas (log. 12 and 13), we now encounter a third saying about a concrete individual person: *John the Baptist*. Together with Jesus, he proclaimed the kingdom of God as the eschatological future of mankind. The solemn saying, the weight of which is supported by two names—Adam and John the Baptist—and by the phrase *among those born of women*, that is, "among all human beings," expresses the great significance of John and reflects Jesus' respect for his former teacher; at the same time, however, the second sentence expresses the superiority of Jesus' concept of the kingdom of God to the teaching of John.

His eyes do not fail, which is the probable meaning of the end of sentence 1, may mean that John inherits eternal life[139] but might also mean that he will not need to *cast his eyes down* in the face of God, as was the duty of ordinary people in the presence of rulers or other high-ranking figures.

In the context of the theology of *Gospel of Thomas*, to *become little* means a return to the spiritual being which is elevated above sexuality (see log. 4, 21, 22, 37). The members of the Thomas community are often called children (cf. log. 50), the small, or also the solitary ones (log. 49 and 75), whereas their adversaries are "many"—that is, a crowd without structure (see log. 74 and 75).

B

There are canonical parallels in Matt 11:11; Luke 7:28 (Q). The parallel frame-stories from Matt 11:2–19 and Luke 7:18–35 are quite different in their wording,[140] even though the basic themes are preserved.

Jesus was one of the followers of John the Baptist and was baptized by him. They both proclaimed the apocalyptic last judgment and coming of the kingdom of God. Jesus, however, put more emphasis on the promise of salvation, the Good News (Gr. *euangelion*), while John stressed warning and judgment (Luke 7:33–35 par. [Q]; Matt 3:1 par. [Q]). Apart from his consciousness of a special mission, this was evidently the main reason why Jesus emancipated himself from John.

Since John was a popular figure in Palestine, the followers of Jesus soon started to consider John to be Jesus' forerunner, and since this saying does not mention the function of forerunner, it may be a saying with very ancient origins, perhaps in the life of Jesus indeed.

---

138. The text may be corrupted; the possible translation may be: ". . . so that his eyes do not fail."

139. See the opposite in Lev 26:16.

140. Schrage 1964, 107f.

Literature

Hellhom, David. 1995. "Mighty Minority of Gnostic Christians," in *Mighty Minorities?* (FS J. Jervell) = *Studia Theologica* 49:41–66.

Webb, Robert L. 1991. *John the Baptizer and Prophet* (JSNTS 62). Sheffield: Sheffield Academic Press.

47
41,12b–23

(1) Jesus says:
"It is impossible for a person
to mount two horses and to stretch two bows.
(2) And it is impossible for a servant
to serve two masters.
Or else he will honor the one
and insult the other."
(3) "No person drinks old wine
and immediately desires to drink new wine.
(4) And new wine is not put
into old wineskins, so that they do not burst;
nor is old wine put into (a) new wineskin,
so that it does not spoil it.
(5) And old patch is not sewn onto a new garment,
because a tear will result."

A

Another saying that (in the frame of the *Gospel of Thomas*) stresses the difference and tension between the old and new life of an individual who becomes a disciple of Jesus. The new destroys the *old*, and the spiritual life suppresses the material tendencies.

B

The proverbs in sentence 1 of this combined saying have no parallel in the Synoptics. The proverb in sentence 2 is shorter than its canonical parallel in Matt 6:24; Luke 16:13. Jesus used this proverb to express the idea that human beings must do the will of God with an undivided heart.

Sentences 3 to 5 have a parallel in Mark 2:21–22 parr. The closest parallel is in Luke 5:36–39. Here we read of the man who drinks *old wine* (see sentence 3). In the *Gospel of Thomas*, however, the individual statements follow in a different order: Luke 5:39, 37, 38, and 36.[141]

The addition (*nor is old wine put into a new wineskin*) is a symmetrical creation, and obviously secondary since it is not based in experience. Old wine does not destroy new wineskins.

---

141. See an overview in Plisch 2007, 132.

48	Jesus says:
41,24–27	"If two make peace with one another
	in one and the same house, (then)
	they will say to the mountain:
	'Move away,' and it will move away."

A

Peace with one another means here that two or more people agree in their relation to God. Unlike in the Synoptic parallels, there is nothing here about common petition to God, that is, prayer. Prayer has already been challenged in sayings 6 and 14. The peace consists then in (1) overcoming individual differences, and in (2) common communication with God (cf. log. 22:4–7). Saying 106 is a transformed version of the basic statement (from unity to moving the mountains), where we find an interpretative parallel (unity = peace). There we read not of making peace but of making two into one, so that the two (people) become sons of man ("children of mankind").[142] This means that "making peace" is the same as the return to the original unity of human beings as beings created in God's image.

B

The saying is a conflation of two sayings that are also preserved in Synoptic traditions. The first has its parallel in Matt 18:19 ("if two of you agree on earth about anything you ask, it will be done for you by my Father in heaven"); the second in Matt 21:21b par. (cf. Mark 11:23 parr.): "If you have faith and do not doubt . . . if you say to this mountain, 'Be lifted up and thrown into the sea' it will be done." In the Synoptic tradition it is *faith* that moves the mountains. Faith is a confidence in God which inspires and supports human activity and opens the way toward its source. In the *Gospel of Thomas* the two sayings are combined in order to avoid mention of faith, since in the Thomas group spiritual knowledge and wisdom were more than faith.

In 1 Cor 13:2b Paul relativized this saying of Jesus by stressing the priority of love.

49	(1) Jesus says:
41,27b–30a	"Blessed are the solitary ones, the elect.
	For you will find the kingdom.
	(2) For you come from it (and)
	will return to it."

---

142. A possible alternative translation is suggested by NHD.

A

The *kingdom* (of God) is in this context a place of rest[143] and of close communication with God, as it is in saying 50:2–3. The solitary ones (Gr. *monachos*) is not yet the term for hermits or monks, but for those Christians who possess real wisdom and have attained close communion with God (see log. 4, 16, and 75).[144]

On *finding the kingdom,* see also log. 27. The kingdom of God is here almost identical with the human soul and its divine spark as a hidden trace of the fact that humans are created in the image of God.[145]

B

In the Synoptics we read only once about seeking the kingdom of God (Matt 6:33; Luke 12:31 [Q]—"But strive for the kingdom of God"); the most typical expression is to "enter" the kingdom of God.

The Coptic translation is quite broken.

50
41,30b–42,7a

(1) Jesus says:
"If they say to you"
'Where are you from?'
(then) say to them:
'We have come from the light,
the place where the light has
come into being by itself,
has established [itself]
and has appeared in their image.'
(2) If they say to you: 'Is it you?,'
(then) say: 'We are his children, and
we are the elect of the living Father.'
(3) If they ask you:
'What is the sign of your Father among you?,'
(then) say to them: 'It is movement and repose.'"

A

This saying is a catechetical instruction for a missionary dialogue, for a baptismal interrogation, or even for an encounter with celestial powers and lower gods who try to prevent souls from ascending to the Living One.

The *light,* from which the true disciples of Jesus come, is identical to the image of God in which the humans are created. Only enlightened and wise Christians are aware of it. Since it is light from God, the kingdom of God is the *place where the light has come into being by itself.* The image of God is therefore the light, which

---

143. See also log. 90.
144. See also log. 16:4 and 24, and introduction: The Theology of the *Gospel of Thomas*.
145. Montefiore and Turner 1962, 106f.

reveals itself in human faces and lives. It is divine light, but at the same time is a part of the individual's personality. It is the Holy Spirit that enters into an initiated and wise Christian, and its light opposes the extension of darkness in the world.

The proper identity of a human being is given by his or her relation to God as *Father* (see log. 3:3–5, 111:2–3).

The *sign* of communion with the Father is *movement and repose*. This response is mysterious: it is the paradoxical common denominator of the exhortations to seek, proclaim, search on the one hand, and repose, unity, and peace on the other (log. 48, 60:6, and 90). "Looking for repose" (log. 60:6) or "making peace moves mountains" (log. 48) are logical expressions of the relationship between movement as an instrument to reach repose, and repose as the meaning and inner sense of movement, as the Sabbath (the day of repose) is the inner meaning of workdays (see log. 27).

B

This dialogue is concerned with the source of life and expresses the theology of authentic traditions about Jesus. In many philosophical systems we meet the image of a circle, the center of which is quiet; one of the best known is the definition of the characteristics of God in Aristotle, *Metaph.* 12.7.1072b.

See also the comment on log. 24.

Literature

Pokorný, Petr. 1992. *Die Zukunft des Glaubens: Sechs Kapitel über Eschatologie.* Stuttgart: Calwer, chapter 2.

51	(1) His disciples said to him:
42,7b–12a	"When will the \<resurrection\> of the dead
	take place, and when will the new world come?"
	(2) He said to them: "That (resurrection)
	which you are awaiting has (already) come,
	but you do not recognize it."

A

A short dialogue about the supposedly imminent coming of the kingdom of God responds to questions that contemporaries asked the disciples of Jesus and presents a series of three sayings introduced by the words of the disciples. The dialogue is, in fact, catechetical instruction on how to discuss the problems of the community.

The kingdom of God, here called the *new world*, has a dimension in the present, and this in fact plays an important role in the Gospels and the Epistles as well as in the *Gospel of Thomas*: "The kingdom of the Father is spread out upon the earth, and people do not see it" (log. 113:4; cf. log. 3). Similarly, the *resurrection* in the sense of the general resurrection of all mortals as envisaged by the apocalyptic texts (Dan 12:3; 1 Thess 4:16f.) has to be understood as already taking place, in the sense that the eschatological future of every individual will unfold on the basis of their present behavior. In John 5:25 we read: "I tell you, the hour is coming, and is now here (*has come*), when the dead will hear the voice of the Son of God, and those who hear will live."

B

Jesus proclaimed the imminent coming of the kingdom of God, but he refused to specify a date. "About that day or hour no one knows, neither the angels in heaven, nor the Son, but only the Father" (Mark 13:32). The Lukan tradition concentrated on Jesus as the representative and agent of the kingdom, such that the problem of its time of arrival receded into the background: "In fact the kingdom of God is among you" (Luke 17:21b). The Johannine and Thomasine new interpretation of the eschatological (final and absolute) human hope helped Christians to overcome their disappointment over the delayed coming of God's kingdom by stressing its present dimension. This position is also taken over by one wing of the Pauline schools: ". . . you were also raised with him through faith" (Col 2:12b). The other wing of the Pauline school realized the danger of a pious perfectionism that might lead to judging others, and so rejected as heretical the doctrine that resurrection has already taken place: "Hymenaeus and Philetus . . . swerved from the truth by claiming that resurrection has already taken place" (2 Tim 2:18.[146]

The word *resurrection* (Gr. *anastasis*) in part 1 is almost illegible. It may be that the Coptic scribe originally wrote "repose" (Gr. *anapausis*), which has the same syllables at the beginning and end.

52
42,12b–18a

(1) His disciples said to him:
"Twenty-four prophets have spoken in Israel,
and all (of them) have spoken through you."[147]
(2) He said to them:
"You have pushed away the living (one)
from yourselves, and you have begun[148]
to speak of those who are dead."

---

146. With regard to the resurrection before the death, see the *Gospel of Philip* (NHC II/3; 56,15–20).

147. Possible alternative translations are: "in you," or "about you" (NHD).

148. "Begun" helps to express the Greek tense (aorist), which was obviously present in the Greek original.

A

The question concerns the authority of the Jewish Bible, the Law and the Prophets, in the church as the community of Jesus' disciples.

The answer proclaims that Jesus is not a revived old prophet in the sense of the expected Elijah (Mal 3:23)[149] or Moses (an expectation derived from Deut 18:15). Jesus is one with the *living* God himself (log. 50).

Even in the canonical Gospels Jesus is different from the prophets. His proclaimed resurrection was conceived not as an individual miracle but rather as the revelation of God's creative power and love, which manifests itself at a lower level in the life of nature, such as the growth of a crop (1 Cor 15:12–49) and which is also the basis of the future of other human beings (Rom 6:3–12). This is why Jesus can promise life to others: "Whoever keeps my word will never taste death" (John 8:52b).

Twenty-four is the number of the books of the Law and Prophets, the Jewish Bible, according to the traditional numbering. The books of Samuel and the books of Kings were each considered one book and the so-called Writings, as the third part of the Scriptures, were not included. All the biblical authors were considered to be *prophets*.

The saying does not mean the rejection of the Jewish Bible, as was later the case with Marcion. It rejects only the so-called history of salvation (in German *Heilsgeschichte*) in favor of the immediate voice of the living Jesus.

B

The mainstream church understood the Law and the Prophets (the basic parts of the later Old Testament) as a series of sayings and stories related to the coming of Jesus as Christ, the revelation of God.

The phrase about the *Living One* and the dead from part 2 has its parallel in Luke 24:5: "Why do you look for the living among the dead?" These are both expressions that reflect Easter terminology, with analogies in literary metaphors such as "died with Christ—live with him" (Rom 6:8) or "was dead and is alive" in the parable about the prodigal son in Luke 15:24 and 32. Another kind of indirect parallel is the saying about the proclamation of the kingdom as more important than burying the dead from source Q (Matt 8:22; Luke 9:60).

The second part is quoted by Augustinus Aurelius (Augustine, beginning of the fifth century) in his tractate *Against the Contestants of the Law.*[150]

53	(1) His disciples said to him:
42,18b–23a	"Is circumcision beneficial or not?"
	(2) He said to them: "If it were beneficial,

---

149. On the identification of Jesus with Elijah who was raised from the dead, see Mark 6:15 parr. and 8:28 parr.

150. See Plisch 2007, 143f.

> their father would beget them circumcised
> from their mother.
> (3) But the true circumcision in the spirit
> has prevailed over everything."[151]

A

In saying 14 we have already encountered a proclamation that radically rejects the cult, or, concretely, the three main principles, of Jewish piety. Here it is one of the commandments of the Jewish Law that is rejected or radically reinterpreted. Thomasine Christianity broke with the synagogue at the end of the first or at the beginning of the second century. The reason was the fear that cult might weaken inner spiritual piety.

Is circumcision beneficial? From Jesus' answer, the reader realizes that *in the spirit* may mean baptism interpreted as spiritual renewal, as we already meet it in the Gospel of John: "No one can enter the kingdom of God without being born of water and Spirit" (John 3:5).

B

The apostle Paul had already interpreted faith as true circumcision (Rom 2:29). Unlike the *Gospel of Thomas,* he did not reject circumcision generally but rejected it as a condition for membership in God's people (see Rom 2:25; cf. Col 2:11). In the most ancient layers of the Synoptic Gospels, Jesus did not reject circumcision.[152] If a saying of Jesus similar to the one in *Gospel of Thomas* 53 had been available at the time of the apostle Paul, he would have quoted it in his argument against those who compelled former pagans (gentiles) to be circumcised as a condition for becoming Christians (Rom 2–4).

The emerging church wished to link closely spiritual baptism (consisting of special gifts from God—Gr. *charisma*) with baptism by water. The Acts of the Apostles is a text that documents this struggle very clearly: see, for example, Acts 8:12, 14–17 (baptism in water quickly complemented by the gift of the Spirit), Acts 10:47 (those who have received the gift of Spirit are baptized as soon as possible), and Acts 2:37–38 (a model of the ideal unity of simultaneously receiving the gift of the Spirit and being baptized). Traditionally, this tendency has been supported by the story of the baptism of Jesus, in which the Spirit descended on Jesus as he ascended from the water after his baptism. This narrative was shaped as the model of true Christian baptism.

54	Jesus says:
42,23b–24	"Blessed are the poor.
	For the kingdom of heaven belongs to you."

---

151. Literally, "has found absolute profit (or use)" (NHD).
152. John 7:22f. does not mean a refusal of circumcision.

A

The beatitude about the *poor* was understood as a protest against the world-view of the possessors. The poor are people like the members of the Thomas community, like the small ones mentioned in saying 46. They are addressed in the second person (*to you*), as in the parallel in Luke 6:20. The beatitude is expressed as a promise to concrete people. Everybody can see who it is that has the real future. The attribute *of heaven* was understood as an expression of the spiritual quality of the promised realm.

B

A beatitude is a *blessing* on people who enter a special space protected by a divinity. "Blessed is the earthly human who saw them (the mysteries)," we read in the Homeric hymn on Demeter (480), referring to those initiated into the Eleusinian mysteries.

Jesus often blessed those who were not specifically qualified in this sense, so that the beatitude was a promise, in this case the concrete proclamation of what would be the transformed social structure of the kingdom of God. The Thomas group identified itself with the poor, and this beatitude helped it build up its inner identity. As with most of the sayings whose Greek version is preserved in P.Oxy. 655,[153] here too we have a saying from the oldest layer of the Jesus tradition.

The only feature this saying has in common with the other parallel in Matt 5:3 is the concluding part of the sentence, where the *kingdom of heaven* is promised. This expression is adopted from orthodox Jewish practice, which did not pronounce God's name.

Other beatitudes well known from Luke 6 have their parallels in sayings 68 and 69.

55
42,25–29a

(1) Jesus says:
"Whoever does not hate his father and his mother
cannot become a disciple of mine.
(2) And whoever does not hate
brothers and his sisters (and)
will not take up his cross as I do,
will not be worthy of me."

A

This saying has its parallel in Luke 14:26–27 (Q). *Hate* is an emphatic and exaggerated expression for "love less than . . . ," as the Q version was interpreted in Matt 10:37. It is a way of speaking quite common in Semitic languages. The shocking impression served as a means of emphasizing the value contrasted with that which should be hated. Here it means that family ties must not prevent the disciple

---

153. Robinson 1999, 65.

of Jesus from taking the path of his spiritual teacher and loving him from the heart. Logion 101:1 is a parallel to this saying, but in its second part it says: "And whoever does [not] love his [father and] his mother as I do, will not be able to be a [disciple] of mine."

The cross was a symbol of suffering, and in the early church it was a symbol of Jesus' death.

B

In the *Gospel of Thomas* the criticism of family relations contributed to the social crisis of Thomas Christianity. In spite of its demanding character, it is still an attractive religious attitude. It offers a simple religious ideology.

A parallel to the second part of log. 55:2 is also to be found in the maxim from Mark 8:34 parr. The *cross* may have been added in the post-Easter period in place of the word "yoke," as in Matt 11:28f.

Here we are in the arithmetic center of the *Gospel of Thomas,* and the reference to the cross may have a deeper function: The cross of Jesus is being interpreted as a way toward the revelation of an alternative world.[154] If this is true, here we are also at the theological center of the *Gospel of Thomas.*

Literature

Diebner, Bernd J. 1995. "Bemerkungen zur 'Mitte' des Thomas-Evangeliums," in C. Fluck, L. Langener, S. Richter, S. Schaten, and G. Wurst, *Divitiae Aegypti* (FS Martin Krause). Wiesbaden: Reichert Verlag.

Pokorný, Petr. 2002. "Stilistische und rhetorische Eigentümlichkeiten der ältesten Jesustradition," in J. Schröter and R. Brucker, eds., *Der historische Jesus: Tendenzen und Perspektiven der gegenwärtigen Forschung* (Beiheft ZNW 114). Berlin/New York: de Gruyter, 393–408.

56	(1) Jesus says:
42,29–32	"Whoever has come to know the world has found a corpse.
	(2) and whoever has found (this) corpse, of him the world is not worthy."

A

The true knowledge of the *world*, such as is given to spiritually developed individual, leads to a shocking discovery: The world is a *corpse*, a cadaver. This is not only a metaphor expressing the tension between the absurdities of the visible world and the harmony of original God's creation. It is a statement based on pragmatic

---

154. Diebner 1995, 77ff.

speculation about human beings and the world (anthropology and cosmology): the life of humans is sustained by eating animals—the carcasses, the cadavers. And the only visible prospect of those who concentrate on eating the dead, is death.

The Thomas Christian who is able to recognize this character of the world[155] is superior to it in its present form, and the world is in this sense *not worthy of him*, since he and all those like him belong to the divine side. And yet, at least some of the Christians can become something like the soul of the body of the world and change the carcass into a living being: "When they shake off their intoxication from wine, then they will change the mind" (log. 29), since the spirit came into being because of the body. This is a paradox of Thomas theology. In log. 29 indeed, we read that "it is a wonder of wonders."

B

If this saying has an authentic core, it is probably Jesus' metaphorical characterization of the present life of human society as the opposite of the kingdom of God—the source of life. In saying 80 we find what is probably the same saying in a different and obviously better translation: The world is a body. In the anthropology of the Judaism of the time, the body received its life through the soul, but the soul came from the spirit of God. The readers of the *Gospel of Thomas* may soon have come to understand the body as a corpse or carcass, but it is probable that originally it was meant as body, which needs the soul and the Spirit, and that it was supposed that the Christians might mediate that animation of the body by their witness.

In the *Gospel of Philip* (73,19) the world is compared to a corpse-eater. All that is being eaten in the world is mortal.

57
42,32b–43,7a

(1) Jesus says:
"The kingdom of the Father
is like a person who had a (good) seed.
(2) His enemy came by night.
He sowed darnel among the good seed.
(3) The person did not allow (the servants)
to pull up the darnel. He said to them:
'Lest you go to pull up the darnel (and then)
pull up the darnel (and then) pull up
the wheat along with it.'[156]
(4) For on the day of the harvest
the darnel will be apparent[157] and
will be pulled up (and) burned."

---

155. For the theme of knowing the world, see also log. 67, 110, and 111.

156. The text is not quite clear, and the scribe may have omitted one line. The main argument remains the same in all alternative translations.

157. Or "visible" (NHD).

A

The parable warns against the premature judgment and rejection of the others and proclaims that God's judgment is the last judgment (*harvest*) indeed and will be impartial and just. The spiritually initiated people have various gifts, but no human is called to judge the others.[158] That is why the farmer concerned is an example of prudent, wise, or sensible people, as they are mentioned, for example, in log. 76:2 or 8:1.

B

This parable has its parallel in Matt 13:24–30. Here, in log. 57, we find a slightly shorter version: Matt 13:26–28 has no parallel here. What is most striking is that the allegorical explanation from Matt 13:36b–43 is missing too. It is an allegorical ecclesiastic interpretation relating the parable to the true (*good seed*) and false (*darnel*, weeds) Christians. This led some scholars[159] to the conclusion that the parable must have been taken over from a tradition independent of Matthew.

The tendency toward spiritual interpretation of a basically apocalyptic parable, as we indicated in part A, is frequent in the *Gospel of Thomas;* and we also find it in saying 20.[160]

58	Jesus says:
43,7b–9a	"Blessed is the person who has struggled.
	He has found life."

A

This saying expresses the promise of human activity and work as the price of life. In the Thomas community it may also have been understood as an illustration of the spiritual maxim dealing with the relation between movement and repose, as it is mentioned in log. 50:3. The *Gospel of Thomas* understands such activity as the overcoming of drunkenness (shaking off intoxication)[161] or the search for the kingdom of God (log. 27, 92, and 94) and in saying 107:2–3 as the search for the lost big sheep.

B

The proverb may have a meaning similar to that of the originally military proverb: "Those who try to make their life secure will lose it, but those who lose their life will keep it (Luke 17:33 par. [Q]; Mark 8:35 parr.). Jesus may have recalled it when he had to cope with the risk to his own life.

There are some rather indirect parallels in the New Testament, that is, 1 Pet

---

158. A later Gnostic interpretation considers the darnel to be the body and the good seed to be the spirit (Clement of Alexandria, *Exc. ex Theod.* § 53—a Valentinian system, according to Ptolemaios).

159. Cullmann 1960; Hunzinger 1960.

160. Patterson 1993, 211f.

161. See log. 28:4.

3:14; Jas 1:12; Acts 14:22b: "It is through many persecutions that we must enter the kingdom of God." The ninth *Psalm of Thomas,* verse 7, may possibly contain a quotation of this saying.

Labor, effort, or struggling (Copt. *hise,* which also means the suffering of martyrdom) appeared occasionally as a virtue in Gnostic writings (*Apocryphon of James,* NHC I/2, 4,22—5,23).

Literature

Beardslee, William. 1979. "Saving One's Life by Losing It," *Journal of the American Academy of Religion* 47:57–72.
Koschorke, Klaus. 1978. *Die Polemik der Gnostiker gegen das kirchliche Christentum* (NHS 12). Leiden: Brill. See excursus V (on the theme of suffering in Gnosticism).
Pokorný, Petr. 2002. "Luk 17,33 und ein (damals) bekanntes Sprichwort," in *For the Children: Perfect Instruction* (FS H.-M. Schenke; NHMS 54). Leiden/Boston: Brill, 387–98 (on the theme of losing and gaining life).

59	Jesus says:
43,9b–12a	"Look for the Living One while you are alive,
	so that you will not die and (then) seek to see him.
	And you will not be able to see (him)."

A

A parallel to the exhortation from log. 38. To *look for the Living One* and *you are alive* are two corresponding expressions. It means that the human being's fate in terms of eternal life will be decided during his earthly life. But for the Thomas community it hinted at a still higher truth: To look for the Living One means to reach eternal life (*you will not die*); see log. 111:2: "Whoever is living from the Living One will not see death," and especially the next saying 60.[162]

B

Look for the Living One while you are alive is a bridge to the next saying concerning the Samaritan with the lamb.

60	(1) <He saw> a Samaritan
43,12b–23a	who was trying to take away a lamb
	while he was on his way to Judea.
	(2) He said to his disciples:

---

162. Cf. the *Gospel of Philip* (NHC II/3; 52,15–18).

"That (person) is stalking the lamb."[163]
(3) They said to him:
"So that he may kill it (and) eat it."
(4) He said to them:
"As long as it is alive he will not eat it,
but (only) when he has killed it (and)
it has become a corpse."
(5) They said: "Otherwise he cannot do it."
(6) He said to them: "You too,
look for a place for your repose
so that you may not become a corpse
(and) get eaten."

A

This strange saying offers the key to the understanding of the saying on the world as a corpse (log. 56). The *lamb* will not be eaten as long as it lives. The conclusion is that those who are alive indeed, that is, are linked with the source of life (log. 13, 50, and 59), will not be swallowed by the unclean power and will not die. Otherwise they would become a *corpse* like the slaughtered lamb. It is a sophisticated theory, since the lamb cannot resist being *stalked* and *killed*. But the answer may be that in the moment when the man with lamb was observed, the *stalked* lamb was still a living lamb. The wise person has to identify him or herself with the *living lamb* and by a wise decision it has a chance to survive. It can act (*Look for . . .*)—that is, undergo conversion and achieve the new status of those who are linked with the Living One (*place of repose*). Otherwise, their fate will be death indeed.[164]

Repose (Gr. *anapausis*) is an expression for salvation derived from the biblical Sabbath—the day of rest, the seventh day of the Jewish calendar (Exod 20:8–11—linked with the creation of the world), Deut 5:12–15—linked with the exodus from Egypt). In early Christian literature it often denotes the life free of earthly struggle (log. 58). The term *place* also has an eschatological connotation (cf. log. 24—a place where Jesus is).

B

Logion 60 could be considered a further part of log. 59: they are linked by common themes and by apparent literary continuity.[165]

The whole dialogue poses problems for translators, since the text seems to have been corrupted or misunderstood by the scribe or the original translator himself. Most scholars believe that the word *saw* has been omitted at the beginning. The Berlin group (NHD) regards the first sentence as expressing an attempt (Lat.

---

163. Literally, "That (person) is around the lamb."
164. Turner in Montefiore and Turner 1962, 63; Dembska and Myszor 1979.
165. Kasser 1961, ad loc.

de conatu) as it is rendered in the English translation. There are also a number of words missing in part 2.

It is not necessary, however, to theorize textual corruptions. It is possible that what we have here is the skeleton of a dialogue, which had to be filled out in the process of narration. The text seems to be derived from notes aiding oral transmission. A similar phenomenon can be observed, for example, in the Pauline version of the institution of the Lord's Supper (1 Cor 11:24—"This is my body for you").

The setting is not clear. A Samaritan walking with a lamb to *Judea* probably intended to sacrifice it in the Temple of Jerusalem, but we have no evidence of Samaritans sacrificing in Jerusalem after their temple at Mount Gerizim was destroyed by the Jewish ruler John Hyrcanus. It is also improbable that somebody would go from Samaria to Judea to sell a single lamb. The translation, according to which the lamb was stolen (see the translation of the NHD), is more logical. But why should a single lamb be transported to Judea? The scene seems to have been created as a background for Jesus' closing exhortation from part 6, which has its indicative parallel in sayings 7, 11, and 56. It may have been part of the Thomas liturgy similar to the liturgy of one of the Pauline groups, in which we hear: "Sleeper awake! Rise from the dead and Christ will shine on you" (Eph 5:14).

Literature

Laausma, Jon. 1997. *"I Will Give You Rest"* (WUNT 2/98). Tübingen: Mohr Siebeck.

61	(1) Jesus says:
43,23b–34a	"Two will rest on a couch.
	The one will die, the other will live."
	(2) Salome said: "(So) who are you, man?
	You have got a place on my couch
	as a \<stranger\>[166] and you have eaten from my table."
	(3) Jesus said to her:
	"I am he who comes from the one
	who is (always) the same.
	I was given some of that which is my Father's;
	(4) I am your disciple!"
	(5) Therefore I say: "If someone becomes \<like\> (God),
	he will become full of light.
	But if he becomes one, separated (from God),
	he will become full of darkness."

---

166. The translation is based on a reconstruction of the Greek source. The translator could read the Greek *hōs xenos* ("as a stranger") as *hōs ek henos* ("as from one").

A

The first part expresses, in a way similar to saying 16, the weight, authority, and impartiality of the last judgment.

The following dialogue is linked with the first part by the motif of *couch* in the sense of a place at the table (*you have eaten from my table*). It introduces the theme of life and of living in proximity to God. The scene of sentences 2 and 3 supposes table fellowship, its participants reclining on couches around a low table or a carpet. Jesus obviously came to the dinner at Salome's house unexpectedly: *You have got a place on my couch.* In antiquity, table fellowship usually also expressed an inner link between the participants. Like Socrates, Jesus often presented his teaching on such occasions (e.g., Mark 2:15–17).

The content of Jesus' revelation (sentence 3) is his close relation to God, who *is the same.* This may mean that God is reliable, because of his identity over time (this presupposes the Greek *ek tou isou*),[167] but the Coptic *oua* may also express his uniqueness,[168] the fact that he cannot be compared with any other. This means that Jesus' authority consisted in his unity with God, that he participates in his power: *I was given some of that which is my Father's.*" He revealed himself as the Son of the Supreme One.[169] Sentence 3b recalls the revelatory hymn of Jesus from the source Q: Matt 11:27; Luke 10:22 (Q); cf. John 13:3. If we accept the text reconstruction of the Berlin translators,[170] Jesus may have been considered as a *stranger* since Salome has not yet attained the full knowledge of the Divine.

Salome should be Salome of Zebedee, the mother of James and John,[171] and according to some later traditions she was also the aunt of Jesus (cf. John 19:25 with Mark 15:45f.). She proclaimed herself to be Jesus' *disciple* (sentence 4).[172] It follows that 61:5a expresses what will be given to such disciples who are "worthy" of his mysteries: They will be *full of light*.[173] Whereas those who are *separated* (Copt. *pōš*),[174] obviously[174] separated in their minds from God and living an "earthly" life,[175] *will become full of darkness*—they will lose their orientation in life.[176]

B

This small collection of sayings consists of three main units: an apocalyptic saying (sentence 1), the revelatory speech of Jesus framed by a discussion with Salome (sentences 2–4), and the concluding maxim proclaimed by Jesus (sentence 5).

---

167. As does the translation of NHD; a possible corruption commented on in the edition by Layton 1989, 74 note) with reference to H.-J. Polotsky.

168. Uro 1998, 51 ("someone special").

169. Meyer 1992, 47.

170. See note 166 above.

171. This is the most common understanding of Mark 15:40.

172. See above introduction: on theology and ecclesiology in *Gospel of Thomas*.

173. See log. 24:3; 33:2–3; and Matt 6:22.

174. The text is not quite clear.

175. Later development in *Gospel of Philip* (NHC II/3, 52,15–18).

176. In the *Apocryphon of John* (NHC II/1; 31,35–37) such a person is cursed.

The memory of the tradition of Jesus' table fellowship serves here merely as the setting for his self-revelation in the Thomas sense.

62
43,34b–44,2a

(1) Jesus says:
"I tell my mysteries to those who
[are worthy] of [my] mysteries."
(2) "Whatever your right hand does,
your left hand should not know
what it is doing."

The first part is almost illegible

A

Again we have here a tandem of two sayings: The first serves as expression of the inner identity of the Thomas community in relation to the outer world, but also in relation to the other followers of Jesus. The people who keep to the heritage of Thomas know that they are children of the living God, as expressed in log. 3:4. *Those who are worthy of mysteries* are those who are addressed in the prologue and in the first saying and whose next representative is Salome from the preceding saying. The mystery is God who is close to human beings, even if they in their blindness do not see it. This is the only place where the Greek term *mysterion* is used, even if it is presupposed in the whole *Gospel of Thomas* as a theological concept of the revelation of hidden truth (prologue and the first saying). The mystery can be discovered by a wise, prudent, or sensible person, who has true knowledge.

The second sentence has a parallel in Matt 6:3, where it appears as an instruction on how to give alms. *Not know* means that giving alms should be self-evident, done without any publicity, not as a special act of giving alms but spontaneously, just as God's love affects wise human beings. It is in this sense that we should also interpret log. 14:3 (cf. log. 6 and 104).

B

Irenaeus reported the later speculation of the Valentinians concerning this saying, that is, that the right hand represents the spiritual area and the left hand the mundane area, but this is a later Gnostic development.[177]

63
44,2b–10a

(1) Jesus says:
"There was a rich person
who had many possessions.
(2) He said: 'I will use my possessions
so that I might sow, reap, plant (and)

---

177. *Adv. haer.* 1.5.1; see Gärtner 1961, 115.

> fill my storehouses with fruit
> so that I will not lack anything.'
> (3) This is what he was thinking in his heart.
> And in that night he died.
> (4) Whoever has ears should hear."

A

Sayings 63 through 65 criticize a style of life orientated toward safeguarding external good conditions and wealth. Saying 63 is an example (a parable in the broader sense) of a bad calculation in life, well known from Luke 12:16–20. It is an image of life without the prospect of God's promise—a life in which the human *heart* cares for mundane *possessions*. It is dramatically depicted through reproduction of an inner monologue (Lat. *soliloquium*). The *Gospel of Thomas* rejects care for possessions and a high valuation of wealth in sayings 54 and 63–65.[178]

The effect of the parable is built upon the contrast between the care and organizing work of the protagonist and the unforeseeable limit of his life. The length of the description of the care (twenty-one words in Coptic) and of the unexpected death (five words) underscores the impact of the story. We may consider it a masterpiece of a pragmatic argument in Jesus tradition.

For the exhortation in sentence 4, see the comment to the parallel in log. 8. The most important New Testament parallels are Mark 4:9 and Rev 2:7.

B

An alternative interpretation sees in the rich man the positive figure of a person who was able to do a great deal of work before he died.[179] The many possessions may be compared to the big fish or the pearl. Nevertheless, the fact that in his death he is entirely isolated from what he intended during his life speaks in favor of an interpretation similar to that of Luke 12. The difference is that in Luke 12 the protagonist is a rich farmer, while here he has more possessions and is probably a businessman. Since "dealers and merchants" are condemned in the next saying (64:12), the protagonist of this parable will be a negative figure, too.

Compared with Luke 12:16–21, this is a shorter version,[180] totally concentrated on the simple plot itself. This makes it immensely effective, especially the abrupt ending.

The text is not influenced by the Lukan parallel, so log. 63 must have been taken from an independent source. This is the only saying with a parallel in material that is singular to Luke.[181]

---

178. See the commentary.

179. Schrage 1964a, 132f.

180. Eighty Greek words in Luke and thirty-three Coptic words here; forty-one words in the reconstructed Greek text.

181. Schürmann 1968, 232f., observed some minor lexical similarities between the preceding verses in Luke 12:13ff. on the one hand and the Coptic text of saying 72 on the other. He deduced that

64	(1) Jesus says:
44,10b–35	"A person had guests.
	And when he had prepared the dinner,
	he sent his servants so that he
	might invite the quests.
	(2) He came to the first (and) said to him:
	'My master invites you.'
	(3) He said: 'I have bills against some merchants.
	They are coming to me this evening.
	I will go (and) give instructions to them.
	Excuse me from the dinner.'
	(4) He came to another (and) said to him:
	'My master has invited you.'
	(5) He said to him: 'I have bought a house,
	and I have been called (away) for a day.
	I will not have time.'
	(6) He went to another (and) said to him:
	'My master invites you.'
	(7) He said to him: 'My friend is going to marry,
	and I am one who is going to prepare the meal.
	I will not be able to come.
	Excuse me from the dinner.'
	(8) He came to another (and) said to him:
	'My master invites you.'
	(9) He said to him: 'I have bought a village.
	Since I am going to collect the rent,
	I will not be able to come. Excuse me.'
	(10) The servant went away.
	He said to his master: 'Those whom you invited
	to dinner have asked to be excused.'
	(11) The master said to his servant:
	'Go out on the roads.
	Bring (back) whomever you find,
	so that they might have dinner,'
	(12) Dealers and merchants,
	[will] not enter the places of my Father."

A

The parable expresses the inner structure of human hope: the communion with God (the host) and with other people (guests) in the Age to Come. It also demon-

---

the editor of the *Gospel of Thomas* was familiar with the text of Luke and may have taken this parable from Luke as well.

strates the depth of Jesus' proclamation of the kingdom of God and the fatal consequences of a refusal or indifference toward the invitation.

As in all the versions, the parable deals with obstacles to reaching the meal in the kingdom of God. In all versions the problem is that the invited guests have a scale of values in which the table fellowship of the host does not occupy the highest position. The unconditional invitation is therefore not accepted. The potential guests excuse themselves politely (*I will not be able . . . excuse me*), but they all decline.

In the *Gospel of Thomas* it is business (*dealers and merchants*) that prevents them from coming. Only sentence 7 (wedding of a friend) seems to be a personal or strictly social affair. But the editor of the *Gospel of Thomas* considered preparing a banquet as an activity obviously associated with a business relationship between the guest and his friend. In any case the concluding sentence from part 11 is unambiguous. In the Jewry of the time business was a morally controversial occupation because of the danger of illegal profit. A critical attitude toward business expressed a conservative distance from city civilization (Sir 26:29–27:2). For the Thomas community, business was in addition to this a dangerous occupation on principle, since it was related to possessions. As such, business tended to be an obstacle on the way toward conversion, spiritual renewal, and reaching the kingdom of the heavenly *Father*.

The new strategy of the host, who eventually invites people who lived outside the city (*on the roads*), was understood as a prophetic image of the pagan mission, as it was at least in the other two versions.

The word *places* (Gr./Copt. *topos*) in the concluding part is an eschatological term; see log. 4 and 60:6.

B

This is the longest saying in the *Gospel of Thomas*. It has a parallel in Luke 14:14–24 and in Matt 22:2–10 (the longest, extended version), the Thomas version being just a little shorter than the Lukan one. The two Synoptic versions are so different from each other that some exegetes doubt whether they belong to the same source Q, but since most of the differences between the two Synoptic versions can be explained by the editorial and theological intentions of the Gospel writers, especially Matthew, we can still suppose that both Gospel writers took the parable from their common source. In Matthew we find an additional scene about the two kinds of guests that enjoyed the dinner—a theme that has its analogy, for example, in the adoring and doubting disciples of Jesus according to Matt 28:17. Similarly, the many servants who invite the guests (another difference from Luke and Thomas), remind the reader of Christian missionaries as they are described in Matt 10:11–14 or 28:19f. As regards the version from the *Gospel of Thomas*, we may generally say that it "contains about as much primary and as much secondary material as the other(s)."[182] Some elements that could be explained as dependent on

---

182. Koester and Robinson 1971, 132.

the Synoptic versions[183] may have been added during translation into Coptic. On the whole, the version in the *Gospel of Thomas* may contain several independent and old features,[184] is more colorful, and includes interesting details.

65

45,1–16a

(1) He said:

"A [usurer][185] owned a vineyard.
He gave it to some farmers
so that they would work it (and)
he might receive its fruit from them.
(2) He sent his servant so that the farmers
might give him the fruit of the vineyard.
(3) They seized his servant, beat him (and)
almost killed him.
The servant went (back and) told his master.
(4) His master said:
'Perhaps <they> did not recognize <him>.'[186]
(5) He sent another servant,
(and) the farmers beat that other one as well.
(6) Then the master sent his son (and) said:
'Perhaps they will show respect to my son.'
(7) (But) those farmers,
since they knew that he was the heir of the vineyard,
seized him (and) killed him."

A

If our interpretation is correct, the protagonist who sends his servants is in this case a negative figure, and the two parables, log. 64 and 65, represent two different attitudes. Both parables warn against greed: in log. 64 it is the greed of the invited persons; here it is the greed of the owner of the vineyard. The protagonist is a greedy landowner, one of a group of rich cosmopolitan businessmen who influenced the economy of the Eastern Mediterranean during the later hellenistic and early imperial period, that is, also in the time of Jesus. He is termed a *usurer*. Such individuals exploited the farmers (peasants) who received land for colonization and turned them into fully dependent laborers: They *would work* and *he might receive*

---

183. This was the thesis of the first period of research (e.g., Grant and Freedman 1960, 158f.; for an overview of the discussion, see Nordsieck 2004.

184. Schürmann 1968, 236.

185. Only the beginning of the word is legible. It may be "a good man" (Gr. *chrēstos*) or "a usurer" (*chrēstēs*). The NHD group decided for the second alternative, which corresponds to the proposed intention of the parable.

186. The text is damaged; the other possible reconstruction is "Perhaps he did not recognize them" (NHD).

. . . *fruit from them*. This was his idea. But the farmers surprised him: they did not pay him anything and even beat his agents. Eventually he sent his *son*, since a son was a valid representative of his father from the legal point of view. The revolting farmers acted consistently and killed the son. The hearer/reader may learn how foolish it is to rely on possessions. The usurer lost both: his possessions and his son. This is the tragic end of greedy people. In the Jesus tradition, this usurer is a relative of the rich fool (Luke 12:13–21; log. 63). The concluding eschatological exhortation of log. 63 underscores the key character of this story. Do not rely on possessions; do not trust in mammon (Luke 16:13 par. [Q]). The motivation is not moralistic, but pragmatic. To rely on possessions is foolish; it is a miscalculation.

B

This was the interpretation of the parable offered by Dehandshutter (1974) and supported by Kloppenborg (2006). It is a surprising interpretation, since in the parallel in the Gospel of Mark (Mark 12:1–12; parallels Matt 21:33–46; Luke 20:9–19), in which the same actors appear and the plot is almost the same, the general intention is fundamentally different. The laborers are killed (they lose their life) and the vineyard is given to others. The lord is a positive key person (God) and his murdered son is a metaphorical expression for Jesus and his role as it appears in those Christian confessions that speak about his sacrificial death. As a whole the story is in fact an allegory. The son is mentioned as the "beloved (Gr. *agapētos*) son" (Mark 12:6), as Jesus is called at his baptism (Mark 1:11) and transfiguration (9:7). Other interpretations were blocked by the fact that the traditional understanding was fixed in common Christian consciousness, in which it demonstrates the omniscience of Jesus, who foresees his own violent death. The critical scholarship of the twentieth century accepted this interpretation and, on the basis of its understanding of the story as allegorical, considered this text to be a creation of Christian communities.[187] The christological (Markan) understanding was so influential that it overshadowed the older and obviously more original version. Here it was the greed of the landlord that was the cause of his failure. The action of the tenants was pragmatic, since discovery of the murderers of a person who came from far away[188] was quite difficult. Their action was criminal, but the parable stressed the failure of the possessor, not the morality of the murderers. This is a theme that appears in the Jesus tradition several times, for example, in the parable on the dishonest steward (Luke 16:1–9) or in the *Gospel of Thomas* in the parable on the terrorist (log. 98).

The fact that the Thomas version does not seem to be formulated as a polemic against the christological (Markan) version suggests that saying 65 is not only different in its intention but also independent of the Synoptic version of the story.[189] The attribute *usurer* (in Coptic/Greek *ourōme ᵉnchrēstēs*—literally, "a man—usurer") would seem to be the decisive evidence in favor of this interpretation, if it

---

187. "Gemeindebildung" (Bultmann 1979, 191).

188. There are records of possessors of vineyards in Palestine who lived in Egypt. In Pap. Londonensis 2661 we have a letter from a trustee, who gives his master in Egypt a report on his tenants who take care of eighty thousand vine trees.

189. Crossan 1991, chapter 13; Patterson 1993, 48ff., 228nn.

were well attested. Unfortunately the text is damaged, and since a similar adjective *chrēstos* means "good" or "ordered," the decision for the translation as "userer" is based only on an inner analysis of the parable, in which nothing speaks in favor of the possessor as a positive figure.

A special problem is presented by the fact that the following log. 66 reproduces a saying (a quotation from Psalm 118) that in Mark 12:10–11 is immediately attached to the parable. Mark 12:9 serves as a bridge between the parable and the scriptural quotation. The fact that in the *Gospel of Thomas* both units follow in the same sequence might call into question the theory of the independent origin of the version from saying 65. However, the editor of the *Gospel of Thomas* may have known the parable from Mark (or Luke) and from an independent source. From Mark he took over the Psalm quotation and from the special source the different version of the parable. However, the quote might also fall into place as a summary of the Thomas understanding of the parable: as a warning demonstrated by an example of reversal of fortunes.[190] Jesus, who did not have any possessions, is the cornerstone of the eschatological order of the kingdom of heaven.

Mark used the attached proverb as the basis for his soteriological interpretation of the parable. At the same time he inserted verse 1b, which enumerates the elements of a good vineyard, as mentioned in the Song of the Vineyard from Isa 5:1–7 in verse 2. In this well-known text the vineyard that does not bring forth fruit allegorically represents "the house of Israel" (v. 7), whereas the owner of the vineyard, the singer, is a positive figure (cf. Jer 2:21). This metaphorical and allegorical tradition of the biblical language supported the christological understanding of the parable as we know it from Mark.[191]

Crossan has also referred to another version of the vineyard parable from the Shepherd of Hermas *Sim.* 5.2.1–8. The parable tells of a lord (Gr. *despotēs*) who had a piece of land that he intended to cultivate and give to his son as his vineyard. He asked his servant (Gr. *doulos*) to watch the piece of land during his absence. The servant cultivated it and turned it into a fruitful vineyard. When he returned home, the lord decided that the servant (and his friends, 2.9–11) would be co-owners of his vineyard together with his son, who gladly consented. Psalm 118 is not mentioned. This is, however, a clear allegory of the church—the vineyard owned by the Son of the Lord and the other people who serve the same Lord.

Having discussed all these alternatives, we cannot exclude the possibility that if another manuscript of the *Gospel of Thomas* is found, it will read "a good man" in the first sentence. We have here a text with two different interpretations reaching obviously back to the pre-Markan traditions. But the interpretation of the parable that we have presented fits better the pre-Easter teaching of Jesus.

---

190. Kloppenborg 1986, 273.

191. Another well-known passage about a vineyard as metaphor is John 15:1–6; cf. *Gospel of Thomas*, log. 40.

Literature

Bultmann, R. 1979. *Die Geschichte der synoptischen Tradition* (FRLANT 29). Göttingen: Vandenhoeck & Ruprecht (ninth edition).

Dehandshutter, Boudewijn. 1974. "La parabole des vignerons homicides (Mc. XII,1–12) et l'évangile selon Thomas," in M. Sabbe, 1974, *L'Évangile selon Marc: tradition et redaction* (BETL 34). Louvain: Louvain University; Gembloux: Duculot, 202–19.

Kloppenborg, John S. 1986. *The Tenants in the Vineyard.* WUNT 195. Tübingen: Mohr Siebeck.

Schramm, Tim, and Kathrin Löwenstein. 1986. *Unmoralische Helden.* Göttingen: Vandenhoeck & Ruprecht, 22–42.

66
45,16b–19a

Jesus says:
"Show me the stone
that the builders have rejected.
It is the cornerstone."

A

The rejected cornerstone is Jesus[192] as teacher of wisdom, but at the same time it is the inner divine substance of humanity that he represents. For the Thomas community, this idea was a help in coping with its marginal position in society as well as in the church.

B

Jesus must have discussed his identity with his disciples several times: Mark 8:27 parr.: "Who do men say that I am," or log. 13: "Compare me and tell me who I am like." The quotation from Psalm 118:22,[193] which he mentioned before in the original interpretation that we have discussed in our commentary on the preceding saying, was one of the texts that helped him to cope with his misfortune (cf. log. 31) and to express his mission.

The verse is a proverb illustrating the reversal of the fortunes of the pilgrims coming to the temple in Jerusalem. Both in Mark 12 and in Luke 20:17–18 it follows on from the parable on the wicked tenants, even if in these cases it is already introduced as a new saying of Jesus. *Jesus was rejected* not only by his death on cross, but above all by the fact that he was not recognized as the Messiah in the sense of a savior—a key figure of human hope. In the "drunken" world he was not recognized as the cornerstone—the main stone of the foundation.

---

192. Similar quotations in a christological sense are in Eph 2:20 and 1 Pet 2:4–6; secondary references are in Hippolytus *Philos.* 5.7.35.

193. In the Septuagint, it is Psalm 117:22.

67	Jesus says:
45,19b–20	"Whoever knows all, if he is lacking everywhere,[194] he is (already) lacking everything."

A

The translation offered above suggests the crucial role of (spiritual) knowledge in the *Gospel of Thomas*. The knowledge has to be identical with overall orientation.

Another possible translation is: Whoever knows all (Copt. *tēr*) but is lacking in himself [195] is lacking everything—a maxim relating to the fact that humans do not know about their inner unity with God, and so are unable to find any orientation in the world and in their lives. This is in some respect an analogy to the Delphic maxim *Gnothi seauton*, "Know yourself," which was originally probably an admonition to consider human mortality, but in later periods was understood as an exhortation to introspection.[196] A similar meaning is given by the translation by Lambdin (1989): "If one who knows all still feels a personal deficiency, he is completely deficient"

B

Another (third possible) translation is "Who knows all,[197] but is lacking in one (*ua*), his knowledge is principally lacking." The knowledge is either full, that is, is insight into the substance of all, or it is no knowledge at all. There is no "almost perfect" knowledge.[198] This resembles the teaching of the earlier Stoics with their theory about perfect distance from the world (Gr. *epochē*). Anyone who is not entirely free of the influence of the contingent events in this world is not free at all.

68	(1) Jesus says:
45,21–24a	"Blessed are you when(ever) they hate you (and) persecute you. (2) But they (themselves) will find no place there where they have persecuted you."

---

194. Probably a textual corruption.

195. In Coptic, the NHD team considers a scribal error to be one possibility and also suggests the alternative reading *ouaafᵉr* ("is lacking in himself," "<he> is utterly lacking") instead of *oua afᵉr* ("everywhere, he is . . .").

196. Kasser 1961.

197. In this case *tērf* is understood as an adjective (Crumm 1931, 424).

198. Interpretation offered by Plisch 2007, 176.

A

In logion 66 we read about the mysterious power of the rejected—of those who know their own divine core, and the same truth is now expressed from the point of view of the rejected minority. The opposition of the world confirms that the message and style of life of the persecuted is a part of the way toward the true end, the fulfillment and salvation. The reason for the persecution of the group is not indicated, but obviously it was its self-understanding as the elect possessing a special knowledge. The *place* is an eschatological term denoting the area of repose (log. 60:6) and life (log. 4). Life itself comes from the Father (log. 64:12) and penetrates into human souls (log. 24). The second part may have expressed the universal character of the persecution: ". . . wherever you have been persecuted" (Valantasis 1997). If we add a second negation, which the scribe could have omitted, this meaning would be still more striking: "And no place will be found, where you have not been persecuted." In this respect it is a parallel to log. 58: "Blessed is the person who has struggled (and) has found life." It is a promise for those who suffer.

B

This is a parallel to Matt 5:11 and Luke 6:22 (Q), since the following saying (69) is a slightly different reproduction of the same traditional unit—the beatitudes of Jesus. The opening beatitude (blessing) from Luke 6:20 par. (Q) has its parallel in log. 54. The theme of *persecution* links this saying with the following one.

In the translation offered here by the NHD group the second sentence may relate to the expulsion of Jews (those who *persecute you*) from Jerusalem, renamed Aelia Capitolina (*a place where they have persecuted you*), after the defeat of the Bar Kochba revolt in 132–135. This would mean that the *Gospel* was either composed later than we supposed, or that log. 68:2 has been added in one of the later editions of the *Gospel of Thomas*.

Another way of improving the unclear text is to switch the negation: "But they will find a place there where they have not been persecuted." Such a place would be their community as the preliminary form of the eschatological kingdom.

69	(1) Jesus says:
45,24b—29a	"Blessed are those
	who have been persecuted in their heart.
	They are the ones who have truly come
	to know the Father."
	(2) "Blessed are those
	who suffer from hunger
	to satisfy the belly of the one who wishes it."

A

Persecution is understood here as inner process, as overcoming sleep, drunkenness, or alienation. *To know the Father truly* means a spiritual initiation.[199]

The second blessing is interpreted as a promise for those who voluntarily forgo some of their food in favor of their poor neighbors.[200] To *satisfy the belly* was the unfulfilled wish of the prodigal son from Luke 15:17 (cf. 16:21).

B

The interpretation suggested by NHD scholars as an alternative reading of a supposedly corrupted text is quite probably "Blessed are the persecuted, <insofar as they are pure> in their hearts." This would be an analogy to the version from Matt 5:8.

The second sentence, together with the exhortation to heal the sick (log. 14:4) and other sayings from the social layer S (see introduction—Theology), is a trace of the social character of the kingdom of God in Jesus' proclamation.

These are the last two from the set of beatitudes with parallels in source Q, but they seem to be quoted from a tradition similar to the Lukan version, and the editor obviously did not know the text of Matt 5:6 ("Blessed are those who hunger and thirst for righteousness") which would fit better with his spiritual intention.[201] This means that he took the first part (log. 69:1) from a tradition independent of the text of the Gospel of Matthew, but one that shared some of its ideas.

70
45,29b–33

(1) Jesus says:
"If you bring it into being within you,
(then) that which you have will save you.
(2) If you do not have it within you,
(then) that which you do not have within you
[will] kill you."

A

The mysterious *it* which is *within you* or is missing (*If you do not have it within you*) is most probably the inner being—the "inner man" (Gr. *esō anthrōpos*), as he has already appeared in Paul's concept of the human being (Rom 7:22; 2 Cor 4:16–18; Eph 3:16).

---

199. A later example of this phrase, possible influenced by the *Gospel of Thomas*, is in the Valentinian *Gospel of Truth* (NHC I/3, 24,31): Knowledge is lacking unless it is knowledge of the Father (cf. log. 67).

200. Leipoldt 1967, ad loc.; Patterson (1993), 140f.

201. This is an argument against Schürmann 1968, 236, who believed that the editor took the blessings out of the Synoptic context.

B

Unlike in Paul, here the inner human being is divine in itself; the Divine is a part of human substance, it is produced from it and to revive it is a matter of true self-understanding. This is an idea that differs from the Christian concept of human inner renewal, which is above all a matter of God's grace and compassion. It is rather similar to some later Gnostic ideas: knowledge = salvation.[202]

The text is not fully intelligible. Most probably saying 41 has to be understood as parallel, that is, "in his hand" is the same as *within you.*

---

71   Jesus says:
45,34–35   "I will [destroy this] house,
              and no one will be able to build it (again)
              [except me]."[203]

A

The tension between the piety of Thomas group and the life of the world and human society of that time (and of today as well) was painful and almost unbearable. Jesus is promising a transformation of the given world and human bodies.

B

The logion was originally probably one version of Jesus' sayings about the Temple in Jerusalem (cf. Acts 6:14). He relativized its role by confronting it with the kingdom of God and the new temple as described in Ezekiel 40–47 or perhaps with the direct presence of God with his people as it is mentioned in Rev 21:22. From the New Testament we mostly recall the version that includes reference to the three-day period for construction of the new (eschatological) temple from Mark 14:58 par. (cf. John 2:19).[204] One bridge to the understanding sketched under A may be the Johannine comment on the saying from John 2:19 in John 2:21, according to which the temple is the body of Jesus. Paul related the metaphor of the body as temple to all human bodies (1 Cor 6:19).

Literature

Riley, Gregory J. 1995. *Resurrection Reconsidered: Thomas and John in Controversy.* Minneapolis: Fortress Press, 147f.

---

202. See Irenaeus, *Adv. haer.* 1.21.4; cf. the *Gospel of Mary* 18,16–17 and the *Gospel of Judas* 35,2–10.
203. Reconstruction of a not-wholly-legible text.
204. Riley 1995.

72 46,1–6a	(1) A [person said] to him: "Tell my brothers that they have to divide my father's possessions with me." (2) He said to him: "O man, who made me a divider?" (3) He turned to his disciples (and) said to them: "I am not a divider, am I?"

A

For the editor of the *Gospel of Thomas*, the problem of *possessions* is the classic problem of those who are still "drunk" and express care for "worldly" matters. Jesus' answer is a rhetorical question supposing a negative answer, which is stressed at the end. The reason for his refusal is not only his understanding of possessions as something that may seduce people from obedience to God, but especially the divisive character of the activity mentioned. He is not sent to divide, but to unite.[205]

B

A parallel to Luke 12:13f. The *Gospel of Thomas* has taken it over from a tradition close to source Q.[206] In the early church Jesus soon came to be considered a judge over all humankind (Rom 14:9–10; 2 Tim 4:1). That may be the reason why in Luke the final rhetorical question (*I am not a divider, am I?*) is not included. The *Gospel of Thomas* argues against the image of Jesus as judge, in a way similar to John 3:17 or 8:15–16.[207]

73 46,6b–9a	Jesus says: "The harvest is plentiful but there are few workers. But beg the Lord that he may send workers into the harvest."

A

Sayings 73–75 have one common theme: the difference between much and less—the need for salvation and the limited number of *workers*. Here the workers are the wandering missionaries,[208] and the readers are exhorted to stand at the side

---

205. Plisch 2007, 186.
206. Schürmann 1968, 232.
207. Hedrick 1994, 145f.; Plisch 2007, 186.
208. Schröter 1997, 231f.

of those entering the kingdom. The *harvest* is the installation of the divine kingdom (see log. 21:10). *Beg* is an appeal to pray; the *Lord* is God.

B

The Thomas group was in a minority situation, and such sayings helped its members to cope with their circumstances, as in log. 23: "I will chose you one from a thousand"—an attitude that is different from the later theory of the church as all inclusive, in German *Volkskirche*.

There is again a parallel in the source Q: Matt 9:37f.; Luke 10:2 (Q). See *Acts of Thomas* 147.

---

74   He said:
46,9b–11a   "Lord, there are many around the well
              but there is nothing[209] in the <well>."[210]

A

The meaning is similar to that of the preceding saying. The situation is different from that in log. 28, where Jesus stood unrecognized in the middle of the world. Here there are *many* who feel the need for the water of life, but the *well* (cistern) is not accessible. It may be empty, which is the most probable reading, but it may also mean that *nobody* has entered the well. In any case it means that the mainstream church is unable to mediate access to the living water that Jesus is offering (cf. John 4:4ff., 15). It either does not invite the people to the well, or they are not allowed to enter the source.

B

Despite the general intention, the saying is full of problems: It is not Jesus' saying, but a question asked by somebody who addressed him as "Lord." "Lord" is not the title of Jesus used in the *Gospel of Thomas*, but it was well known as his address. In that case the saying ought to be introducing a dialogue.[211] Since sayings 73, 74, and 75 are bound together by a similar theme, it is probable that they are all similar in shape, and this is why Kasser (1961) suggested that "Lord" could be a part of the introducing sentence, "He, the Lord, said. . . ."

The last word is *šōne,* which in Coptic means "illness." Guillaumont (1959) rightly understood this as a scribal error and translated it as "well" (or "cistern," Copt. *šōte*). Lambdin (1989) translates the beginning of the sentence as ". . . there are many around the drinking trough (which was a part of the well)," since in the

---

209. Or, "nobody."
210. Erroneously, "illness."
211. Plisch 2007.

manuscript we read the Coptic *čōt*[*e*] (drinking trough). The NHD team considers it to be a synonym for well or cistern and translates it as "well." In Origen (*Contra Celsum* 8.15f.) we read: "Why are there many around the well, but nobody (has access to) to the well?" In both cases the word used is the Greek *frear*—well. The sentence most probably concerns the relation of the Thomas group to the great church, which was supposed to lack the water of life, as is attested in third century *Apocalypse of Peter* (NHC VII/3), where the bishops and deacons of the mainstream church are called "dry canals" (79,30).[212]

The reading according to which there is "nobody" in the well is less probable.[213]

---

75 46,11b–13a	Jesus says: "Many are standing before the door, but it is the solitary ones who will enter the wedding hall."

A

This is the third saying about selection, which approximates the sense of Matt 22:14: "For many are called, but few are chosen." The most plausible interpretation is similar to that of log. 74: Only few individuals achieve access to the divine kingdom. The *wedding hall* is a quite common image of the church as the community of God's people; see Mark 2:18–20 parrs., where the earthly presence of Jesus is a time of wedding. Originally, it was a metaphor for eschatological joy, while later it became linked with allegorical elements (e.g., Rev 21:2, 9; Eph 5:33). The *solitary ones* (Gr. *monachoi*) as the opposite of the *many* are the true initiated and personally converted individuals—the ideal members of the Thomas group. For interpretation of this term, see also log. 16 and 49.

B

Many parallel features can be found in the parable of the foolish maidens in Matt 25:1–13. Nevertheless, the difference is clear: as in the preceding saying the obstacle (empty well, *closed door*) is on the human side. The mainstream church is unable to open the door as it is unable to offer the water of life. This means that the Matthean version of the parable of the wedding garment (Matt 22:1–14) and the logion on the narrow gate (Luke 13:24 par. [Q]) cannot be considered parallels here either.

The later Christian Gnostic concept of the sacrament of the bridal chamber

---

212. See a similar polemic against heretics in 2 Pet 2:17.

213. According to Gillabert, Burgeois, and Haas 1985, 229, it could mean that nobody has descended so deep into the well that the heavens became his or her only horizon.

from the *Gospel of Philip* (NHC II/3; 67,15–18; 82,2–6) is a secondary development.

76

46,13b–22a

(1) Jesus says:

"The kingdom of my Father is like a merchant
who had merchandise and found a pearl.
(2) The merchant is prudent. He sold the goods (and)
bought for himself the pearl alone.
(3) You too look for his treasure
which does not perish,
that stays where no moth can reach it to eat it
and no worm destroys it."

A

The merchant is characterized as *prudent*—a similar attribute to that of the "sensible" fisherman in log. 8. In Hellenistic Jewish literature this denotes an individual who is spiritually initiated.[214] The fisherman likewise abandoned all his catch and concentrated only on a big fish—the real treasure. In fact the large fish and the (precious) *pearl* are the human soul with its divine core.

The conclusion is a moral exhortation that includes the code for deciphering the allegory. It is almost identical to Matt 6:19f.; Luke 12:33 (Q). The difference is that in the latter the place of the real treasure is in the heavens, which are not mentioned here, because it is believed that the real treasures and pearls can be stored in human souls. *Moth* and *worm* are symbols of the destruction of possessions and of human beings themselves.

B

The parable that we know from the set of Jesus parables in Matt 13 (13:5f.) is turned into an allegory here and combined with the saying on the true treasure (Luke 12:33 parr. [Q]) in 76:3.[215]

The description of the merchant's activity is shorter here than in Matthew. The reader does not know that the pearl was more precious than the rest of the merchant's merchandise. According to Matt 13:45 the pearl was fine and of great value, and the merchant sold all his possessions in order to buy it. Here he sold only all his other merchandise.

A classical example of a developed image of the pearl as human soul is the "Song of the Pearl" from the *Acts of Thomas* 108–13.[216]

---

214. *Sentences of Sextus,* nos. 309 and 310; in NHC XII/1 this originally Greek collection of sayings is also attested in Coptic translation; for further evidence, see Montefiore 1960–61, 60.

215. See Hedrick 1994, 127f.; Plisch 2007, 194.

216. For the Gnostic image of the pearl, see the Naassene sermon in Hippolytus *Philos.* 5.8.32.

| **77**
46,22b–28a | (1) Jesus says:
"I am the light that is over all.
I am the All.
The All came forth out of me.
And to me the All has come.
(2) Split a piece of wood, I am there.
(3) Lift the stone, and you will find me there." |

77:2–3 = P.Oxy 1, 27b–30

A

The saying extols Jesus as the mediator of *all* creation in the style of the "I am" sayings of Jesus as we know them from the Gospel of John (esp. John 8:12). The revelation of Jesus is an absolute value and expresses the meaning of all Being—all creation.[217] Here we have another document of the theological conclusion born from the depth of faith, but the stress here is more on the omnipresence of Jesus. The opening metaphor of light is an old expression of the experience of Jesus' new presence.[218]

The second part is another expression of the same experience. It is not pantheistic but panentheistic language that is employed: God is not identical with the *All*, but is present in all parts of it.

B

The sentence about the All coming back to Jesus is unclear: The All has been lost (see the sayings about the All as cadaver in log. 56 and 80) and its return consists in the revelation brought through Jesus.[219]

Sentences 2 and 3 may have expressed the idea that human beings may still encounter God in heavy work. This would be an opposite view of the skeptical opinion expressed in Eccl 10:9,[220] where we read: "Whoever quarries stones will be hurt by them; and whoever splits logs will be endangered by them.[221]

In the 1960s the cosmic dimension of Jesus' being and impact was discovered in ecumenical discussions as a way of expressing Jesus' value for all humans, all history, and even for the meaning of cosmos. The German systematic theologian Jürgen Moltmann quoted these sayings in one of his latest studies on the "cosmic Jesus."[222]

---

217. 1 Cor 8:6; cf. Col 1:15f.; John 1:1ff.; and Heb 1:2b.

218. See log. 24, 32, 50, 61, and John 1:9 and 8:12; from the texts from Qumran, see, e.g., 1QS 3.20–21.

219. The Coptic *p-terf,* which we translated as "all," can also be translated as "whole," which may be related to the church. This is, however, quite improbable.

220. Jeremias 1948, 80f.

221. Leipoldt 1967, 18.

222. J. Moltmann, "The Resurrection of Christ and the New Earth," *Communio viatorum* 49 (2007): 141–49.

78	(1) Jesus says:
46,28b–47,3a	"Why did you go out to the countryside?
	To see a reed shaken by the wind,
	(2) and to see a person dressed in soft clothing
	[like your] kings and your great men?
	(3) They are dressed in soft clothing
	and will not be able to recognize the truth."

A

Two rhetorical questions, each of them expecting a negative answer. A *reed* is a metaphor for weakness, because the wind can bend it. This could be an example of escape from the problems of society into nature. It could also be a demonstration of powerlessness,[223] the lack of external power so typical for Jesus. The alternative reason for the coming of so many people to Jesus is the expectation of a (messianic) ruler, a king *dressed in soft clothing.* The scene is meant to evoke the life of Jesus, the time of his teaching the crowds. Why did they come? And, what expectation is the right one? The answer (part 3), is that the savior is not a rich king, and a person's significance cannot be judged by the way he is dressed. Many well-dressed people do not recognize the truth (the mystery, the light), whereas the persecuted have this ability (log. 69:1, "truly," in both cases Copt. *me*—truth).

B

In the Synoptic parallel Luke 7:24f.; Matt 11:7f. (Q) this theme is related to John the Baptist, who is recalled in log. 46. The sayings may both have been taken from a common older tradition and reshaped for their new contexts.

79	(1) A woman in the crowd said to him:
47,3b–12a	"Hail to the womb that carried you
	and to the breasts that fed you."
	(2) He said [her]: "Hail to those
	who have heard the word of the Father
	(and) have truly kept it.
	(3) For there will be days when you will say:
	'Hail to the womb that has not conceived
	and to these breasts that have not given milk.'"

---

223. Cf. Matt 12:20.

A

The first part, the praise of the *womb* and *breasts* of Jesus's mother, is an indirect expression of the woman's high regard for Jesus. Jesus corrects her statement by reminding her of the will of God.

Sentence 3 is the praise of barren women in rejoinder by Jesus—a contradictory image that reminds the hearer of the apocalyptic sufferings to come at the end of this age, when the suffering of the children will be a terrible experience for their mothers. The visible world is indeed very dangerous.

B

The saying is composed of two units (sentence 1–2 and 3), each having its parallel in Luke 11:27–28 and 23:29.[224] The *Gospel of Thomas* and the Gospel of Luke probably drew the material independently from the same tradition.[225] This does not mean, of course, that the Coptic translator knew the text of the Gospel of Luke. Since sentence 3 as well as Luke 23:29 belongs to the apocalyptic tradition, the editor of the *Gospel of Thomas* must have been aware of this dimension of the Jesus tradition. He/she also tried to interpret it.

In the Synoptic tradition Jesus's warning is linked with the idea of apocalyptic suffering as the prelude to the coming kingdom of God.

By "*hail*" the NHD group translated the Coptic *neeiat;* by "blessed"—the Greek *makarios* taken over in Coptic.

80
47,12b–15a

(1) Jesus says:
"Whoever has come to know the world
has found the body.
(2) But whoever has found the body,
of him the world is not worthy."

A

The idea of the *body* (Gr. *sōma*) as a metaphor for the *world* is a new step in the knowledge presented by the *Gospel of Thomas*. In log. 56 the world has been characterized as a corpse (Gr. *ptōma*), but in log. 29 we read about the wonder of incarnation, according to which the spirit can take up residence in the body and unite with its soul (the individual human body as well as the body of the world). This is the mystery of incarnation. The Thomas group interpreted it in a way that differed from the mainstream church, but did not deny it. In log. 60 we read about the living lamb that will become a corpse as soon as it is killed. Conversely, the spirit of

---

224. According to Schröter 1997, 139, the editor of the *Gospel of Thomas* may have combined texts from the Synoptic Gospels.

225. Schürmann (1968, 231) supposes that Luke and Thomas took this saying from source Q and Matthew omitted it.

God can reanimate the corpse of the world. Through the action of the spirit even a corpse can become a living organism, and so it can always be seen as a body.[226]

B

Many translators, including the NHD group, believe that here we have an analogy to log. 56 and that the reading *sōma* is the result of scribal error: The scribe read *ptōma* as *psōma* and understood it as *p* (Coptic article) + *sōma*.

The interpretation inspired by Valantasis (1997) that we presented under A in the commentary to log. 56 is still quite probable.

81
47,15b–17a

(1) Jesus says:
"Whoever has become rich should be king.
(2) And the one who has power
should renounce (it)."

A

Since the *Gospel of Thomas* rejects wealth and riches (see log. 54, 63, and 64), to *become rich* may be understood in two ways only. First, it may be an ironic description of a way of life necessarily orientated to the acquisition of political power,[227] since possessions always tend to become an instrument of obtaining power and rule over other people. Logion 81:1 would then be describing a career that needs to be rejected.[228]

The second interpretation might be a spiritual one, since the *king* over All is the one who finds the meaning of Jesus' sayings.[229] Poverty then means a life in the world without the spirit of God (see log. 3:5 and 29:3).

The second part speaks about ruling and being king. This is language that is used consistently in the *Gospel of Thomas*: to be king in the Father's kingdom means to participate in his intentions and in his rule, the rule of God that is free of violence or political power.

B

In Luke 6:20 the kingdom of God is promised to the poor, and the spiritually oriented groups, probably forerunners of the Thomas community, saw themselves as kings. Many followers of Jesus believed that the promise given by Jesus meant not only that they would participate in the kingdom of God but that they would rule with him, as expressed in Luke 22:29–30 par. [Q]: "I assign to you, as my Father assigned to me, a kingdom, that you may eat and drink at my table in my kingdom, and sit on thrones judging the twelve tribes of Israel."

"Kingdom of God" connects this saying with the following one.

---

226. See the commentary on log. 56.
227. The Coptic "do a king" can simply mean "to rule."
228. Plisch 2007.
229. Valantasis 1997.

82	(1) Jesus says:
	"The person who is near me is near the fire.
	(2) And the person who is far from me
	is far from the kingdom."

A

Fire with its transforming and purifying power[230] signifies the presence of God as the holy one[231] and as the righteous judge.[232] This is why the spirit of God as sign of a new age was seen as a kind of fire.[233] In sayings such as log. 82 all these incandescent functions of fire are present: Holiness, transforming power, purification, and renewal, but especially the coming of the kingdom of the Father as a rupture in history, which has to undergo the judgment of God. It is an expression of a deep hope—as serious and dangerous as all encounters with God can be,[234] but still the deepest hope, coming from the other side and opening up a new time and space of life. The next related saying is log. 10 with its Synoptic parallel in Luke 12:49f.[235] It is one of the best-attested sayings of Jesus.[236]

B

What we have said justifies us in considering this saying to be part of one of the ancient Jesus traditions.[237]

Literature

Hedrick, Charles W. 2002. "An Anecdotal Argument for the Independence of the *Gospel of Thomas* from the Synoptic Gospels," in H.-G. Bethge, S. Emmel, K. L. King, and I. Schletterer, *For the Children: Perfect Instruction* (FS H.-M. Schenke; NHMS 54. Leiden/Boston: Brill, 113–26.

83	(1) Jesus says:
47,19b–24a	"The images are visible to humanity,
	but the light within them is hidden in the image.

---

230. See Matt 3:10 par.; John 15:6.
231. Deut 4:24; Isa 33:14.
232. Luke 3:16f. par. [Q]; Matt 5:22; 13:30; Rev 21:8, etc.
233. Luke 24:32; Acts 2:3.
234. See the widespread image of Zeus with lightning.
235. Cf. Luke 12:51–53 par. [Q] with parallel in log. 16.
236. E.g., Didymus (†394) *Comm. Ps.* 88:8 (Klostermann 1910, 5f.); *Gospel of the Savior* 107,43–48; for further evidence see Plisch 2007.
237. Hedrick 2002, 121–24.

(2) { }[238] The light of the Father will reveal itself,
but his image is hidden by his light."

A

This saying has a Platonic background[239] and anticipates some Gnostic ideas—see log. 5.[240] Spiritual ideas have their images (Gr. *eikōn*) in earthly objects (see Gen 1:27f.), but the light of these ideas is *hidden*.[241] We cannot deduce from seeing the individual objects that there is a world of ideas. The light of the heavenly Father is accessible through his revelation. It shines so intensely (log. 33 and 61) because it is inner enlightenment that plays the decisive role. Without this light even Jesus would not be recognized as the Son.[242]

B

Plisch (2007) has supported this interpretation by a reconstruction of the original text: he argues for the possibility that the word "humanity" (Copt. *p-rōme*) was omitted (a frequent scribal error). If this were to be the case, the structure of the argument would become clearer:

The images of the humans
   are visible to the humans
   but the light within them is hidden in the image.
The light of the Father
   will reveal itself
   but the image (of the Father) is hidden by his light.

This means: What is visible in the world originates from God, but is not the revelation of his light. The light of the Father is accessible by a spiritual enlightenment integrally connected with Jesus as his revelation; Jesus of Nazareth as the image of the Father (see 2 Cor 4:5; Col 1:15) is understandable only through the light of the revelation that is "over all" (log. 77:1), and this light is mediated by the sayings of Jesus as the Living One to those who look for the "very treasure" (log. 76:3).[243] The theme "image" links this saying with the following one.

Valantasis mentioned a parallel from Porphyry's *Life and Works of Plotinus*: Plotinus refused to have his portrait painted because he believed that the icon would overshadow his teaching.

---

238. In the manuscript, the second part is attached by means of a genitive (of); see Leipoldt 1967.

239. See the commentary on log. 7 and Turner 1962, 98.

240. See also the commentary on log. 22.

241. This motif is developed in *Hypostasis of the Archons* (NHC II/4, 87,11–33).

242. Cf. *Gospel of Philip* (NHC II/3; 67,9–27).

243. See similar speculation in later texts such as Irenaeus, *Adv. haer.* 2.7.6.

A Gnostic myth corresponding to these ideas is expressed in the *Hypostasis of the Archons* (NHC II/4, 87,11–33).[244]

84	(1) Jesus says:
47,24b–29a	"When you see your likeness you are full of joy.
	(2) But when you see your likeness
	which came into existence before you—
	they neither die nor become manifest—
	how much will you bear?"

A

Formulated as it is in the second person, the saying has a deep personal appeal. The first sentence refers to the origin of the human being as a creation in the likeness of God,[245] as presented in Gen 1:26. This is a joyful discovery for each follower of Jesus.

The second part is introduced by a "but" and is shaped as a rhetorical question summing up deeper reflection on the human and the divine. When we see our individual human egos reflected back in an earthly mirror the sight may be encouraging, but when we are confronted by the deeper mirror—the assignment given to each us from God—the experience may be quite depressing.

To put it another way: What is visible in the world originates from God, but is not the revelation of his light. To be confronted with his revelation in the words of Jesus is startling, provoking, and inspiring.

In the tradition of the mainstream church all this is closely connected with God's judgment.

B

Logion 84 is based on theological and philosophical speculation. We know that Gnosis developed from speculation about Gen 1:26.[246] Plisch was the first scholar to suggest that we should understand the first part of the logion to relate to the visible image or mirror image of the individual person (most people like to look at their own reflection), while the second sentence relates to confrontation with the ideal individual human being, and so reveals the depth of human alienation.

The connection with the previous saying is obvious.

85	(1) Jesus says:
47,29b–34a	"Adam came from a great power and great wealth.
	But he did not become worthy of you.

---

244. Schenke 1962, 61–62 (the text is quoted according to the pages of the first edition, not after the pages of the codex itself).

245. Here, Copt. *eine*.

246. Ménard 1975, 184f.

(2) For if he had been worthy,
(then) [he would] not [have tasted] death."

A

Adam was accorded an extraordinary position in the *great wealth* of the whole creation of God as the Creator, that is, of the *great power*. Indeed, a tradition elevating the status of Adam was widespread in Judaism (see, e.g., Sirach 49:16). Yet according to the logion he is not worthy of *you*, that is, the readers of the *Gospel of Thomas* from the Thomas community.

The difference between Adam and the Thomas reader is explained in the second part: Adam is lower than the initiated disciples of Jesus, since he *tasted death*.[247] He died because he did not know the words of Jesus as the Living One and their meaning, as indicated in log. 1 and 18:3. He left paradise and the tree of life (log. 19:3–4).

Thus, the scale of proximity to the divine center of life is as follows: God—Jesus as the Living One—his converted followers (the Thomas group)—Adam—other humans. This idea was a part of the self-understanding of the Thomas group as a new human race, higher than the race of Adam.

B

In the New Testament, Adam appears as the negative image (antitype) of Christ.[248]

Literature

Brandenburger, Egon. 1962. *Adam und Christus* (WMANT 7). Neukirchen: Neukirchener Verlag.

86
47,34b–48,4a

(1) Jesus says:
"[The foxes have] their holes
and the birds have their nest.
(2) But the son of man
has no place to lay his head down (and) to rest."

A

The proverb, quoted most probably by Jesus himself, expresses the vulnerability and even the homelessness of human beings compared with the rest of the

---

247. For the phrase "to taste death," see log. 1 and Mark 9:1
248. See, e.g., Rom 5:12–17; for further discussion, see Brandenburger 1962.

creation. The words were already attributed to Jesus in the oldest tradition of source Q: Matt 8:20; Luke 9:58. According to the Thomas community it was necessary to stress that humankind had no home in this world: "You, too, look for a place for your repose so that you may not become a corpse and get eaten" (log 60:6).

B

Son of man—a semitic expression for the individual human being—was used in the earliest Christian literature as the title of an apocalyptical being coming from God himself (see, e.g., Luke 12:8). The *Gospel of Thomas* does not, however, use christological titles. The editor understood the expression son of man to mean human being in the religious sense, that is, a member of the Thomas community.

Literature

Jens Schröter 1997: 227, 229–31.

87	(1) Jesus said:
48,4b–7a	"Wretched the body that hangs on a body.
	(2) And wretched is the soul
	that depends on these two."

A

The *body* is human being in its material and visible dimension. If a human being is dependent (only) on another human being, it has no hope. The saying is shaped as a twofold sapiential "woe." *Wretched* (Gr. *talaipōros*) is the counterpart and opposite of "blessed" (Gr. *makarios*).

The second sentence explains the wisdom of saying 7 as we have interpreted it: Blessed is the body that depends on the soul (log. 7:1), but *wretched* is the soul that depends on the body (7:2 in our interpretation).

What can a human being do to avoid such frustration? According to the specific Thomas theology, the solution is concentration on union with the divine spirit, and living life as a "solitary" one (see log. 4, 11, 22:4ff.).

B

A simplified parallel is to be found in log. 112.

88	(1) Jesus says:
48,7b–12	"The messengers[249] are coming to you
	and the prophets,

---

249. Alternative translation: "angels" (Gr. *angelos*).

and they will give you what belongs to you.
(2) And you, in turn, give to them
what you have in your hands (and) say to yourselves:
'When will they come
(and) take what belongs to them?'"

A

The *messengers* (angels) and the prophets are the wandering missionaries and Christian prophets. They may come to visit the Thomas community as well. The members of the community should offer them *what they have in their hands*, their material possessions, and they should support them.

B

The scene could obviously relate to the visit of wandering missionaries (maybe from the Thomas group) to a Christian community. The community ought to feed and support the messengers from their possessions, and ought to be aware of this duty in advance (*When will they come . . .*). A similar instruction for apostles and prophets is documented in *Didache* 11. This is the interpretation suggested by Plisch, and seems to be the most persuasive.[250]

A different interpretation, suggested by Valantasis (1997), is more spiritual. According to this, the angels (see note on the *messengers*) and the prophets from the Jewish Bible (the later Christian Old Testament) offer the Syriac Thomas Christians all the promises of the Scriptures, but their prophecies and promises concern what the initiated Christians already know from the "living Jesus," and it is the duty of the initiated to offer this knowledge to those who represent the Jewish precursors of Jesus. In this respect they are higher than the angels[251] and *prophets*.[252]

89
48,13–16a

(1) Jesus says:
"Why do you wash the outside of the cup?
(2) Do you not understand
that the one who created the inside
is also the one who created the outside?"

A

For a Jew, to wash the *outside of the cup* meant to fulfill an extra(?) surplus prescription formulated by additional rabbinic tradition.[253] The intention was to

---

250. It belongs to the layer of social sayings (S), see introduction, Theology of the *Gospel of Thomas*.

251. See this motif in 1 Cor 6:3.

252. Luke 10:24.

253. See H. L. Strack and P. Billerbeck, *Kommentar zum Neuen Testament aus Talmud und Midrasch*. 6 vols. (Munich: Beck, 1922–1961): 1:934ff.

protect the "great" commandment from transgression. The *cup* is a metonym for the utensils to which the purity law related.

The second sentence is probably a metaphorical interpretation of the inner purity of human beings. The inner and outer (bodily) aspects of human life are interrelated. The argument that there is only one Creator (*who created*) corresponds to the Hebrew and Christian tradition, and is not influenced by Gnostic or pre-Gnostic speculation in which the Creator was an inferior deity.

B

The saying has parallels in Luke 11:39–40 and Matt 23:25f. (probably Q), and the version in the *Gospel of Thomas* is only a little shorter.

The two statements might be understood literally as a rejection of the Jewish purity laws, as was evidently the intention in the ancient tradition about Jesus.[254] This is improbable, however, because only the additional prescriptions are rejected.

The possibility of a switch from a literal to a metaphorical meaning as proposed under A cannot be ruled out, since in the parallel from Matt 23:25f., the criticism of cultic piety is combined with criticism of Pharisaic morality ("inside they are full of extortion and rapacity"), but the transition between sentence 1 and sentence 2 is still far from smooth. Most probably the awkwardness has been caused by corruption of the text (Plisch).

90
48,16b–20a

(1) Jesus says:
"Come to me, for my yoke is gentle
and my lordship is mild.
(2) And you will find repose for yourselves."

A

A well-known proclamation attested only here and in Matt 11:28–30 (longer version). It is based on impressive paradoxes (oxymorons) such as *gentle yoke*[255] and *mild lordship* (in Matthew, "burden"). The intended meaning is that the hardships on the way of life as taught by the living Jesus find sufficient compensation in God's love, promise, and joy of salvation. *Repose* (Gr. *anapausis*) was a metaphor for salvation in the Thomas group (log. 50, 51, 60; cf. log. 86 and log. 90) and later in Gnosticism. In Heb 4:9–10 we already find *katapausis*, a synonym, with the same metaphorical meaning.

---

254. Leipoldt 1967, 18f.

255. The yoke is a symbol of the position of the animal as subject and the domination of the human over the animal.

B

Originally this was a sapiential saying (cf. Sir 51:26–27) related to wisdom itself. We do not know when it was linked with the Jesus tradition. Jesus may have quoted it himself.

91	(1) They said to him:
48,20b–25a	"Tell us who you are
	so that we may believe in you."
	(2) He said to them:
	"You examine the face of sky and earth;
	but the one who is before you,
	you have not recognized,
	and you do not know
	how to test this opportunity."

A

This saying is in fact the central part of a dialogue dealing with the very identity of Jesus. In sentence 1 the disciples or/and some other people ask about Jesus' identity to establish whether they should *believe* him. The second part is Jesus' answer. Essentially the situation is the same as when his adversaries asked him for a sign from heaven. Jesus refuses to declare his identity, on the grounds that it is implicit in his teaching.

In sentence 2, Jesus refuses to answer and he mentions *testing* (*peirazō*; Luke 12:56, *dokimazō*). The questioners are unaware of their experience, both of nature and, by analogy, of Jesus and his teaching. "Many times you have desired to hear these words" (log. 38). Clearly they should have realized on the basis of his sayings that Jesus represents the kingdom of his Father and should have realized that they are (could be) his children (log. 3:3–4). The opportunity (or "right moment")[256] to recognize this truth ("There will be days when you will seek me and you will not find me"—log. 38:2) is now. It is not the time of Jesus' earthly life, but the time of reading the text.

B

There is a parallel in Luke 12:54–56 and par. (Q) and in Mark 8:11–13. In the Jesus tradition, the opportunity is related to the coming of the kingdom proclaimed by Jesus (see the context in Luke 12). According to the *Gospel of Thomas*, in the proclamation of Jesus, even in written form, the kingdom of the Father penetrates into the present, as expressed in log. 113.

To *examine* is the first expression from the semantic field (the cognate expressions) of "seeking," which is the common theme of one of the larger clusters of sayings, including log. 91–94.[257]

---

256. The other possible way of translating the Greek-Coptic *kairos* according to NHD.
257. See Myszor 1979, 78.

92	(1) Jesus says:
48,25b–30a	"Seek and you will find.
	(2) But the things
	you asked me about in past times,
	and what I did not tell you in that day,
	now I am willing to tell you,
	but you do not seek them."

A

The saying exhorts the readers to *seek* the truth of life and assures them that this is possible and urgently necessary. As the reader already knows, the truth is contained in the words of Jesus.

The second part is spoken from the point of view of the living Jesus as eternal Word of God. His existence includes his preexistence. In this past he did not teach people about the matters that they wished to know (*asked me*), that is, the words of life, such as the sayings in the *Gospel of Thomas*. A brief reference is made to the history of salvation (*that day*), thus helping the hearers to find an orientation in history as it is expressed in log. 38:1. *Now*, that is, when reading these lines, the hearers should not miss the opportunity (see log. 91:2); they should *seek* the words of the living Jesus, even if most people, who are not initiated into the mysteries of life (cf. log. 62:1), do not seek them.

B

Sayings 92 to 94 have parallels in Matt 7:6–8, and both the *Gospel of Thomas* and Matthew evidently took them from a similar cluster of sayings in oral tradition or in one of the early textual units. The parallel to the first part of log. 92 is in Matt 7:7, which mentions three acts of active relationship to God from the human side (ask, seek, knock). Here we read only of *seek*ing, which is a typical theme in the *Gospel of Thomas*. Knocking is mentioned in the next saying, but asking (in prayer) is not mentioned, most probably because the *Gospel of Thomas* is critical of prayer (log. 14:2). The second part has no parallel in Matthew 7.

93	(1) "Do not give what is holy to the dogs,
48,30b–33a	lest they throw it upon the dunghill.
	(2) Do not throw pearls to swine,
	lest they turn <them>[258] into [mud]."[259]

---

258. In the manuscript this is erroneously singular; NHD.

259. The last words are practically illegible. They can be restored in different ways, but the meaning remains the same.

A

The *holy* and the pearl are metaphors for the message concerning the soul and the potential of the divine spirit to dwell within it. This was the content of the gospel as it was proclaimed by Christian missionaries—their most precious commodity, as it is expressed in log. 76. In the *Acts of Thomas* we read the famous "Hymn of the Pearl" (108–13), which expresses this truth in poetic form.

The saying is a warning against misuse of the gospel and an admonition to proclaim the gospel in a careful way that avoids the possibility of misunderstanding or ridicule. *Dogs* and *swine* are people who are not among the seekers, and who are spoken of in log. 92 as people who have not "ears to hear" (log. 8 and others).

B

Both parts of this saying use metaphors taken from the animal world. The first is realistic, since *holy* denoted the meat from the sacrifices in the temple, and so to throw such remains to the dogs would be sacrilegious. Originally, it may have been a warning against such misuse of the remains of the sacrifices.

The second part is hyperbole, because to throw pearls to swine would make no sense. The proverb style[260] supports the idea that Jesus already used both words as metaphors.

This saying, which (in the Coptic manuscript) is not introduced by the phrase "Jesus says,"[261] has its New Testament parallel in Matt 7:6. The differences in local color support the conclusion that it is taken from an older tradition. In *Didache* 9:5 (about 110 A.D.), Matt 7:6 is quoted as a justification for excluding nonbaptized individuals from participation in the eucharistic feast.

Literature

Elliott 1999: 439–511 (on *Acts of Thomas*).

---

94 48,33b–34	(1) Jesus says: "The one who is seeking will find. (2) [The one who knocks], to that one will be opened,"

A

The saying is the positive counterpart of the preceding one. The *seeking*[262] holds a divine promise, for "The word is near you, on your lips and in your heart"

---

260. See Haenchen 1961, 51; cf. Beardslee 1972, 100.
261. The other cases are log. 27 and 101, probably also 62:2 and 69:2.
262. See the commentary on log. 2 and 92; and Zöckler 1999, 65.

(Rom 10:8). Through the special inspiration and instruction of the living Jesus, God can be discovered in the human heart. This corresponds to the theology of the *Gospel of Thomas*.

B

Compared with the parallel in logion 92, here we read not only about *seeking*, but also about the other expressions of active interest in *finding*—finding what? The kingdom of the Father (log. 9:1) represented by Jesus—(the one who is before you; log. 91:2). In the parallels to these sayings that can be found in "Q" there is reference to three active expressions of interest in the kingdom: Who asks receives, who searches finds, who knocks the door will be opened: Luke 11:10; Matt 7:8.

By connecting this saying with the preceding one, the editor argues that the dogs and swine from log. 93 are those who do not ask, search, and knock.

---

95   (1) [Jesus says:]
                  "You have money, do not lend (it) out at interest.
                  (2) Rather, give [it] to the one
                  from whom you will not get it (back)."

A

The saying proposes a fundamental alteration in the attitude toward money. Money should not serve to enlarge the possessions of the owner, but should be a means to strengthen the community by reducing social differences. Money is not abandoned, but simply acquires a new function. The main intention behind this practice is not social need, however, but primarily the liberation of the followers of Jesus from the seductive spell of possessions, as indicated in log. 64—the parable of the great feast: "Dealers and merchants will not enter the places of my Father" (64:12).

B

To lend money at interest was forbidden by the Law (Exod 22:25), and this prohibition is also presupposed in Matt 5:42; Luke 6:30 (Q) ("Give to everyone who begs from you") and especially in Luke 6:34 ("If you lend to those from whom you hope to receive, what credit is that to you?). Leipoldt (1967) draws attention to the *Revelation of Peter* from the beginning of the second century,[263] where we read the first Christian prohibition of lending money at interest. Here we can see how the social dimension of Thomas theology (S) is the other side of the more important theme of distancing believers from society.

In saying 109 there is a positive reference to interest, but this is a parable, indeed one of the "immoral" parables where some of the principles valid among

---

263. Coptic version 31; Ethiopic version 10.

sinners are used with a reversed function as models for good actions and the profit they bring. The most striking example of such a parable is saying 98 about a successful terrorist.

96
49,2b–6

(1) Jesus [says]:
"The kingdom of the Father is like [a] woman.
(2) She took a little bit of yeast.
[She] hid it in dough
(and) made it into huge loaves of bread.
(3) Whoever has ears should hear."

A

The saying illustrates the inner power of the Father's kingdom. It is invisible from outside (*she hid* it), but it changes its surroundings. This is a common experience, well documented in the New Testament as well: "Do you not know that a little yeast leavens the whole batch of dough?" asks Paul in 1 Cor 5:6.[264] Nevertheless, here the agent who sets this power in motion is the *woman* who makes use of this power to produce *bread*—a *huge* amount of food for life.

Since this kind of life-giving power is hidden under the surface, the spiritual understanding of the metaphor is evident: the yeast represents the sayings of the living Jesus. They are hidden, but their power will be manifest as the light of the world. Such is the message of sayings 5 and 33.[265]

B

Logia 96–98 are all parables of the kingdom of the Father and may already have formed a group in the oral tradition:[266] Two of them take their imagery from the daily work of women, while the third (log. 98) is about a man from an unexpected area—a terrorist.

Logion 96 has its parallel in Q, in Matt 13:33; Luke 13:20–21. There the kingdom is compared to yeast, but here it is compared with the woman. According to some scholars the latter is the original version,[267] since the role of women in the church was progressively reduced. On the other hand, as we shall see, in the following parable (log. 97) the focus on the woman may be a secondary motif and the presence of women in the central role may be the result of editorial transformation of these parables. Given that here we also find other differences from the Synoptic versions that cannot be explained in terms of the intentions of the editor, it seems probable that these parables have an origin independent of the Synoptics. Logion 114 defends the role of the women among the followers of Jesus (log. 114:3).

---

264. Cf. also Gal 5:6.

265. According to Hippolytus, *Philos.* 5.8.8, in Gnostic speculation, the yeast could mean the divine core of human being.

266. Doran 1987.

267. Cullmann 1966, 585.

For the concluding exhortation see the commentary on log. 8.

Literature

R. Doran. 1987. "A Complex of Parables GTh 96–98," *Novum Testamentum* 29:347–52.

97	(1) Jesus says:
49,7–15a	"The kingdom of the [Father]
	is like a woman
	who is carrying a [jar] filled with flour.
	(2) While she was walking on [a] long way
	the handle of the jar broke (and)
	the flour leaked out [on] the path.
	(3) (But) she did not know (it);
	she had not noticed a problem.[268]
	(4) When she reached her house,
	she put the jar down on the floor
	(and) found it empty."

A

(Explanation 1) The saying is probably a parable of the imperceptible influence of the kingdom of God on earth, as in the parable of the woman who hid a little bit yeast in the dough and made huge loaves of bread (log. 96): *The kingdom . . . is like a woman.* This is an explanation that corresponds to the general theological intentions of the collection and fits with the context of saying 96. Such an interpretation is clearly valid if we consider sentence 3 to be a secondary addition, but even as it stands as a whole the parable may have proclaimed the kingdom that is "inside of you and outside of you" (log. 3:3)—*on the path.* Sentence 3 seems to turn the woman into a negative figure, since she *did not know*: The kingdom of the Father is spread out upon the earth, and people do not see it" (log. 113:4), but ultimately she nonetheless realized her situation when *she reached her house* (sentence 4).[269] The kingdom is not in her hand (see log. 113).[270]

Yet we are obliged to consider a different interpretation, which is suggested by sentence 3 (explanation 2), that is, that the parable warns against losing the kingdom by not *noticing the problem.* The *woman* would then be the opposite of the woman in the preceding saying. She is not engaged in the growth and unexpected coming of the kingdom, and so she loses what she intended to bring *to her house.*

---

268. Another possible reconstruction of the text (K. Nagel) is "she has not noticed it, whereas she exerted herself."

269. The Gnostic interpretation applied the parable to the celestial Adam, who is being kept in the earth in the body of clay (Hippolytus *Philos.* 5.7.36).

270. Plisch 2007, 230.

It is a parable that has not yet been found in any other source. On the one hand, this supports the argument for the *Gospel of Thomas* as an independent document of the Jesus tradition, but, on the other, the nature of the parable has led to doubts about its authenticity, for how could the woman not have noticed the loss when jars were carried on the head?[271] In fact, while big jars were carried in this way, smaller ones designed to contain flour for just one day had only one *handle* and were carried in the hand. Since the handle might have reached from the lip to the bottom and the point at which it was attached to the body of the jar was the most vulnerable, a crack could develop near the bottom and the flour, quite dusty in the high temperature and dry climate, could pour out unnoticed.[272]

All the same, explanation 1 has priority. "The *kingdom of the Father is like a woman . . .*" (sentence 1a).

B

Valantasis (1997) has pointed out one feature that this parable shares with the parable of the sower (log. 9), that is, the corn *on the path*. Here the corn has been milled into flour, but it is still the basic component of bread—the food of life. At least according to some scholars this provides the clue to the intention of the parable: the flour on the path where it would be turned into mud as mentioned in log. 93. This is explanation 3, and the least probable.

Literature

P. Nagel. 2001. "Das Gleichnis vom zerbrochenen Krug. EvThom Logion 97," *ZNW* 92:229–56.

B. B. Scott. 1987. "The Empty Jar, Foundations and Facets," *Forum* 3:77–80, according to Riley 1994:243.

See also the literature on log. 96.

See the figure by Charles McCollough on the cover (as open to as many interpretations as the text of the saying itself).

98	(1) Jesus says:
49,15b–20	"The kingdom of the Father is like a person
	who wanted to kill a powerful[273] person.
	(2) He drew the sword in his house
	(and) stabbed it into the wall
	to test whether his hand would be strong (enough).
	(3) Then he killed the powerful one."

---

271. Kasser 1961.
272. So Plisch 2007.
273. Or "noble" (NHD).

A

This unexpected parable from the life of a terrorist is one of the immoral parables of Jesus, like, for example, the parable of the dishonest manager (Luke 16:1–8), of the usurer and the tenants (log. 65 in one of its interpretations), and in its original intention the parable of the ten pounds (Luke 19:11–27 par. [Q]). These describe the boldness and consequence of bad humans, which suggests that the hearers must use the same qualities in the service of the kingdom of God.

In this case the hearer is supposed to try to act with the same decisiveness and readiness to take action, and must likewise test his own power of discipleship in advance. In this respect there is an indirect parallel with the sayings on the cost of discipleship in Luke 14:28–33: He who intends to build a tower has first to estimate the cost, and a king has to consider whether he has people enough to start a war against another king. So the terrorist (*the person who wanted to kill a powerful person*) had to test whether he was *strong enough*.

B

The application of the parable to spiritual battle against the Evil One[274] and on the side of Jesus, the "stronger" or the "more powerful" one,[275] may have been present from the very beginning, since an openness of intention (polysemy) is a characteristic of any parable and any metaphor: "Put on the whole armor of God, so that you may be able to stand against the wiles of the devil. For our struggle is not against enemies of blood and flesh, but against the rulers, against the authorities, against the cosmic powers of this present darkness, against the spiritual forces of the evil in the heavenly places" (Eph 6:11–12). Nevertheless, the main intention of the parable in its given form is to provoke thought on the cost of discipleship. A certain role is also played by the stress on the suddenness and unexpectedness of the coming of God's judgment and his kingdom: "For as the lightning flashes and lights up the sky from one side to the other, so will the Son of Man be in his day" (Luke 17:24). And the powerful one, relying on his power, may lose his life at an unexpected moment.

Literature

Hunzinger 1964: 209–20.
Schramm and Löwenstein 1986: 53–55.

99
49,21–26

(1) The disciples said to him:
"Your brothers and your mother
are standing outside."
(2) He said to them:

---

274. See also *Acts of Thomas* 147; Hunzinger 1964.
275. Mark 1:7 par.

> "Those here, who do the will of my Father,
> they are my brothers and my mother.
> (3) They are the ones who will enter
> the kingdom of my Father."

A

This well-known saying of Jesus redefines social relations based on biological kinship from the point of view of the kingdom of the Father as the eschatological prospect.

B

The Synoptic parallel is in Mark 3:32–35 (Matt 12:47–50 and Luke 8:20f.).

This version has more features in common with Luke than with Matthew, but it is essentially not dependent on either of them. A similar "combined" version is to be found in *2 Clement* 9:11 and according to Epiphanius[276] in the *Gospel of the Ebionites.*[277] Did the editor of the *Gospel of Thomas* know the *Gospel of the Ebionites?* He is more likely to have known a tradition from which the *Gospel of the Ebionites* also took some of its material.[278] Nor can we exclude the possibility that the few common features were accidental.

In the Synoptic traditions as well as in the *Gospel of Thomas* there are other sayings about true interhuman relations based on common relation to God, or, better, on God's relation to human beings. Some of them sound quite cruel in relation to biological parents: see log. 101 and 105 and their interpretation.

100
49,27–31

(1) They showed Jesus a gold coin and said to him:
"Ceasar's people demand taxes from us."
(2) He said to them:
"Give Caesar (the things) that are Caesar's.
(3) Give God (the things) that are God's.
(4) And what is mine give me."

A

Taxes became a burning issue after 6 A.D., when Judea was incorporated into the Roman province of Syria (Orient) and had to pay the *census*, the tax on every "head," to the Roman imperial administration. This provoked protests among the inhabitants who saw it not only as economic exploitation but also as cultural ("national") humiliation and religious deprivation, since the emperor (*Caesar*)

---

276. *Panarion* 30.14.
277. E. Klostermann 1910, 11.
278. So Vielhauer 1975, 628f.

claimed a divine status, as was common in ancient Egypt and other Near Eastern empires.[279]

Jesus' adversaries used this situation to ask him a question designed to compromise him: "Caesar's people demand taxes from us," that is, "What is your opinion?" If he said, "Pay them," he would be compromised in the eyes of the people; and if he said, "No," he would be considered an enemy of the Roman emperor. According to Mark, he asked the adversaries to produce a Roman *denarius*. It showed the name and the face of the emperor, and so was in fact his possession. In this way Jesus escaped the trap, since the adversaries admitted that paying taxes was simply the logical consequence of their use of the imperial monetary system.

This is the concrete background to the discussion as presented by Mark 12:14–17 and parallels in Matt 22:17–21 and Luke 20:22–25. Here the question is only hinted at, and instead of *denarius* we read of a *gold coin*. The abbreviated story is evidently motivated by the desire to accent a "deeper" understanding of the story, that is, the rejection of earthly power and possessions. The christological part of the answer ("*And what is mine give me*") is also an addition. It expresses the special role of Jesus as the Living One who reveals divine knowledge to his disciples. This is the knowledge of life, which originates from God and therefore belongs to God, whereas only money belongs to the emperor. A topical problem is being presented here as a way of highlighting fundamental alternatives in human life. The same tendency toward generalization can be identified in the version from Papyrus Egerton (frag. 2), where the problem is the support of any earthly rule; Jesus refused to give an answer and reminded his questioners of his teaching.

B

The well-known Synoptic dialogue represents the older version of the saying. The fourth sentence, the christological maxim, is obviously a later addition, assuming an explicit belief about the revelations mediated by the living Jesus.

Literature

Gibson, J. B. 1995. *Temptations of Jesus in Early Christianity* (JSNTS SS 112). Sheffield: Sheffield Academic Press, 294ff., 314.

---

101 49,32–50,1	(1) "Whoever does not hate his [father] and his mother as I do, will not be able to be a [disciple] of mine. (2) And whoever does [not] love his [father and] his mother as I do, will not be able to be a [disciple of mine].

---

279. The protests that it provoked were described by Flavius Josephus (*Jewish War* 2.8.1 = 2.117f.).

(3) For my mother [. . .],[280]
but my true [mother] gave me life."

A

The saying is a provocative exhortation to a reorientation of the values of life. The first part, with its parallel in log. 55:1, instructs the hearer to subordinate his relationship to his biological parents to the higher norm of Jesus' words. *To hate* is a semitic emphatic expression, which warns against considering family relations (*father* and *mother*, in log. 55:2, also brothers and sisters) to be the absolute norm. To this day, the family in the Near East has extraordinary authority and power over its individual members. Here we have an instruction that also arose from the practical problems of the wandering missionaries, and was typical for the Thomas community as well.

The *love* of parents mentioned in the second part, where "love" replaces hate, may reflect a different attitude toward parents, including a Christian witness leading to their salvation; but in the Thomas group it may in fact apply to another mother and father, as we might deduce from the third sentence, where we read about the *true* mother. The true mother may be the Holy Spirit, because the Hebrew word for Spirit (*ruah*) is feminine. God the Father as revealed through Jesus is then the true Father. An explicit proclamation of the Spirit as the mother of Jesus is to be found in the *Gospel of Hebrews* (frags. 2 and 3).[281]

This means that in the third part the *true mother* of Jesus, who gave him *life*, is the Holy Spirit. This would be the meaning of the unreadable section.

B

The first part and log. 55:1 have their parallel in Luke 14:26 par. According to Mark 3:31–35[282] Jesus declared that his true mother and brothers were those who were sitting around him: "Whoever does the will of God is my brother and sister and mother." In the *Gospel of Thomas*, the ethical character of social relations (God's family) is essentially spiritualized.

It seems evident that an older version of the saying, very similar to log. 55, has been transformed in a spiritualized, pre-Gnostic direction.

---

102   Jesus says:
50,2–5a   "Woe to the Pharisees,
                 for they are like a dog sleeping[283]

---

280. The lacuna can be filled as follows: "For my mother, who has [given birth to me, has destroyed me]"; another possibility: "For my mother has [deceived me]" (NHD).

281. In the *Gospel of Philip* (NHC II/3; 55,24–26) we read a polemic against the teaching of Mary's conception by the Spirit, because a woman cannot conceive from a woman. See also the commentary on log. 105.

282. Parallels in Matt 13:1–9 and Luke 8:4–8.

283. Or, "lying" (NHD).

in a cattle trough,
for it neither eats nor [lets] the cattle eat."

A

This a proverb about those who do not wish to allow others even food or possessions that they do not need themselves. The reader/hearer of *Gospel of Thomas* understood it as criticism of the mainstream church which failed to teach the doctrine of the divine core of human beings.

B

The proverb is well known from Greek popular traditions[284] and is still common in Russian and English. Several proverbs from the Jesus traditions are later accretions, but undoubtedly some of them were quoted by Jesus himself. In log. 39 and in Luke 11:52 the Pharisees, the Jewish reform movement, are characterized in a similar way: ". . . you have taken away the key of knowledge; you did not enter yourselves, and you hindered those who were entering."

103	Jesus says:
50,5b–10a	"Blessed the person who knows,
	at which point (of the house)[285]
	the robbers are going to enter,
	so that [he] may arise to gather together
	his [domain] and gird his loin
	before they enter."

A

The saying blesses the person who possesses valuable knowledge: he/she does know where his or her house (kingdom, empire) will be attacked by robbers and can prepare to counter the assault. The *robbers* may be real enemies and the suffering associated with their attacks. Such a situation is always a heavy test of self-understanding and orientation in life. At a more profound level, however, the robber is the "world," as it is expressed in log. 21:6. The *point* at which the robbers may enter is most probably the human soul, which has the potential to be filled with the spirit of God. The knowledge of this treasure is in some respects identical with the treasure itself. The function of the saying within the *Gospel of Thomas* is to warn against the loss of the divine substance, that is, the grateful knowledge of the divine substance. If this is lost the human being may become a carcass, as mentioned in

---

284. Leutsch and Schniedewin 1851.
285. Or, "at what part of the night" (NHD).

log. 56. The problem of what the robbers would win by the attack is outside the scope of the parable.

In any case, compared to the Synoptic parallels—Matt 24:43; Luke 12:39b [Q] for the first part and Luke 12:35 for the second—the stress has changed: it is not the "when," but the "where" that is posed as the problem for the hearers.[286]

B

Originally, the saying was an exhortation to vigilant expectation of the imminent coming of the kingdom of God and the last judgment (cf. 1 Thess 5:2). Even here the *point* (Gr. *meros*) may have originally been understood in the temporal sense.[287] In the given version, however, the kingdom of the Father seems to be represented by an area (space) in which the addressees are already living and which has to be protected. The same shift of emphasis can be observed in the parallel in log. 21:6–9.

This is one of the sayings that may have been influenced by the Lukan parallel,[288] either at the time of the earliest formulation of the *Gospel of Thomas* or when it was translated into Coptic.

104
50,10b–16a

(1) They said to [Jesus]:
"Come, let us pray and fast today!"
(2) Jesus said: "What sin is it that I have committed,
or wherein have I been overcome?
(3) But when the bridegroom comes
out of the wedding chamber,
then one is to fast and pray."

A

The saying proclaims that those who are one with the living Jesus through their obedience to his words do not need to *fast* and *pray*. The main intention is not to reject prayer but to stress the inner power of community with Jesus. This is the idea behind all the sayings that criticize the ritual dimension of religion, such as log. 6 and 14. Prayer is supposed to be necessary as a part of penitence after a person has committed a sin in the sense of individual transgression of a commandment of Law.[289]

---

286. Valantasis 1997.
287. Plisch mentioned Aeschylus's *Agamemnon* 557.
288. Schürmann 1968.
289. See a similar saying of Jesus in the *Gospel of the Nazarenes,* fragment 8 (2).

B

The background to the image of Jesus as bridegroom is anchored in the Synoptic tradition in Mark 2:19–20 parr.[290]

In the sense intended by Jesus, the *wedding* feast was the time of proclamation of the kingdom of God (*today*). The time *when the bridegroom was taken away* was the period after the death of Jesus. Here, *today* is the present time of reading the *Gospel of Thomas,* and the bridegroom's coming *out of the wedding chamber* is an "impossible possibility."[291]

Unlike log. 6, where only the prescribed prayers are rejected, here prayer is rejected absolutely in favor of a meditative mystic union with God through obedience to the words of Jesus. This was a radical step in religious practice and in the liturgy of the community.

105	Jesus says:
50,16b–18a	"Whoever will know father and mother,
	he will be called son of a whore."

A

A mysterious saying that relativizes family ties, as was proclaimed in log. 101 and 55:1. It is formulated in the future tense, that is, it expresses the situation in the face of God (originally at the last judgment) and may apply to biological parents. The meaning would be: "Whoever will know only the earthly father and mother. . . ." But those who recognize biological parents are not *sons of a whore*! According to log. 101 the beloved parents would then be the Spirit and God the Father as represented by Jesus. In that case, earthly people who do not know God as the true, heavenly Father and know only their biological parents would be sons of a whore. In a similar sense, Jesus, according to John 8:39–47, proclaimed that Jews who did not know the deeds of Abraham were illegitimate children.

Another interpretation relies on a particular reconstruction of the text. In 1967 Leipoldt[292] suggested the insertion of a negative at the beginning of the sentence ("Whoever will not know"), believing it to have been omitted in the process of translation. In this case the statement would apply to the spiritual *father and mother,* that is, the heavenly Father as revealed by Jesus and the spirit of God as mother. The intention would be the same, but since "*know*" is used in the *Gospel of Thomas* in a predominantly positive way, this interpretation would be the more plausible one. In the *Gospel of Philip*[293] the Jews, who do not have Jesus, are termed orphans. *Son of*

---

290. A developed version is to be found in Eph 5:28–32.
291. In the *Gospel of Philip* the "wedding chamber" is a special sacrament (NHC II/3; 82,19ff.).
292. This is a reconstruction included in the critical edition of the text in 1967.
293. NHC II/3; 52,21–24.

a whore would be an expression for the same reality. It would be the invective of the Thomas group against those who failed to recognize their spiritual parents.[294]

B

The logion may have been placed here because it develops the theme of spiritual wedding, which appears in the preceding saying.

106
50,18b–22a

(1) Jesus says:
"When you make the two into one,
you will become sons of man.
(2) And when you say:
'Mountain, move away,' it will move away."

A

A parallel to log. 48. Instead of "making peace" it is *making two into one* that is the basis of the great promise. In practice it meant to overcome the difference of sexes—to return to the original unity of human being represented by Adam before Eve was created from his rib (Gen 2:21–25). *Sons of man* are therefore human beings in their original mission as beings created in God's image. The designation of Jesus as Son of Man, which does not occur in the *Gospel of Thomas*, may be assumed here. In the *Gospel of Philip*[295] the true disciples of Jesus are the sons of man and Jesus, the Son of Man.

The second part of the saying consists of the well-attested words of Jesus from Mark 11:23 par. and Luke 17:6 par. (Q)—and in log. 48. The reference to *moving mountains* is a metaphor expressing a power that transcends ordinary human abilities.

107
50,22b–27

(1) Jesus says:
"The kingdom is like a shepherd
who had a hundred sheep.
(2) One of them went astray, the largest.
He left the ninety-nine,
(and) he sought the one until he found it.
(3) After he had labored, he said to the sheep:
'I love you more than the ninety-nine.'"

---

294. See Patterson 1990, 136.
295. Paragraph 120 (NHC II/3; 81,14ff.).

A

In this independent version of a parable (*The kingdom is like*) well known from the source Q (Matt 18:12f.; Luke 15:4–6; cf. Matt 12:11f.) we encounter a special feature: *the sheep* that *went astray* is especially precious, for it was *the largest* and most beloved (*I love you more than the ninety-nine*). It may allegorically represent the spiritually initiated member of the community who has decided to leave the mainstream church and restore his/her personality by embracing the integral life of the "solitary ones" as they are characterized in sayings 4, 11, 22:4, or 75. The *largest* sheep plays a similar role to the big fish in log. 8, or the large branch in log. 20:4. These are individuals who are especially precious, since they are able to leave the flock and look for new ways, which is why the wise central figures such as the wise fisherman in log. 8 or prudent merchant in log. 76:2 value them so highly.

B

The characterization of the sheep as the largest one is something added by the editor of the *Gospel of Thomas*. The big or large ones are the initiated members of the religious elite groups, as they are praised in log. 23: "I will choose you, one from a thousand . . . and you two from ten thousand. And you will stand as a single one." Later this interpretation of older Jesus traditions was to be developed by the Gnostics,[296] but the original intention has not been entirely abandoned here, for in contrast to the parable of the wise or sensible fisherman in log. 8, whereas the other fish were thrown back into the sea, here the other sheep are still loved by the shepherd (sentence 3).[297]

Literature

Bauer, J. B. 1950. "Echte Jesusworte?" in W. C. van Unnik, *Evangelien aus dem Nilsand*. Frankfurt: H. Scheffer, 109–50, esp. p. 143.

Petersen, W. L. 1981. "The Parable of the Lost Sheep in the *Gospel of Thomas* and the Synoptics," *Novum Testamentum* 23:128–47.

Myszor, Wincenty. 1986. "Exegeza propowieści o zagubionej owcy u Ireneusza i gnostików," in *Opuscula I*, Warsaw, 74–201.

108 50,28–30	(1) Jesus says: "Whoever will drink from my mouth will become like me. (2) I myself will become he (3) and what is hidden will be revealed to him."

---

296. Irenaeus *Adv. haer.* 1.8.4; *Gospel of Truth* (NHC I/3; 31,35ff.). The followers of Simon of Gittai (*Apg 8*) considered his mate Helen a lost sheep, too; see Hippolytus, *Philos.* 6.19.2.

297. Leipoldt 1967; Plisch 2007.

A

This, the most mystical saying from the *Gospel of Thomas*,[298] discloses (*revealed*) the mystery of those who are the solitary ones (Gr./Copt. *monachoi*)—they are united with the living Jesus by drinking from his mouth (log. 13:5). This means a union of substance with the giver of the water of life, as it is expressed in John 4:10–14.[299]

B

The image of drinking *from mouth* to mouth may reflect the liturgical kiss common in early Christian congregations (Rom 16:16, etc.).

109	(1) Jesus says:
50,31–51,3	"The kingdom is like a person
	who has a hidden treasure in his field,
	[of which] he knows nothing.
	(2) And [after] he had died,
	he left it to his [son].
	(But) the son did not know (about it either).
	He took over that field (and) sold [it].
	(3) And the one who has bought it came,
	and started to plough,
	(and) [he found] the treasure.
	He began to lend money at interest
	to whom he wished."

A

The parable of the treasure in the field is well known from Matt 13:44. The person who finds the treasure gives all his/her possessions to gain the field. The moral problem is not discussed, since all attention is concentrated on demonstrating the value of the treasure: it is worth more than all human possessions. In this version there are two generations of owners of a field who do not know about the treasure. It is only the new owner who discovers it and wins possessions that enable him to obtain power over others (*He began to lend money at interest*[300] *to whom he wished*).

Both versions contain allegorical features. In the Matthean parable the treasure is the kingdom, while in Thomas the treasure is the divine substance of the human soul unnoticed by generations of people who lack the knowledge and discovered by those who are searching (*started to plough*).

---

298. Plisch 2007, 249..

299. John 7:37–39 can serve as a good commentary; cf. the *Gospel of Philip* (NHC II/3; 58,33–59,6).

300. This does not run counter to the ban on lending at interest, as proclaimed in log. 95, since here it is simply a metaphor for power over others.

B

The fable is known in several cultural milieux, the best-known example is from the *Satires* of Horace (1,6:10–12).

The Thomas version seems to originate from an independent source, but it is more deeply adapted to the ideas of the *Gospel of Thomas* than the Matthean version to the theology of the Gospel of Matthew.

110	Jesus says:
51,4–5	"The one who has found the world
	(and) has become wealthy[301]
	should renounce the world."

A

The one who *found the world* is a person who has discovered the rules of the visible world, who has the knowledge of it and may even manipulate the others, like the "rich" person in log. 81, who derives power from his wealth (log. 81:2). Yet if he or she truly knows the world and its rules, that is, if he or she has recognized that the world is a carcass in a spiritual sense (log. 80; cf. 56), the only logical reaction is to *renounce* (Gr./Copt. *arneomai*) or even to reject[302] it. This basic experience following from religious knowledge is expressed in a humorous and even playful way.[303]

B

The saying makes it impossible for the preceding saying (109:3) to be literally interpreted as a blessing for the rich on the grounds of their earthly possessions.

The last sayings were selected and adapted by the editor to serve as summaries of some of the principal ideas of the *Gospel of Thomas*.

111	(1) Jesus says:
51,6–10a	"The heavens will roll up before you, and the earth.
	(2) And whoever is living from the Living One
	will not see death."
	(3) Does not Jesus say:[304]
	"Whoever has found himself, of him the world
	is not worthy"?

---

301. Possibly, "The one who <will> find the world (and) has become wealthy" (NHD).
302. An alternative translation suggested the NHD group.
303. Valantasis 1995.
304. Obviously an elliptical sentence (in which a part is omitted).

A

The apocalyptic vision of the heavens *rolled up* like a scroll,[305] to which Jesus himself referred, especially in his sayings about the Son of Man,[306] and which was common in the earliest period of Christianity[307] is quite unusual in the *Gospel of Thomas*. The editor was evidently familiar with apocalyptic traditions, mentioning the unexpected coming of the kingdom, as attested in sayings 21:5 and 103. On the other hand, even in these cases too the editor or the earlier traditions transformed the themes to serve the idea of salvation as a process of inner mystic transformation of human personality.[308]

The second sentence seems to return to the beginning of the *Gospel of Thomas*, where in the *incipit*, the opening sentence or the title of the book, we read of the "living Jesus" (according to log. 37, he is the "son of *the Living One*"). On the other hand, in sayings 3:4 and 50:2 the "living Father" is God himself, and so he may be meant here too. The living Jesus would then be a mediator in the sense of mystic mediation as described in log. 108.

The last part is mysterious and has perhaps been mutilated by the scribe or copyist. It might be understood as a rhetorical question about the theory of salvation from the world through the discovery of one's own divine substance (*of him the world is not worthy*; cf. log. 67). In logion 1 life is promised to those who find the meaning of the sayings from the *Gospel of Thomas*. This would mean that what is discovered in the "*self-finding*" is participation in the divine power that works in the living Jesus, the very mystagogue himself—the power of God as the "living Father."

B

The third part is a paradoxical literary construction: Jesus supports his argument from parts 1 and 2 by quoting Jesus! This has obviously resulted from an attempt to interpret the first two statements through an additional saying of Jesus—in a way that is awkward in literary effect.[309]

The relationship of this saying to logion 1 supports the conclusion that the last sayings of the *Gospel of Thomas* were intentionally selected and adapted as a summary of the main ideas of this mysterious text.

112	(1) Jesus says:
51,10b–12a	"Woe to the flesh that depends on the soul.
	(2) Woe to the soul that depends on the flesh."

---

305. Rev 6:14; Heb 1:12 (here the heavens will be rolled up like a clothing) or *Oracula Sibyllina* 3:82f.

306. E.g., Matt 24:26–28; Luke 17:23–24, 37.

307. E.g., 1 Thess 1:10.

308. See a similar transformation of the apocalyptic expectations in John 5:24f.

309. According to Plisch 2007 this must have happened after the *Gospel of Thomas* was composed.

A

The saying expresses the antagonism between the flesh (matter) on one side and the spirit dwelling in the human soul on the other. It is an analogy to saying 87.

The second sentence expresses reality from the point of view of the soul. The saying about the happy lion (log. 7:1) would seem to claim the opposite. In fact, the statement from 7:1 is formulated from the human point of view: the lion representing the "flesh" will be transformed into a human being. Here, in log. 112:1 the same process is seen from the point of view of the flesh. The flesh that depends on the soul does not function as flesh, and ceases to be "flesh."

B

The Gr./Copt. word *sarx* is used for body here, and *sōma* in log. 87. *Sarx* does not include the dimension of matter as organism and can simply denote "meat"; in Pauline theology it is a synonym for sinfulness. The body is defined in a similar way in log. 29 dealing with the incarnation of God in Jesus. Since the concluding sayings each deal with some major idea of the *Gospel of Thomas*, the anthropology dominated by the dichotomy soul–flesh (matter) was evidently one of the main ideas of the Thomas group. It was not simply a dualist anthropology. Flesh and soul may coexist, but human hope and all attention should be concentrated on the soul, in and through which the divine spirit can be discovered and recognized as the power of life.

A synopsis of related sayings:

Log. 87	Log. 112
(1) Wretched the body that hangs to a body.	(2) Woe to the soul that depends on the flesh.
(2) And wretched is the soul that depends on these two.	(1) Woe to the flesh that depends on the soul.
Log. 7	
(1) Blessed is the lion that a person will eat and the lion will become human.	(Log. 7:2 And anathema is the person whom a lion will eat and the lion will become human.)

113 51,12b–18a	(1) His disciples said to him: "The kingdom—on what day will it come?" (2) "It will not come by watching (and waiting for) it. (3) They will not say: 'Look, here!' or 'Look, there!' (5) Rather the kingdom of the Father is spread out upon the earth, and people do not see it."

A

This saying is analogous to saying 3 and a proclamation similar to Luke 17:20f. It expresses the present (realized) eschatology of the group.

B

It was necessary to stress the idea of present salvation precisely because the editor of the *Gospel of Thomas* must have been aware of the tradition of the future, apocalyptic eschatology of God's judgment and the coming of the kingdom. The idea of perfect salvation served as a spiritual antidote. The idea of a resurrection that has already come, expressed in log. 51, is a different formulation of the same problem.

114
51,18b–26

(1) Simon Peter said to them:
  "Let Mary go away from us,
  for women are not worthy of life."
(2) Jesus said: "Look, I will draw her in
  so as to make her male,
  so that she too may become a living male spirit
  being similar to you."
(3) (But I say to you):
  "Every woman, if she makes herself male,
  will enter the kingdom of heaven."

A

Peter's surprising words clearly refer to *Mary* Magdalene. They prompt Jesus to intervene and reveal an important and general truth:

Despite her feminine gender, Mary will be attracted (Copt. *sok*; Greek probably *elkyo* as in John 12:32) to the spiritual side, the side of Jesus. Here the feminine gender can be transformed into masculine, as it was at the beginning with Adam as the single human being (Gen 2).[310] This is an idea mentioned in log. 22:5, where we have commented on it. The masculine was considered to be spiritual, and the feminine material.[311] In the ancient traditions Jesus communicated with women and women were his disciples (cf. Luke 8:2–3), while women had an important role in the early church (e.g., Rom 16:1), but by the end of the first century the mainstream church as well as several esoteric groups were curtailing the role of women in the life of Christian communities. Here, in sentence 1, Peter tells the other disciples of Jesus that *Mary* should *go away* from them, that is, that she should be excluded from the group of disciples of Jesus and leaders of the Christian communities.[312]

---

310. See *On the Origin of the World* (NHC II/5; 109,1ff.).
311. See Meyer 1992.
312. According Leipoldt 1967, 77, this is an "alien tone."

We do not know whether the narrator supposed that Jesus was actually among those addressed by Peter, but in any case in 114:2 Jesus deals with the problem of Mary, as we mentioned above, and in sentence 3 he formulates a general statement[313] about the access of women to the kingdom of God:[314] Any *woman can enter the kingdom of heaven* if she *makes herself male*. The human being can take active steps to his/her salvation: can search the kingdom, hear the voice of the living Jesus, answer his call, and *be drawn* by him to his side.[315]

This provided a practical justification for the role of women in the Thomas community, as we can trace that role in the *Acts of Thomas*. Even more, Mary can become the real disciple, just as Salome was according to saying 61:4, whereas the disciples (except James and Thomas)[316] often did not understand Jesus.

B

Like the preceding saying, this opens with a question from the side of Jesus's disciples. The question and the two answers given by Jesus, one particular and one general, evoke the impression of a scene[317] similar to that of John 20:11–18—when Jesus revealed himself to Mary Magdalene as the Living One. In fact it is a model of communication with Jesus: a group (said *to them*) has problems; its speaker (*Peter*) suggests a solution; but Jesus is the key figure, and having accepted his solution, the members of the group reshape their relations. *Mary* and Peter, two people from the group closest to Jesus, may have been discussed as possible spiritual leaders. The *Gospel of Mary* from the second century reflects her authority in early Christianity, but the real authority remains Jesus himself. *Living* male spirit means living in the sense of eternal life, of salvation as it can be understood from log. 4:1 or 11:2–3, to live as Salome lived (log. 61:4) and as Mary can live.

Another implication is that women are full members of the community. In most translations the solution given is that by a mysterious intervention of Jesus Mary will became male, but the Berlin group (H.-B. Bethge) has suggested a better translation. The word *hoout,* "male, masculine," is related to *pneuma* (Gr./Copt. "spirit") by means of the particle *in* (*inhout*), expressing the idea that "male" is an attribute of "spirit." Jesus will "draw" her to the spiritual, "male" part. The practical implication is that biological gender plays no role in human destiny,[318] but the

---

313. This is a new statement, not the ground or cause for accepting Mary. The particle *če* introducing the third part is not used in a causal sense but is an elliptic introduction of sentence 3. In the translation, it is expressed by the inserted introduction of direct speech.

314. Plisch (2007, 264) noticed that Jesus' disputation about the children and the kingdom of God in Mark 10:13–16 has the same structure: first he accepts a child, and then a general statement follows.

315. For later speculation on transforming the spiritual role of gender, see, e.g., Clement of Alexandria, *Exc. ex Theod.* 21.3 from a Valentinian setting; see also Kosnetter 1965, 40.

316. See log. 13 and 14 and the introduction, on the theology of the *Gospel of Thomas*, ecclesiology; for log. 114 see Brankaer 2005, 151ff.

317. The scene is also shaped in this way by, e.g., saying 61.

318. BG 8502,1, the *Gospel of Mary* 18:9–10. In the *Gospel of Mary* 17:15–18:12 we find a developed version of this scene from the *Gospel of Thomas*, log. 114.

condition for the realization of that idea was the abolition of marriage[319] for the elect members of the community. This was ultimately to contribute to the extinction of the community.

Some of the earlier translations follow the basic intention of the saying,[320] but the solution proposed by the Berlin group is the most persuasive.

Literature

Brankaer, Johanna. 2005. "L'ironie de Jésus das le *LOGION* 114 de l'*Évangile de Thomas*," *Apocrypha* 16:149–62.

Buckley, J. J. 1985. "An Interpretation of Logion 114 in the *Gospel of Thomas*," *Novum Testamentum* 27:245–72.

Drijvers, H. J. W. 1970. "Edessa und das jüdische Christentum," *Vigiliae Christianae*, 4–33.

Kosnetter, J. 1965. "Das Thomasevangelium und die Synoptiker," in *Wissenschaft im Dienste des Glaubens* (FS H. Peichl), 29–40. Vienna.

Meyer, Marvin W. 1985. " 'Making Mary Male' The Categories 'Male' and 'Female' in the *Gospel of Thomas*," *New Testament Studies* 33:554–70.

———. 2002. "*Gospel of Thomas* Logion 114 Revisited," in *For the Children: Perfect Instruction* (FS H.-M. Schenke), 101–11. Leiden/Boston: Brill.

Schüngel, P. 1994. "Ein Vorschlag. EvTho 114 neu zu übersetzen," *Novum Testamentum* 36:394–401.

THE TITLE OF THE BOOK   The Gospel according to Thomas
51, 27–28

It is possible that the title at the end was added only in the last Greek version, in layer three, as we described it in the introduction. The editor adopted the early Christian title of "Gospel." The Gospels originated as anonymous books whose author was supposed to be identical with their protagonist—Jesus himself. That is why the additional titles, which were all cast in the same literary form, mention the Gospel writers only as editors and bearers of traditions, as expressed by the term "*according to*" (Gr./Copt. *kata*). The scrolls of the Gospels stored in the libraries of individual Christian communities could then be distinguished from one another by the names of the Gospel writers. This must have happened at the beginning of the second century.[321] The term *euangelion*, "gospel," for these books is derived from

---

319. See Drijvers 1970, 18ff.
320. Esp. Schüngel 1994.
321. Hengel 1984, 8ff., 14ff.

Mark 1:1. Mark decided to add to the oral Easter gospel (Rom 1:1; 1 Cor 15:1), the proclamation of the resurrection of Jesus, the life story of Jesus culminating with his cross and resurrection. "The Gospel according to . . ." makes the reader aware of the fact that there is only one Gospel. The *Gospel according to Thomas* took over this type of title, even though it has a different literary form; and unlike the canonical Gospels and, for example, the *Gospel of Peter,* it does not build the hope it offers on Easter. The term *euangelion* came to refer to books ("Gospels" in the plural) in the second part of the second century. Earlier, even in, for example, "The Gospel according to Matthew," the "Gospel" (*euangelion*) meant the oral proclamation. According to Mark 1:14–15, *euangelion* was also the proclamation of Jesus about the kingdom of God, and so the editor of the *Gospel of Thomas* may have felt entitled to adopt such a title on these grounds (see the section in the introduction on the gospel as oral message and as book, and on the title of the *Gospel of Thomas*).

From Interpretations to the Interpreted

We have now concluded our successive interpretation of the *Gospel of Thomas,* the purpose of which was to discover its spiritual milieu and its theology. At the beginning, however, we indicated that our study of the *Gospel of Thomas* has a second purpose, which is to use this text as a source in Jesus research. Our critical analysis of this dimension of the *Gospel of Thomas,* which may be understood as a modern aid to memory, has not resulted in the discovery of any sensational facts about Jesus' life or teaching. Nevertheless, in some of the sayings we have observed features of traditions that may lead back to the real words of Jesus himself, and may in some cases have been taken from sources independent of the Synoptics. The chance that these are authentic increases according to the rule of two or more independent testimonies. Since many such sayings cannot be explained as statements evoked by the immediate needs of the church, the criterion of dissimilarity to other attested traditions of that period can support their possible claim to authenticity. Nor can the criterion of plausibility be used as an argument against the most ancient origin of such sayings, for there is little to suggest that the symbolic language of these sayings was not familiar or comprehensible in the Jewish and Jewish Hellenistic Palestinian (Galilean) milieu of Jesus's (?) time. In the ears of the intended original audience the sayings of the *Gospel of Thomas* were sometimes startling, but understandable.

The *Gospel of Thomas* shares with the canonical Gospels the proclamation of the kingdom of God, even if in its interpretation the future expectation has been bracketed off, and what predominates is the proclamation of a kingdom already present in a spiritual sense. The shocking impact of the original proclamation of the kingdom is still recognizable in saying 2 and in the intensity of the effort to reinterpret the original proclamation of the kingdom of God as a phenomenon representing the absolute horizon of history. Theoretically, this could be a trick of perspective, as several scholars from the Third Quest have proposed,[322] suggesting that apocalyptic expectations were retrospectively ascribed to Jesus by his followers in their post-Easter enthusiasm. Once we admit that Jesus proclaimed the kingdom of God, however, it is practically impossible to relegate the social and even cosmic dimensions of his proclamation to the later period as secondary accretions. In the introduction we indicated that his exorcisms, sayings on the last judgment, and some mysterious sayings such as Luke 12:49 par. (Q) with their surprising parallel in saying 16:1–2 cannot be excluded from the earliest strata of the Jesus tradition.

The fact that Jesus was compelled to formulate the relationship of his proclamation to the political authorities (Mark 12:13–17 parr.) confirms the social character of his message as well as his consciousness of a special (messianic?) mission entrusted to him by God. The saying on the relationship to political power was preserved in the Synoptic tradition and in the Papyrus Egerton (frag. 2, recto), and also in the *Gospel of Thomas* log. 100.

The absence of messianic titles in the *Gospel of Thomas* undoubtedly reflects the theology of the Thomas group—its tendency to see Jesus as the One who is the mediator of life from the Living One to human beings. The root cause may, however, be that Jesus himself originally tried to distance himself from this kind of messianic reverence.

Finally, the method of conserving Jesus' teaching in individual sayings as in the wisdom traditions and prophetic proclamation is obviously more ancient than the method of setting his teaching in a biographical frame, as invented by Mark. All the same, the biographic frame conserved the ancient layer of the Jesus tradition more effectively than collections of his sayings.

The Interpreted must be the source of the feedback of all interpretations. Some traces of his teaching are recognizable in the *Gospel of Thomas*.

---

322. See introduction.

Bibliography

Text Editions

Robinson, James R., ed. 1974. *The Facsimile Edition of the Nag Hammadi Codices. Codex II.* Published under the auspices of the Arab Republic of Egypt and UNESCO. Leiden: Brill.

Attridge, H. W. 1989. *See below under* Koester 1989.

Bethge, Hans-Gebhard, Christina-Maria Franke, Judith Hartenstein, Uwe-Karsten Plisch, Hans-Martin Schenke, and Jens Schröter. 1996. *Das Thomas Evangelium/ The Gospel According to Thomas.* The Coptic text, with German and English translation, in Kurt Aland, 1996. *Synopsis quattuor evangeliorum.* Stuttgart: Deutsche Bibelgesellschaft, 519–46. *The English translation of the Berlin group is used as the basis for this commentary.*

Gillabert, É., P. Bourgeois, and Y. Haas. 1985. *Évangelie selon Thomas.* Paris.

Grenfell, Bernhard P., and Arthur S. Hunt. 1898. *The Oxyrhynchus Papyri.* Part I. London: Egypt Exploration Fund.

———. 1904. *The Oxyrhynchus Papyri.* Part IV. London: Egypt Exploration Fund.

Guillaumont, A., H.-Ch. Puech, G. Quispel, W. Till, and Y. A. al Masíh, eds. 1959. *The Gospel According to Thomas. Coptic Text Established and Translated.* Leiden: Brill.

Klostermann, Erich. 1910. *Apocrypha II. Evangelien.* Kleine Texte 8. Bonn: Marcus and Weber Verlag. Edition of related texts.

Koester, Helmut. 1989. [Introduction—Helmut Koester; Translation—Thomas O. Lambdin; Critical Edition—Bentley Layton; Greek Fragments—Harold W. Attridge] *The Gospel according to Thomas,* pp. 37–128 in B. Layton, *Nag Hammadi Codex II, 2-7 together with P.Oxy. 1. 654. 655,* I (=NHS 20). Leiden: Brill, 1989.

Lambdin, Thomas O. 1989. *See* Koester 1989.

Layton, Bentley. 1989. *See* Koester 1989.

Leipoldt, Johannes. 1967. *Das Evangelium nach Thomas* (=TU 101), Berlin: Academia.

Meyer, Marvin W., and Harold Bloom. 1992. *The Gospel of Thomas: The Hidden Sayings of Jesus.* San Francisco: Harper & Row.

Nagel, Peter. 1970. *Das Wesen der Archonten aus Codex II der gnostischen Bibliothek von Nag Hammadi. Koptischer Text, deutsche Übersetzung, Konkordanz und Indizes von P. Nagel.* Wissenschaftliche Beiträge der Martin-Luther-Universität Halle-Wittenberg 6 K3. Halle (Saale): Martin-Luther-Universität.

Plisch, Uwe-Carsten. *See* Commentaries and Translations.

160   *Bibliography*

Commentaries and Translations (Marked by *); and Secondary Literature

Allison, Dale C. 1998. *Jesus of Nazareth: Millenarian Prophet.* Minneapolis: Fortress Press.

*Attridge, Harold W. *See above,* Text Editions.

Arnal, W. 1995. "The Rhetoric of Marginality: Apocalypticism, Gnosticism, and Sayings Gospels," *Harvard Theological Review* 88:471–94.

Baarda, Tjitze. 1983. *Early Transmission of Words of Jesus: Thomas, Tatian, and the Text of the New Testament.* Amsterdam: Free University Press.

*Blatz, Beate. 1987. "Das koptische Thomasevangelium." Pp. 93–113 in W. Schneemelcher, *Neutestamentliche Apokryphen I.* Fifth edition. Tübingen: Mohr Siebeck.

Beardslee, William A. 1972. "Proverbs in the *Gospel of Thomas,*" in D. E. Aune, ed., *Studies in New Testament and Early Christian Literature* (FS A. P. Wikgren). SupplNovT 33. Leiden: Brill.

*Bloom, Harold. *See* Meyer and Bloom 1992.

Borg, Marcus J. 1994. *Jesus in Contemporary Scholarship.* Valley Forge, PA: Trinity Press International.

Brankaer, Johanna. 2004. *Je ne suis pas ton maître: Role et signification des disciples dans l'Evangile de Thomas.* NHC II,2. Louvain: Faculté de Théologie.

Brown, Raymond. 1962–63. "The *Gospel of Thomas* and St. John's Gospel." *New Testament Studies* 9:155–77.

Cameron, Ron. 1985. "*Gospel of Thomas.*" Pp. 535–40 in *The Anchor Bible Dictionary.* New York: Doubleday.

———. 1988. *See under* Fallon and Cameron.

Charlesworth, James H. 1974. "Tatian's Dependence upon Apocryphal Traditions." *Heythrop Journal* 15:15–16.

———. 1995. *The Beloved Disciple.* Valley Forge, PA: Trinity Press International.

Crossan, John D. 1973. *In Parables: The Challenge of the Historical Jesus.* San Francisco: Harper & Row.

———. 1991. *The Historical Jesus.* San Francisco: Harper & Row.

Crum, W. E. 1939. *A Coptic Dictionary.* Oxford: Clarendon Press.

Cullmann, Oscar. 1960. "Das Thomasevangelium und die Frage nach dem Alter der in ihm enthaltenen Tradition." In idem, *Vorträge und Aufsätze.* Tübingen/ Zürich: Zwingli.

Davies, Stevan L. 1983. *The Gospel of Thomas and Christian Wisdom.* New York: Seabury.

DeConick, April D. "The Original *Gospel of Thomas.*" *Vigiliae Christianae* 56:167–99.

*Dembska, Albertyna, and Wincenty Myszor. 1979. *Teksty z Nag Hammadi,* Warsaw: Akademia teologii katolickej.

Dodd, Charles D. 1936. *The Parable of the Kingdom.* Third edition. London: Religious Book Club.

Doran, R. 1987. "A Complex of Parables GTh 96–98." *Novum Testamentum* 29:347–52.

Dormeyer, Detlev. 2002. *Das Markusevangelium als Idealbiographie von Jesus Christus dem Nazarener.* SBS 43. Stuttgart: Katholisches Bibelwerk.

Downing, Francis G. 1988. *The Christ and the Cynics.* Sheffield: Sheffield University Press.

Drijwers, H. J. W. 1970. "Edessa und das jüdische Christentum." *Vigiliae Christianae* 24:4–33.

Dunn, James D. G. 2003. *Jesus Remembered.* Grand Rapids: Eerdmans.

*Dus, Jan A., and Petr Pokorný, eds. 2001. *Neznámá evangelia.* Novozákonní apokryfy 1. Praha: Vyšehrad.

Ebner, Michael. 1998. *Jesus ein Weisheitslehrer.* HBS 15. Freiburg: Herder.

*Elliott, J. K. 1999. *The Apocryphal New Testament.* Revised reprint of the 1993 edition. Oxford: Oxford University Press (on the *Gospel of Thomas,* see pp. 123–47).

Fallon, Francis T., and Ron Cameron. 1988. "The *Gospel of Thomas*: A Forschungsbericht and Analysis." *Aufstieg und Niedergang der römischen Welt.* Edited by H. Temporini and W. Haase. Berlin, 1972–. II,25.6, 4195–4251.

*Fieger, Michael. 1991. *Das Thomasevangelium: Einleitung, Kommentar und Systematik.* NTAbh 22. Münster: Aschendorff.

Franzmann, Majella. 1996. *Jesus in the Nag Hammadi Writings.* Edinburgh: T&T Clark.

Garitte, G. 1960. "Les 'Logoi' d'Oxyrhynque sont traduie du Copte." *Le Muséon* 73:335–49.

*Gärtner, Bertil E. 1961. *The Theology of the Gospel according to Thomas.* London: Collins.

Grant, Robert M., and David N. Freedman. 1960. *The Secret Sayings of Jesus.* Garden City, NY: Doubleday.

Grenfell, Bernhard P., and Arthur S. Hunt. 1897. *ΛΟΓΙΑ ΙΗΣΟΥ: Sayings of Our Lord.* London: Frowde.

———. 1904. *New Sayings of Jesus and Fragment of a Lost Gospel from Oxyrhynchus.* London: Frowde.

*Haenchen, Ernst. 1961. *Die Botschaft des Thomas-Evangeliums.* Berlin: Töpelmann.

Haufe, Christof. 1972. "Erwägungen zum Ursprung der sogenannten Parabeltheorie Markus 4,11–12." *Evangelische Theologie* 32:413–21.

Hedrick, Charles W. 1994. *Parables as Poetic Fictions: The Creative Voice of Jesus.* Peabody, MA: Hendrickson.

Hengel, Martin. 1984. "Die Evangelienüberschriften." In *Sitzungsberichte der Heidelbergem Akademie der Wissenschaften.* PH 1984/3. Heidelberg: C. Winter.

Hunzinger, Claus-Hunno. 1964. "Unbekannte Gleichnisse im Thomas-Evangelium." Pp. 209–30 in W. Eltester, ed., *Judentum—Urchristentum—Kirche* (FS J. Jeremias) (=BZNW 26). Berlin: de Gruyter.

————. 1960. "Aussersynoptisches Traditionsgut im Thomas-Evangelium." *Theologische Literaturzeitung* 85:843–46.

Jervell, Jakob. 1960. *Imago Dei* (FRLANT N.F. 58). Göttingen: Vandenhoeck & Ruprecht.

Jonas, Hans. 1954. *Gnosis und spätantiker Geist 2,1*. Göttingen: Vandenhoeck & Ruprecht.

*Kaestli, Jean-D. 1979. "L'Évangile de Thomas." *Études theologiques et religieuses* 54:375–96.

*Kasser, Rudolph. 1961. *L'Évangile selon Thomas*. Neuchâtel.

Khosroyev, Alexander. 1995. *Die Bibliothek von Nag Hammadi: Einige Probleme des Christiantums in Aegypten während der ersten Jahrhunderte.* (Arbeiten zum spätantiken und koptischen Aegypten 7. Altenberge: Oros Verlag.

Kloppenborg, John S., Marvin W. Meyer, Stephen J. Patterson, and Michael G. Steinhauser. 1990. *Q Thomas Reader.* Sonoma, CA: Polebridge Press.

Klijn, A. F. J. 1972. "Christianity in Edessa and the *Gospel of Thomas.*" *Novum Testamentum* 14:70-77.

Körtner, Ulrich J. H. 1983. *Papias von Hierapolis* (FRLANT 133). Göttingen: Vandenhoeck & Ruprecht.

Koester, Helmut. 1980A. *Einführung in das Neue Testament.* Berlin/New York: de Gruyter.

————. 1980B. "Gnostic Writings as Witnesses for Development of the Saying Tradition." Pp. 238–62 in B. Layton, ed., *The Rediscovery of Gnosticism* (STR 41). Leiden: Brill.

————. 1990. *Ancient Christian Gospels.* Cambridge MA: Trinity Press International.

Koschorke, Klaus. 1978. *Die Polemik der Gnostiker gegen das kirchliche Christentum* (NHS 12). Leiden: Brill.

*Layton, Bentley. *See under* Text Editions.

*Leipoldt, Johannes. *See under* Text Editions.

*Lelyveld, Margaretha. 1987. *Les Logia de la vie dans l'Évangile selon Thomas* (=NHS 34). Leiden: Brill.

von Leutsch, E. L., and F. G. Schneidewin, eds. 1965. *Corpus paroemigraphorum graecorum I–II* (1839). Second edition. Hildesheim.

Lindemann, Andreas. 1980. "Zur Gleichnisinterpretation im Thomas-Evangelium." *Zeitschrift für die neutestamentliche Wissenschaft* 71:214-43.

Lövenstein, K. *See under* Schramm.

Mack, Burton L. 1988. *A Myth of Innocence: Mark and Christian Origins.* Philadelphia: Fortress Press.

McArthur, H. K. 1959–60. "The Dependence of the *Gospel of Thomas* on Synoptics." *Expository Times* 7:286–87.

Markschies, Christoph. 2001. *Gnosis. An Introduction.* English translation. London/New York: T&T Clark.

Martyn, J. Louis. 1979. *History and Theology in the Fourth Gospel.* New York and Evanston: Harper & Row.

Ménard, J. É. 1972. "Les problèmes de l'Évangile selon Thomas." Pp. 59–73 in

Essays on the Nag Hammadi Texts in Honor of Alexander Böhlig (NHS 3). Leiden: Brill.

*———. 1975. *L'Évangile selon Thomas* (NHS 5). Leiden: Brill.

———. 1981. "La tradition synoptique et l'Évangile selon Thomas." Pp. 411–26 in *Überlieferungsgeschichtliche Untersuchungen.* Berlin: Akademie Verlag.

Metzger, Bruce. 1987. *The Canon of the New Testament.* Oxford: Clarendon.

*Meyer, Marvin W. *See under* Text Editions.

———. 1990. *See under* Kloppenborg.

———. 1991. "The Beginning of the *Gospel of Thomas.*" *Semeia* 82:161–71.

Montefiore, Hugh. 1960-61. "A Comparison of the Parables of the Gospel according to Thomas and of the Synoptic Gospels." *New Testament Studies* 7:220-48.

———, and Henry E. W. Turner. 1962. *Thomas and the Evangelists* (SBTh 35). Naperville, Ill.: Allenson.

*Morrice, William G. 1997. *Hidden Sayings.* London: SPCK.

*Myszor. *See under* Dembska.

*Nordsieck Reinhard. 2004. *Das Thomasevangelium.* Neukirchen: NeukirchenerVerlag.

Pagels, Elaine. 2003. *Beyond Belief: The Secret Gospel of Thomas*, New York: Random House.

Patterson, Stephen J. 1990A. "The *Gospel of Thomas* and the Historical Jesus." Pp. 614–66 in *Society of Biblical Literature Seminar Papers* 29. Atlanta, GA: Scholars Press.

———. 1990B. *See under* Kloppenborg.

———. 1993. *The Gospel of Thomas and Jesus.* Sonoma, CA.

Perrin, Nicholas. 2002. *Thomas and Tatian: The Relationship between the Gospel of Thomas and the Diatessaron* (AcBib 5). Atlanta, GA: Society of Biblical Literature.

*Plisch, Uwe-Carsten. 2000. Pp. 93–122 (*comments on selected sayings only) in *Verborgene Worte Jesu: Verworfene Evangelien.* Berlin: Evangelische Hauptbibelgesellschaft.

———. 2007. *Das Thomasevangelium: Originaltext mit Kommentar.* Stuttgart: Deutsche Bibelgesellschaft.

Pokorný, Petr. 1990. "Die Herrenworte im Thomasevangelium und bei Paulus." Pp. 157–64 in P. Nagel, ed. *C. Schmidt–Colloquium.* Halle: Martin-Luther-Universität.

———. 1985. "Das Markus-Evangelium." *Aufstieg und Niedergang der römischen Welt.* Edited by H. Temporini and W. Haase. II,25,3, 1969–2035

———. 1987. *The Genesis of Christology.* Edinburgh: T&T Clark.

———. 1998. *Píseň o perle: Tajné knihy starověkých gnostiků*, Praha: Vyšehrad (original edition, 1986).

*———. "Tomášovo evangelium (translation and commentary)." Pp. 77–153 in Dus and Pokorný 2001.

Popkes, Enno Edzard. 2006. "Das Menschenbild des Thomasevangeliums." Habilitationsschrift, Jena: Universität. (To be published in the series WUNT, Tübingen: Mohr Siebeck.)

Porter, Stanley E. 2000. Pp. 126–80, esp. 150ff. in *Criteria for Authenticity in Historical Jesus Research*. JSNTS 191. Edinburgh: T&TClark.

Puech, Henri Ch. 1978. "Doctrines ésotériques et thèmes gnostiques dans l'Évangile selon Thomas." Pp. 93–248 in *En quête de la gnose II*. Paris.

Quispel, Gilles. 1957. "The *Gospel of Thomas* and the New Testament." *Vigiliae Christianae* 11:189–207.

———. 1959. "L'Évangile selon Thomas et Diatessaron." *Vigiliae Christianae* 13:87–117.

———. 1967. *Makarius, das Thomasevangelium und das Lied von der Perle* (=NovTSuppl. 15). Leiden: Brill.

———. 1975. *Tatian and the Gospel of Thomas*. Leiden: Brill.

Ricouer, Paul. 1990. *Amour et justice*. Tübingen: Mohr Siebeck.

Riley, Gregory J. 1994. "The *Gospel of Thomas* in Recent Scholarship." *Current Research: Biblical Studies* 2:227-52.

Robinson, James M. 1971. "LOGOI SOPHON: On the Gattung of Q." Pp. 71–113 in idem and H. Koester, *Trajectories through Early Christianity*. Philadelphia: Fortress Press.

———. 1979. "The Discovery of Nag Hammadi Codices." *Biblical Archeologist* 42:206–24.

———, ed. 1987. *The Nag Hammadi Library in English*. Third edition. San Francisco: Harper.

Robinson, James R. 1999. "A Written Greek Sayings Cluster Older than Q: A Vestige." *Harvard Theological Review* 92:61–77.

Rudolf, Kurt. 1987. *Gnosis*. Second edition. Göttingen: Vandenhoeck & Ruprecht.

Schenke, Hans-Martin. 1962. *Der Gott Mensch in der Gnosis*. Berlin: Evangelische Verlagsanstalt.

———. 1998. "On the Compositional History of the *Gospel of Thomas*." In *The Institute for Antiquity and Christianity Occasional Papers 40*. Claremont, CA: Institute for Antiquity and Christianity.

*———, Hans-Gebhard Bethge, and Ulrike U. Kaiser. 2001. *Nag Hammadi Deutsch. 1*. Band: NHC I,1–V,1 (CS NF 8). Berlin/New York: de Gruyter.

*Schneemelcher W. *See under* Blatz.

*Schrage,Wolfgang. 1964a. *Das Verhältnis des Thomas-Evangeliums zur synoptischen Tradition und zu den koptischen Evangelienübersetzungen* (=BZNW 29). Berlin: Töpelmann.

———. 1964b. "Evangelienzitate in Oxyrhynchus-Logien und im koptischen Thomas-Evangelium." Pp. 251–68 in *Apophoreta* (FS E. Haenchen). Berlin: de Gruyter.

Schramm, Tim, and Kathrin Löwenstein. 1986. *Unmoralische Helden* Göttingen: Vandenhoeck & Ruprecht.

Schröter, Jens. 1997. *Erinnerung an Jesu Worte. Studien zur Rezeption der Logienüberlieferung in Markus, Q und Thomas* (WUNT 76). Neukirchen: Neukirchener Verlag.

Schürmann, Heinz. 1968. "Das Thomasevangelium und das lukanische Sondergut."

Pp. 228–47 in idem, *Traditionsgeschichtliche Untersuchungen zu den synoptischen Evangelien* Düsseldorf: Patmos.

Sieber, John H. 1990. "The *Gospel of Thomas* and the New Testament." Pp. 64–73 in G. J. E. Goehring, Ch. W. Hedrick, J. T. Sanders, and H.-D. Betz, eds., *Gospel Origins and Christian Beginnings* (FS J. M. Robinson). Sonoma, CA.

Steinhauser, Michael G. 1990. *See under* Kloppenborg.

*de Suarez, Philippe. 1974. *L'Évangelie selon Thomas: traduction, présentation et commentaires de Philippe de Suarez*. Marsanne: Métanoïa.

Theissen, Gerd, and Annette Marz. 1996. *Der historische Jesus*. Göttingen: Vandenhoeck & Ruprecht.

Tripp, D. H. 1980–81. "The Aim of the '*Gospel of Thomas*.'" *Expository Times* 92:41–44.

Tuckett, Christopher M. 1986. *Nag Hammadi and the Gospel Tradition*. Edinburgh: T&T Clark.

———. 1995. "Das Thomasevangelium und die synoptischen Evangelien." *Berliner theologische Zeitschrift* 12:186–200.

Turner, Nigel E. *See under* Montefiore.

Uro, Risto, ed. 1998. *Thomas at the Crossroads: Essays on the Gospel of Thomas*. Edinburgh: T&T Clark.

*Valantasis, Richard. 1997. *The Gospel of Thomas*. London/New York: Routledge.

———. 1999. "Is the *Gospel of Thomas* Ascetical? Revisiting an Old Problem with a New Theology." *Journal of Early Christian Studies* 7:55–81.

Vielhauer, Philipp. 1975. *Geschichte der urchristlichen Literatur.* Berlin/New York: de Gruyter.

Voorgang, Dietrich. 1991. *Die Passion Jesu und Christi in der Gnosis*. Frankfurt am Main: F. Lang.

Vouga, Francois. 1994. *Geschichte des frühen Christentums*. Tübingen/Basel: Francke.

Walls, A. F. 1960–61. "The References to Apostles in the *Gospel of Thomas*." *New Testament Studies* 7:266–70.

Wood, John Halsey Jr. 2005. "The New Testament Gospels and the *Gospel of Thomas*: A New Direction." *New Testament Studies* 51:579–95.

Vielhauer, Philipp. 1975. *Geschichte der urchristlichen Literatur*. Berlin/New York: de Gruyter.

Wilson, Robert McL. 1995. "The *Gospel of Thomas* Reconsidered." Pp. 331–36 in C. Fluck et al., eds., *Divitiae Aegypti* (FS M. Kraus). Wiesbaden: Reichert Verlag.

Zöckler, Thomas. 1999. *Jesu Lehren im Thomasevangelium* (NHMS 47). Leiden/ Boston: Brill.

Index of Subjects and Themes

Index of Ancient Sources